The DLM Early Childhood
**EXPRESS**

# Teacher's Edition

## Unit 7
## The Earth and Sky

*Nell Duke • Douglas Clements • Julie Sarama • William Teale*

McGraw Hill **Wright Group**

The **McGraw·Hill** Companies

## Authors

**Nell K. Duke**
*Professor of Teacher Education and Educational Psychology and Co-Director of the Literacy Achievement Research Center* Michigan State University, East Lansing, MI

**Douglas H. Clements**
*Professor of Early Childhood and Mathematics Education* University at Buffalo, State University of New York, New York

**Julie Sarama**
*Associate Professor of Mathematics Education* University at Buffalo, State University of New York, New York

**William Teale**
*Professor of Education* University of Illinois at Chicago, Chicago, IL

## Contributing Authors

**Kim Brenneman, PhD**
*Assistant Research Professor of Psychology at Rutgers University, National Institute for Early Education Research* Rutgers University, New Brunswick, NJ

**Peggy Cerna**
*Early Childhood Consultant* Austin, TX

**Dan Cieloha**
*Educator and President of the Partnership for Interactive Learning* Oakland, CA

**Paula Jones**
*Early Childhood Consultant* Lubbock, TX

**Bobbie Sparks**
*Educator and K-12 Science Consultant* Houston, TX

**Rita Abrams**
*Composer, Lyricist, Educator, Author, and two-time Emmy Award winner* Mill Valley, CA

**Image Credits: Cover** (sprockets) Photodisc/Getty Images, (wheels)felinda/istockphoto, (all other)The McGraw-Hill Companies; **18-19** Jeff R Clow/Getty Images; **19 24** Royalty-Free/Masterfile; **25** D. Hurst/Alamy; **30** Masterfile Royalty-Free Div.; **32** Eileen Hine; **46 48** Steve Mack; **50** Royalty-Free/CORBIS; **54** Daniel Griffo; **56-57** Steve Mason/Getty Images; **57** Royalty-Free/Masterfile; **62** Royalty-Free/CORBIS; **63** ER Productions Ltd/Blend Images/CORBIS; **64** John Kurtz; **68** Dave & Les Jacobs/Getty Images; **70** Holli Conger; **74** The McGraw-Hill Companies, Inc.; **77** Tim Beaumont; **80** Gen Nishino/Getty Images; **82** Melissa Iwai; **84** Thomas Allen / Getty Images; **86** (all)The McGraw-Hill Companies, Inc/Ken Karp photographer; **88** Mike Wesley; **92** Stockbyte/Getty Images; **94-95** Royalty-Free/CORBIS; **95** Mike Powell/Getty Images; **100** Digital Vision/Getty Images; **101** JGI/Jamie Grill/Getty Images; **102** Ariel Skelley/Getty Images; **105** Stockbyte/Getty Images; **110** Digital Vision/Getty Images; **112** The McGraw-Hill Companies, Inc. / Ken Cavanagh Photographer; **113** Christophe Lehenaff/Photolibrary; **118** Masterfile Royalty-Free Div.; **120** Laura Gonzalez; **124** The McGraw-Hill Companies, Inc.; **126** Jan Bryan-Hunt; **130** Ingram Publishing/Alamy; **132-133** Yi Lu/CORBIS; **133** Jose Luis Pelaez Inc/Getty Images; **138** IMAGEMORE Co, Ltd./Getty Images; **139** Thinkstock/Wonderfile/Getty Images; **140** Stockdisc / Getty Images; **144** Valeria Cis; **146** Melissa Iwai; **150** Central Stock/Fotosearch; **156** The McGraw-Hill Companies, Inc./Mazer Creative Services; **158** Steve Mack; **162** Melissa Iwai; **162** The McGraw-Hill Companies, Inc./Jacques Cornell photographer; **163** Ingram Publishing/Alamy; **164** Holli Conger; **171** (r)The McGraw-Hill Companies, Inc./Ken Cavanagh photographer; **172** Dave & Les Jacobs/Getty Images; **178** D. Berry/PhotoLink/Getty Images; **181** (t)Steve Mack, (c)Ingram Publishing/Alamy, (b)Daniel Griffo; **183** (t)Susan LeVan/Getty Images, (b)Laura Gonzalez; **185** Mike Wesley; **186** (t)The McGraw-Hill Companies, Inc., (b)Eileen Hine; **192** Photodisc Collection/Getty Images; **BackCover** (all wheels)felinda/istockphoto, (pencil)Andy Crawford/Getty Images, (rust wicker)Comstock/CORBIS, (bell)Stockbyte/Getty Images, (webcam)Medioimages/Photodisc/Getty Images, (pencilmirror)Yasuhide Fumoto/Getty Images, (U3roof)Ryan McVay/Getty Images, (elephant)PhotoLink/Getty Images, (looking glass) CMCD/Getty Images, (alligator) Siede Preis/Getty Images, (alligatorbelly)Ryan McVay/Getty Images, (U5traincar)83owl/Getty Images, (toothbrush)Raimund Koch/Getty Images, (U8traincar)Ryan McVay/Getty Images, (brush)Brand X Pictures/PunchStock, (all other)The McGraw-Hill Companies.

*The McGraw-Hill Companies*

# www.WrightGroup.com

## Wright Group

Send all inquiries to:
Wright Group/McGraw-Hill
P.O. Box 812960
Chicago, IL 60681

ISBN  978-0-07-658085-9
MHID  0-07-658085-7

3 4 5 6 7 8 9  WEB  16 15 14 13 12 11

### Acknowledgment

*Building Blocks* was supported in part by the National Science Foundation under Grant No. ESI-9730804, "Building Blocks— Foundations for Mathematical Thinking, Pre-Kindergarten to Grade 2: Research-based Materials Development" to Douglas H. Clements and Julie Sarama. The curriculum was also based partly upon work supported in part by the Institute of Educational Sciences (U.S. Dept. of Education, under the Interagency Education Research Initiative, or IERI, a collaboration of the IES, NSF, and NICHHD) under Grant No. R305K05157, "Scaling Trajectories and Technologies" and by the IERI through a National Science Foundation NSF Grant No. REC-0228440, "Scaling Up the Implementation of a Pre-Kindergarten Mathematics Curricula: Teaching for Understanding with Trajectories and Technologies." Any opinions, findings, and conclusions or recommendations expressed in this material are those of the authors and do not necessarily reflect the views of the funding agencies.

### Reviewers

Tonda Brown, *Pre-K Specialist*, Austin ISD; Deanne Colley, *Family Involvement Facilitator*, Northwest ISD; Anita Uphaus, *Retired Early Childhood Director*, Austin ISD; Cathy Ambridge, *Reading Specialist*, Klein ISD; Margaret Jordan, *PreK Special Education Teacher*, McMullen Booth Elementary; Niki Rogers, *Adjunct Professor of Psychology/Child Development*, Concordia University Wisconsin

# Table of Contents

## Getting Started with *The DLM Early Childhood Express*

*The DLM Early Childhood Express* is a holistic, child-centered program that nurtures each child by offering carefully selected and carefully sequenced learning experiences. It provides a wealth of materials and ideas to foster the social-emotional, intellectual, and physical development of children. At the same time, it nurtures the natural curiosity and sense of self that can serve as the foundation for a lifetime of learning.

The lesson format is designed to present information in a way that makes it easy for children to learn. Intelligence is, in large part, our ability to see patterns and build relationships out of those patterns, which is why *DLM* is focused on helping children see the patterns in what they are learning. It builds an understanding of how newly taught material resembles what children already know. Then it takes the differences in the new material and helps the children convert them into new understanding.

Each of the eight Teacher Edition units in *DLM* is centered on an Essential Question relating to the unit's theme. Each week has its own more specific focus question. By focusing on essential questions, children are better able to connect their existing knowledge of the world with the new concepts and ideas they are learning at school. Routines at the beginning and end of each day help children focus on the learning process, reflect on new concepts, and make important connections. The lessons are designed to allow children to apply what they have learned.

### ✗✗✗ Social and Emotional Development
Social-emotional development is addressed everyday through positive reinforcement, interactive activities, and engaging songs.

### Language and Communication
All lessons are focused on language acquisition, which includes oral language development and vocabulary activities.

### Emergent Literacy: Reading
Children develop literacy skills for reading through exposure to multiple read-aloud selections each day and through daily phonological awareness and letter recognition activities.

### Emergent Literacy: Writing
Children develop writing skills through daily writing activities and during Center Time.

### Mathematics
The math strand is based on **Building Blocks,** the result of NSF-funded research, and is designed to develop children's early mathematical knowledge through various individual and group activities.

### Science
Children explore scientific concepts and methods during weekly science-focused, large-group activities, and Center Time activities.

### Social Studies
Children explore Social Studies concepts during weekly social studies-focused, large-group activities, and Center Time activities.

### Fine Arts
Children are exposed to art, dance, and music through a variety of weekly activities and the Creativity Center.

### Physical Development
*DLM* is designed to allow children active time for outdoor play during the day, in addition to daily and weekly movement activities.

### Technology Applications
Technology is integrated throughout each week with the use of online math activities, computer time, and other digital resources.

### 🔲 English Language Learners
Today's classrooms are very diverse. *The DLM Early Childhood Express* addresses this diversity by providing lessons in both English and Spanish. The program also offers strategies to assist English Language Learners at multiple levels of proficiency.

# Flexible Scheduling

## With *The DLM Early Childhood Express*, it's easy to fit lessons into your day.

### Typical Full-Day Schedule

| | |
|---|---|
| 10 min | Opening Routines |
| 15 min | Language Time |
| 60-90 min | Center Time |
| 15 min | Snack Time |
| 15 min | Literacy Time |
| 20 min | Active Play (outdoors if possible) |
| 30 min | Lunch |
| 15 min | Math Time |
| | Rest |
| 15 min | Circle Time: Social and Emotional Development |
| 20 min | Circle Time: Content Connection |
| 30 min | Center Time |
| 25 min | Active Play (outdoors if possible) |
| 15 min | Let's Say Good-Bye |

### Typical Half-Day Schedule

| | |
|---|---|
| 10 min | Opening Routines |
| 15 min | Language Time |
| 60 min | Center Time |
| 15 min | Snack Time |
| 15 min | Circle Time (Literacy, Math, or Social and Emotional Development) |
| 30 min | Active Play (outdoors if possible) |
| 20 min | Circle Time (Content Connection, Literacy, Math, or Social and Emotional Development) |
| 15 min | Let's Say Good-Bye |

## Welcome to *The DLM Early Childhood Express.*

Add your own ideas. Mix and match activities. Our program is designed to offer you a variety of activities on which to build a full year of exciting and creative lessons.

Happy learning to you and the children in your care!

# Themes and Literature

With **The DLM Early Childhood Express,** children develop concrete skills through experiences with music, art, storytelling, hands-on activities and teacher-directed lessons that, in addition to skills development, emphasize practice and reflection. Every four weeks, children are introduced to a new theme organized around an essential question.

Literature selections and cross-curricular content are linked to the theme to help children reinforce lesson concepts. Children hear and discuss an additional read-aloud selection from the *Teacher Treasure Book* at the beginning and end of each day. At the end of each unit, children take home a *My Theme Library Book* reader of their own.

## Unit 1: All About Pre-K
### Why is school important?

| | Focus Question | Literature |
|---|---|---|
| Week 1 | What happens at school? | Welcome to School / Bienvenidos a la escuela |
| Week 2 | What happens in our classroom? | Yellowbelly and Plum Go to School / Barrigota y Pipón van a la escuela |
| Week 3 | What makes a good friend? | Max and Mo's First Day at School / Max y Mo van a la escuela |
| Week 4 | How can we play and learn together? | Amelia's Show and Tell Fiesta/Amelia y la fiesta de "muestra y cuenta" |
| Unit Wrap-Up | My Library Book | How Can I Learn at School? / ¿Cómo puedo aprender en la escuela? |

## Unit 2: All About Me
### What makes me special?

| | Focus Question | Literature |
|---|---|---|
| Week 1 | Who am I? | All About Me / Todo sobre mí |
| Week 2 | What are my feelings? | Lots of Feelings / Montones de sentimientos |
| Week 3 | What do the parts of my body do? | Eyes, Nose, Fingers, and Toes / Ojos, nariz, dedos y pies |
| Week 4 | What is a family? | Jonathan and His Mommy / Juan y su mamá |
| Unit Wrap-Up | My Library Book | What Makes Us Special? / ¿Qué nos hace especiales? |

## Unit 3: My Community
### What is a community?

| | Focus Question | Literature |
|---|---|---|
| Week 1 | What are the parts of a community? | In the Community / En la comunidad |
| Week 2 | How does a community help me? | Rush Hour, / Hora pico |
| Week 3 | Who helps the community? | Quinito's Neighborhood / El vecindario de Quinito |
| Week 4 | How can I help my community? | Flower Garden / Un jardín de flores |
| Unit Wrap-Up | My Library Book | In My Community / Mi comunidad |

## Unit 4: Let's Investigate
### How can I learn more about things?

| | Focus Question | Literature |
|---|---|---|
| Week 1 | How can I learn by observing? | Let's Investigate / Soy detective |
| Week 2 | How can I use tools to investiagte? | I Like Making Tamales / Me gusta hacer tamales |
| Week 3 | How can I compare things? | Nature Spy / Espía de la naturaleza |
| Week 4 | How do objects move? | What Do Wheels Do All Day? / ¿Qué hacen las ruedas todo el día? |
| Unit Wrap-Up | My Library Book | How Can We Investigate? / ¿Cómo podemos investigar? |

## Unit 5: Amazing Animals
### What is amazing about animals?

|         | Focus Question | Literature |
|---------|----------------|------------|
| Week 1 | What are animals like? | *Amazing Animals*<br>*Animales asombrosos* |
| Week 2 | Where do animals live and what do they eat? | *Castles, Caves, and Honeycombs*<br>*Castillos, cuevas y panales* |
| Week 3 | How are animals the same and different? | *Who Is the Beast?*<br>*Quien es la bestia?* |
| Week 4 | How do animals move? | *Move!*<br>*¡A moverse!* |
| Unit Wrap-Up | **My Library Book** | *Hello, Animals!*<br>*¡Hola, animales!* |

## Unit 6: Growing and Changing
### How do living things grow and change?

|         | Focus Question | Literature |
|---------|----------------|------------|
| Week 1 | How do animals grow and change? | *Growing and Changing*<br>*Creciendo y cambiando* |
| Week 2 | How do plants grow and change? | *I Am a Peach*<br>*Yo soy el durazno* |
| Week 3 | How do people grow and change? | *I'm Growing!*<br>*Estoy creciendo!* |
| Week 4 | How do living things grow and change? | *My Garden*<br>*Mi jardin* |
| Unit Wrap-Up | **My Library Book** | *Growing Up*<br>*Creciendo* |

## Unit 7: The Earth and Sky
### What can I learn about the earth and the sky?

|         | Focus Question | Literature |
|---------|----------------|------------|
| Week 1 | What can I learn about the earth and the sky? | *The Earth and Sky*<br>*La Tierra y el cielo* |
| Week 2 | What weather can I observe each day? | *Who Likes Rain?*<br>*¿A quién le gusta la lluvia?* |
| Week 3 | What can I learn about day and night? | *Matthew and the Color of the Sky*<br>*Matias y el color del cielo* |
| Week 4 | Why is caring for the earth and sky important? | *Ada, Once Again!*<br>*¡Otra vez Ada!* |
| Unit Wrap-Up | **My Library Book** | *Good Morning, Earth!*<br>*¡Buenos días, Tierra!* |

## Unit 8: Healthy Food/Healthy Body
### Why is healthy food and exercise good for me?

|         | Focus Question | Literature |
|---------|----------------|------------|
| Week 1 | What are good healthy habits? | *Staying Healthy*<br>*Mantente sano* |
| Week 2 | What kinds of foods are healthy? | *Growing Vegetable Soup*<br>*A sembrar sopa de verduras* |
| Week 3 | Why is exercise important? | *Rise and Exercise!*<br>*A ejercitarse, ¡uno, dos, tres!* |
| Week 4 | How can I stay healthy? | *Jamal's Busy Day*<br>*El intenso día de Jamal* |
| Unit Wrap-Up | **My Library Book** | *Healthy Kids*<br>*Niños sanos* |

# Tools for Teaching

The **DLM Early Childhood Express** is packed full of the components you'll need to teach each theme and enrich your classroom. The *Teacher Treasure Package* is the heart of the program, because it contains all the necessary materials. Plus, the *Teacher's Treasure Book* contains all the fun components that you'll love to teach. The *Literature Package* contains all the stories and books you need to support children's developing literacy. You'll find letter tiles, counters, and puppets in the *Manipulative Package* to connect hands-on learning skills with meaningful play.

Alphabet Wall Cards
(English and Spanish)

ABC Picture Cards
(English and Spanish)

## Teacher Treasure Package

This package contains all the essential tools for the teacher such as the *Teacher's Treasure Book*, *Teacher's Editions*, technology, and other resources no teacher would want to be without!

Sequence Cards
(English and Spanish)

Oral Language Development Cards
(English and Spanish)

Photo Library
CD-ROM

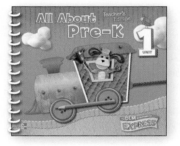
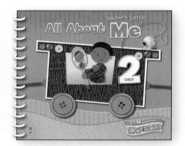

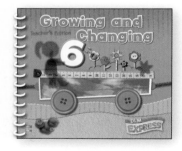

▲ Each lesson's instruction uses a variety of cards to help children learn. **Alphabet Wall Cards** and **ABC Picture Cards** help build letter recognition and phonemic awareness. **Oral Language Development Cards** teach new vocabulary, and are especially helpful when working with English Language Learners. **Sequencing Cards** help children learn how to order events and the vocabulary associated with time and sequence.

▲ There is one bilingual **Teacher's Edition** for each four-week theme. It provides the focus questions for each lesson as well as plans for centers and suggestions for classroom management.

▶ The bilingual **Teacher's Treasure Book** features 500+ pages of the things you love most about teaching Early Childhood, such as songs, traditional read alouds, folk tales, finger plays, and flannelboard stories with patterns.

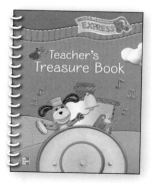

▶ An **ABC Take-Home Book** with blackline masters is provided for each letter of the English and Spanish alphabets.

ABC Take-Home Book
(English and Spanish)

▶ Flip charts and their Audio CDs support the activities in each lesson. Children practice literacy and music skills using the **Rhymes and Chants Flip Chart,** which supports oral language development and phonological awareness in both English and Spanish. An Audio CD is included and provides a recording of every rhyme or chant. The **Making Good Choices Flip Chart** provides illustrations to allow students to explore social and emotional development concepts while facilitating classroom activities and discussion. 15 lively songs recorded in both English and Spanish address key social emotional development themes such as: joining in, helping others, being fair, teasing, bullying, and much more. The **Math and Science Flip Chart** is a demonstration tool that addresses weekly math and science concepts through photos and illustrations.

▶ Other key resources include a **Research & Professional Development Guide,** and a bilingual **Home Connections Resource Guide** which provides weekly letters home and take-home story books.

# Building Blocks

**Building Blocks,** the result of NSF-funded research, develops young children's mathematical thinking using their bodies, manipulatives, paper, and computers.

**Building Blocks** online management system guides children through research-based learning trajectories. These activities-through-trajectories connect children's informal knowledge to more formal school mathematics. The result is a mathematical curriculum that is not only motivating for children but also comprehensive.

▶ **DLMExpressOnline.com** includes the following:

- e-Books of student and teacher materials

- Audio recordings of the **My Library** and **Literature Books** (Big/Little) in English and Spanish

- Teacher planning tools and assessment support

# Tools for Teaching

## Literature Package

This package contains the literature referenced in the program. Packages are available in several variations so you can choose the package that best meets the needs of your classroom. The literature used in the program includes expository selections, traditional stories, and emergent readers for students. All literature is available in English or Spanish.

▶ *My Library Books* are take-home readers for children to continue their exploration of unit themes. (English and Spanish)

▶ *Concept Big Books* are nonfiction selections that introduce the essential questions for each unit and help children make connections between their background knowledge and unit themes. (English and Spanish)

▶ The *ABC Big Book* helps children develop phonemic awareness and letter recognition. (English and Spanish)

▶ The **Big Books** and **Little Books** reinforce each week's theme and the unit theme. Selections include stories originally written in Spanish, as well as those written in English.

▶ The stories in the **Big Books and Little Books** are recorded on the **Listening Library Audio CDs**. They are available in English and Spanish.

# Manipulative Package

This package contains fun tools for children to play and learn with in the classroom.

| | |
|---|---|
| Two Puppets | Pattern Blocks |
| Alphabet Letter Tiles (in English and Spanish) | Shape Sets |
| Transportation and Farm Animal Counters | Connecting Cubes |
| Two-Color Counters | Jumbo Hand Lenses |
| Step-by-Step Number Line | Magnetic Wands |
| Balance Scale | |

# A Typical Weekly Lesson Plan

Each week of *The DLM Early Childhood Express* is organized the same way to provide children with the structure and routines they crave. Each week begins with a weekly opener that introduces the focus question for the week and includes a review of the week's Learning Goals, the Materials and Resources needed for the week, a Daily Planner, and a plan for the Learning Centers children will use throughout the week.

Each day's lesson includes large-group Circle Time and small-group Center Time. Each day includes Literacy, Math, and Social and Emotional Development activities during Circle Time. On Day 1, children explore Science. On Days 2 and 4, they work on more in-depth math lessons. On Day 3, Social Studies is the focus. Fine Art or Music/Movement activities take place during Circle Time on Day 5.

You will find the **Program Materials** and **Other Materials** needed for each day on the Materials and Resources page.

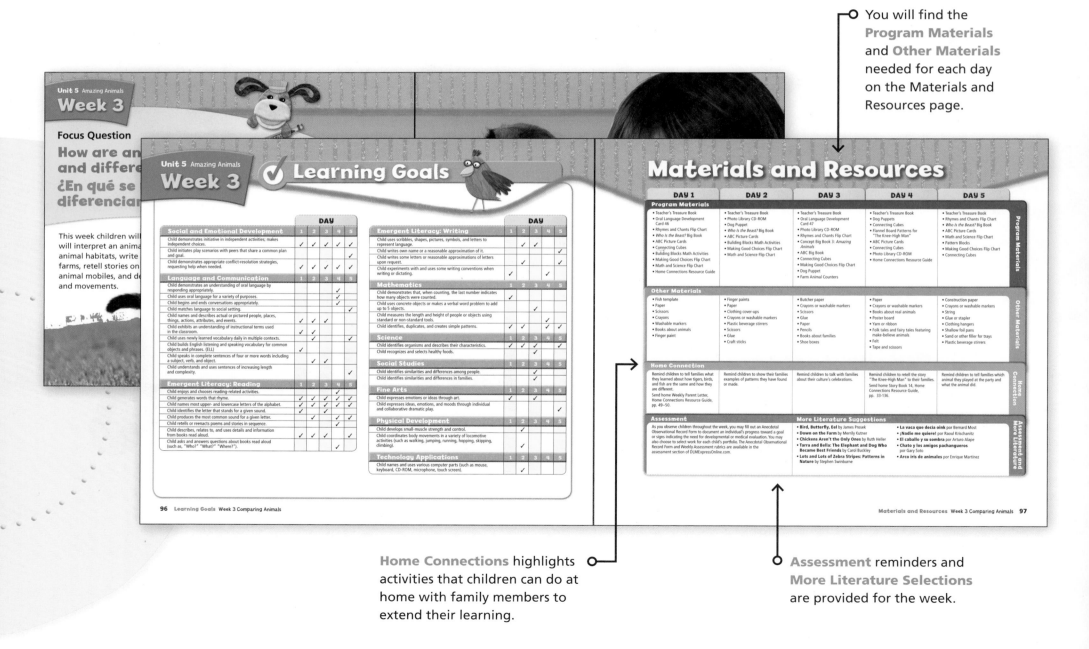

**Home Connections** highlights activities that children can do at home with family members to extend their learning.

**Assessment** reminders and **More Literature Selections** are provided for the week.

The **Daily Planner** provides a Week-at-a-Glance view of the daily structure and lesson topics for each week.

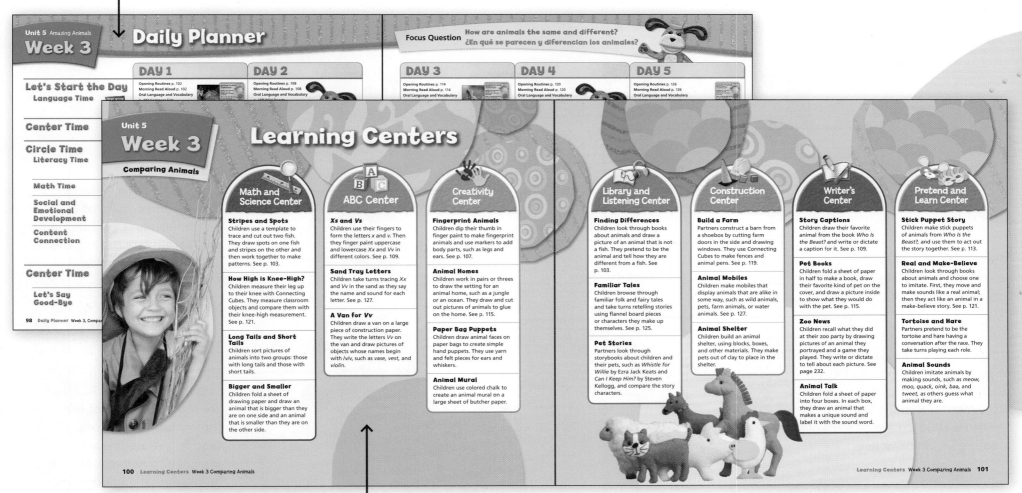

**Learning Centers** should be used throughout the week during Center Time. This page provides an overview of center activities to set up for children. Additional information about some center activities is provided in the daily lessons. The Learning Centers are intended to remain open for the entire week. These centers provide the opportunity for children to explore a wide range of curricular areas.

# Lesson Overview

Our **Teacher's Editions** are organized by theme, week, and day. Each day's lesson is covered in six page spreads. The lessons integrate learning from the skill domain areas of: Social Emotional Development, Language and Communication, Emergent Literacy Reading and Writing, Mathematics, Science, Social Studies, Fine Arts, Physical Development, and Technology.

Each day begins with **Opening Routines** and a **Read Aloud** selection. This structured time helps children settle into their day.

The **Learning Goals** met by the lesson are listed on each page.

**Observational Checks** at point of use help to focus learning. These informal assessment questions help to ensure children are meeting lesson objectives.

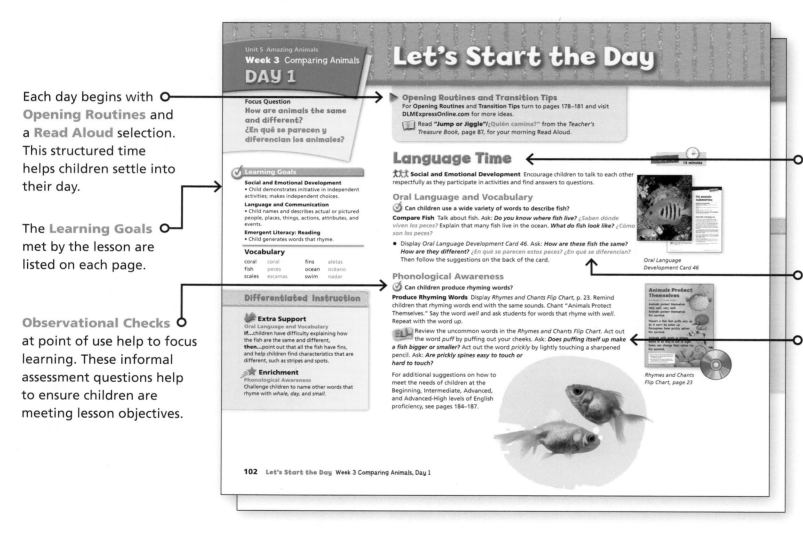

Unit 5 Amazing Animals
**Week 3** Comparing Animals
**DAY 1**

**Focus Question**
How are animals the same and different?
¿En qué se parecen y diferencian los animales?

✓ **Learning Goals**

**Social and Emotional Development**
• Child demonstrates initiative in independent activities; makes independent choices.
**Language and Communication**
• Child names and describes actual or pictured people, places, things, actions, attributes, and events.
**Emergent Literacy: Reading**
• Child generates words that rhyme.

**Vocabulary**

| coral | coral | fins | aletas |
|-------|-------|------|--------|
| fish | peces | ocean | océano |
| scales | escamas | swim | nadar |

**Differentiated Instruction**

**Extra Support**
*Oral Language and Vocabulary*
If...children have difficulty explaining how the fish are the same and different,
then...point out that all the fish have fins, and help children find characteristics that are different, such as stripes and spots.

**Enrichment**
*Phonological Awareness*
Challenge children to name other words that rhyme with *whale, day,* and *small.*

## Let's Start the Day

▶ **Opening Routines and Transition Tips**
For **Opening Routines** and **Transition Tips** turn to pages 178–181 and visit DLMExpressOnline.com for more ideas.

Read **"Jump or Jiggle"/¿Quién camina?"** from the *Teacher's Treasure Book,* page 87, for your morning Read Aloud.

## Language Time

15 minutes

👫👫 **Social and Emotional Development** Encourage children to talk to each other respectfully as they participate in activities and find answers to questions.

### Oral Language and Vocabulary

✓ Can children use a wide variety of words to describe fish?

**Compare Fish** Talk about fish. Ask: *Do you know where fish live? ¿Saben dónde viven los peces?* Explain that many fish live in the ocean. *What do fish look like? ¿Cómo son los peces?*

● Display *Oral Language Development Card 46.* Ask: *How are these fish the same? How are they different? ¿En qué se parecen estos peces? ¿En qué se diferencian?* Then follow the suggestions on the back of the card.

*Oral Language Development Card 46*

### Phonological Awareness

✓ Can children produce rhyming words?

**Produce Rhyming Words** Display *Rhymes and Chants Flip Chart,* p. 23. Remind children that rhyming words end with the same sounds. Chant "Animals Protect Themselves." Say the word *well* and ask students for words that rhyme with *well.* Repeat with the word *up.*

ELL Review the uncommon words in the *Rhymes and Chants Flip Chart.* Act out the word *puff* by puffing out your cheeks. Ask: *Does puffing itself up make a fish bigger or smaller?* Act out the word *prickly* by lightly touching a sharpened pencil. Ask: *Are prickly spines easy to touch or hard to touch?*

For additional suggestions on how to meet the needs of children at the Beginning, Intermediate, Advanced, and Advanced-High levels of English proficiency, see pages 184–187.

*Animals Protect Themselves*

*Rhymes and Chants Flip Chart, page 23*

102 Let's Start the Day Week 3 Comparing Animals, Day 1

**Language Time** is the first large-group activity of the day. It includes Oral Language and Vocabulary Development as well as Phonological Awareness activities.

Instructional questions are provided in both **English and Spanish.**

Tips for working with **English Language Learners** are shown at point of use throughout the lessons. Teaching strategies are provided to help children of of all language backgrounds and abilities meet the lesson objectives.

**Center Time** provides additional information for teacher-guided small-group activities and suggestions for independent activities children will complete during weekly Center Rotation.

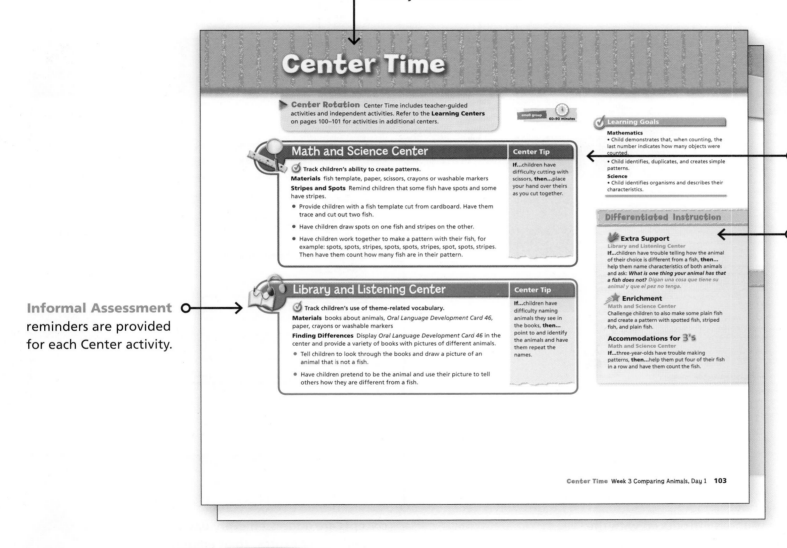

# Center Time

▶ **Center Rotation** Center Time includes teacher-guided activities and independent activities. Refer to the **Learning Centers** on pages 100–101 for activities in additional centers.

*small group* — **60-90 minutes**

## Math and Science Center

☑ Track children's ability to create patterns.

**Materials** fish template, paper, scissors, crayons or washable markers

**Stripes and Spots** Remind children that some fish have spots and some have stripes.

● Provide children with a fish template cut from cardboard. Have them trace and cut out two fish.

● Have children draw spots on one fish and stripes on the other.

● Have children work together to make a pattern with their fish, for example: spots, spots, stripes, spots, spots, stripes, spot, spots, stripes. Then have them count how many fish are in their pattern.

**Center Tip**

**If...**children have difficulty cutting with scissors, **then...**place your hand over theirs as you cut together.

## Library and Listening Center

☑ Track children's use of theme-related vocabulary.

**Materials** books about animals, *Oral Language Development Card 46*, paper, crayons or washable markers

**Finding Differences** Display *Oral Language Development Card 46* in the center and provide a variety of books with pictures of different animals.

● Tell children to look through the books and draw a picture of an animal that is not a fish.

● Have children pretend to be the animal and use their picture to tell others how they are different from a fish.

**Center Tip**

**If...**children have difficulty naming animals they see in the books, **then...**point to and identify the animals and have them repeat the names.

### ☑ Learning Goals

**Mathematics**
• Child demonstrates that, when counting, the last number indicates how many objects were counted.
• Child identifies, duplicates, and creates simple patterns.

**Science**
• Child identifies organisms and describes their characteristics.

### Differentiated Instruction

**Extra Support**
Library and Listening Center
**If...**children have trouble telling how the animal of their choice is different from a fish, **then...**help them name characteristics of both animals and ask: *What is one thing your animal has that a fish does not? Digan una cosa que tiene su animal y que el pez no tenga.*

**Enrichment**
Math and Science Center
Challenge children to also make some plain fish and create a pattern with spotted fish, striped fish, and plain fish.

**Accommodations for 3's**
Math and Science Center
**If...**three-year-olds have trouble making patterns, **then...**help them put four of their fish in a row and have them count the fish.

Center Time Week 3 Comparing Animals, Day 1    **103**

**Center Tips** are provided for center support.

**Differentiated Instruction** offers suggestions for modifications to activities for children who may need Extra Support or Enrichment, as well as Accommodations for 3's and Special Needs.

**Informal Assessment** reminders are provided for each Center activity.

# Lesson Overview

Children have **Literacy Time** every day. During this time, children listen to and discuss a second Read Aloud from a nonfiction **Concept Big Book** or a **Big Book/Little Book** literature selection.

**Building Blocks** online activities are provided each week during Math Time.

Children work in large groups on 15 minute math activities during daily **Math Time.**

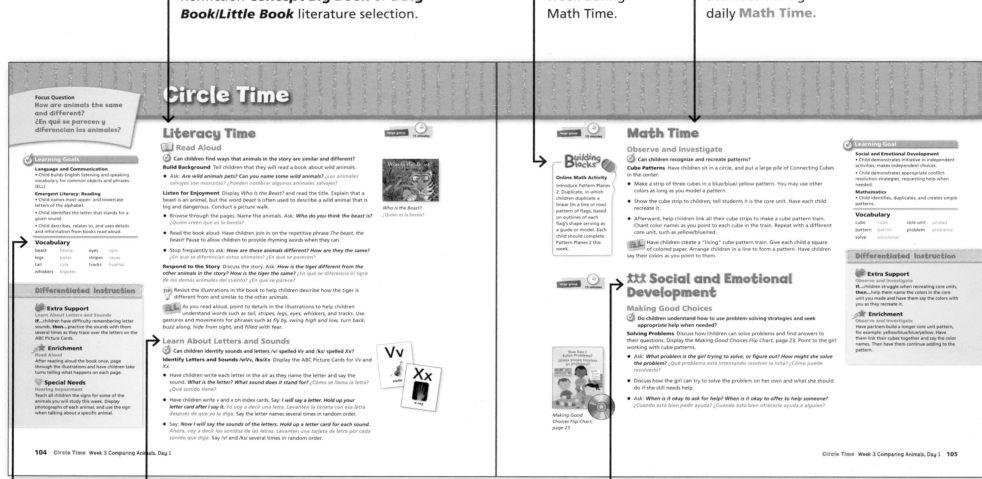

## Circle Time

**Focus Question**
How are animals the same and different?
¿En qué se parecen y diferencian los animales?

### Learning Goals

**Language and Communication**
• Child builds English listening and speaking vocabulary for common objects and phrases. (ELL)

**Emergent Literacy: Reading**
• Child names most upper- and lowercase letters of the alphabet.
• Child identifies the letter that stands for a given sound.
• Child describes, relates to, and uses details and information from books read aloud.

**Vocabulary**

| beast | bestia | eyes | ojos |
|---|---|---|---|
| legs | patas | stripes | rayas |
| tail | cola | tracks | huellas |
| whiskers | bigotes | | |

### Differentiated Instruction

**Extra Support**
*Learn About Letters and Sounds*
**If**...children have difficulty remembering letter sounds, **then**...practice the sounds with them several times as they trace over the letters on the ABC Picture Cards.

**Enrichment**
*Read Aloud*
After reading aloud the book once, page through the illustrations and have children take turns telling what happens on each page.

**Special Needs**
*Hearing Impairment*
Teach all children the signs for some of the animals you will study this week. Display photographs of each animal, and use the sign when talking about a specific animal.

## Literacy Time

### 📖 Read Aloud

🔵 Can children find ways that animals in the story are similar and different?

**Build Background** Tell children that they will read a book about wild animals.

• Ask: *Are wild animals pets? Can you name some wild animals? ¿Los animales salvajes son mascotas? ¿Pueden nombrar algunos animales salvajes?*

**Listen for Enjoyment** Display *Who Is the Beast?* and read the title. Explain that a beast is an animal, but the word *beast* is often used to describe a wild animal that is big and dangerous. Conduct a picture walk.

• Browse through the pages. Name the animals. Ask: *Who do you think the beast is? ¿Quién creen que es la bestia?*

• Read the book aloud. Have children join in on the repetitive phrase *The beast, the beast!* Pause to allow children to provide rhyming words when they can.

• Stop frequently to ask: *How are these animals different? How are they the same? ¿En qué se diferencian estos animales? ¿En qué se parecen?*

**Respond to the Story** Discuss the story. Ask: *How is the tiger different from the other animals in the story? How is the tiger the same? ¿En qué se diferencia el tigre de los demás animales del cuento? ¿En qué se parece?*

**TIP** Revisit the illustrations in the book to help children describe how the tiger is different from and similar to the other animals.

**ELL** As you read aloud, point to details in the illustrations to help children understand words such as *tail, stripes, legs, eyes, whiskers,* and *tracks.* Use gestures and movements for phrases such as *fly by, swing high and low, turn back, buzz along, hide from sight,* and *filled with fear.*

### Learn About Letters and Sounds

🔵 Can children identify sounds and letters /v/ spelled *Vv* and /ks/ spelled *Xx*?

**Identify Letters and Sounds** /v/*Vv*, /ks/*Xx* Display the ABC Picture Cards for *Vv* and *Xx*.

• Have children write each letter in the air as they name the letter and say the sound. *What is the letter? What sound does it stand for? ¿Cómo se llama la letra? ¿Qué sonido tiene?*

• Have children write *v* and *x* on index cards. Say: *I will say a letter. Hold up your letter card after I say it. Yo voy a decir una letra. Levanten la tarjeta con esa letra después de que yo la diga.* Say the letter names several times in random order.

• Say: *Now I will say the sounds of the letters. Hold up a letter card for each sound. Ahora, voy a decir los sonidos de las letras. Levanten una tarjeta de letra por cada sonido que diga.* Say /v/ and /ks/ several times in random order.

*large group* 15 minutes

*Who Is the Beast?*
*¿Quién es la bestia?*

**Vv**
violin

**Xx**
x-ray

## Math Time

*large group* 15 minutes

### Observe and Investigate

**Social and Emotional Development**

🔵 Can children recognize and recreate patterns?

**Building Blocks**

**Online Math Activity**
Introduce Pattern Planes 2: Duplicate, in which children duplicate a linear (in a line or row) pattern of flags, based on outlines of each flag's shape serving as a guide or model. Each child should complete Pattern Planes 2 this week.

**Cube Patterns** Have children sit in a circle, and put a large pile of Connecting Cubes in the center.

• Make a strip of three cubes in a blue/blue/ yellow pattern. You may use other colors as long as you make a pattern.

• Show the cube strip to children; tell students it is the core unit. Have each child recreate it.

• Afterward, help children link all their cube strips to make a cube pattern train. Chant color names as you point to each cube in the train. Repeat with a different core unit, such as yellow/blue/red.

**ELL** Have children create a "living" cube pattern train. Give each child a square of colored paper. Arrange children in a line to form a pattern. Have children say their colors as you point to them.

### 👥 Social and Emotional Development

**Making Good Choices**

🔵 Do children understand how to use problem-solving strategies and seek appropriate help when needed?

**Solving Problems** Discuss how children can solve problems and find answers to their questions. Display the *Making Good Choices Flip Chart*, page 23. Point to the girl working with cube patterns.

• Ask: *What problem is the girl trying to solve, or figure out? How might she solve the problem? ¿Qué problema está intentando resolver la niña? ¿Cómo puede resolverlo?*

• Discuss how the girl can try to solve the problem on her own and what she should do if she still needs help.

• Ask: *When is it okay to ask for help? When is it okay to offer to help someone? ¿Cuándo está bien pedir ayuda? ¿Cuándo está bien ofrecerle ayuda a alguien?*

*Making Good Choices Flip Chart, page 23*

### Learning Goal

**Social and Emotional Development**
• Child demonstrates initiative in independent activities; makes independent choices.
• Child demonstrates appropriate conflict-resolution strategies, requesting help when needed.

**Mathematics**
• Child identifies, duplicates, and creates simple patterns.

**Vocabulary**

| cube | cubo | core unit | unidad |
|---|---|---|---|
| pattern | patrón | problem | problema |
| solve | solucionar | | |

### Differentiated Instruction

**Extra Support**
*Observe and Investigate*
**If**...children struggle when recreating core units, **then**...help them name the colors in the core unit you made and have them say the colors with you as they recreate it.

**Enrichment**
*Observe and Investigate*
Have partners build a longer core unit pattern, for example: yellow/blue/blue/yellow. Have them link their cubes together and say the color names. Then have them continue adding to the pattern.

**Vocabulary** is provided in English and Spanish to help expand children's ability to use both languages.

Children learn about **Letters and Sounds** every day. The sound is introduced with the letter. Children also practice letter formation.

**Social and Emotional Development** concepts are addressed every day to help children better express their emotions and needs, and establish positive relationships.

**Circle Time** is devoted to longer activities focusing on different cross-curricular concepts each day. Day 1 is Science Time. Days 2 and 4 are Math Time. On Day 3, children have Social Studies Time. Fine arts are covered in Art Time or Music and Movement Time on Day 5.

An end-of-the-day **Writing** activity is provided each day.

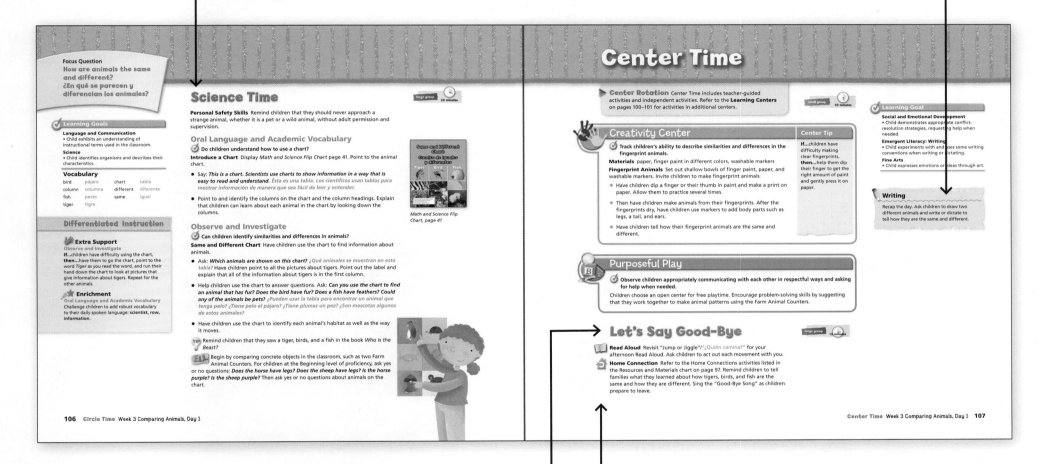

**Let's Say Good-Bye** includes the closing routines for each day. The Read Aloud from the beginning of the day is revisited with a focus on skills practiced during the day.

Each day provides a **Home Connection.** At the start of each week, a letter is provided to inform families of the weekly focus and offer additional literature suggestions to extend the weekly theme focus.

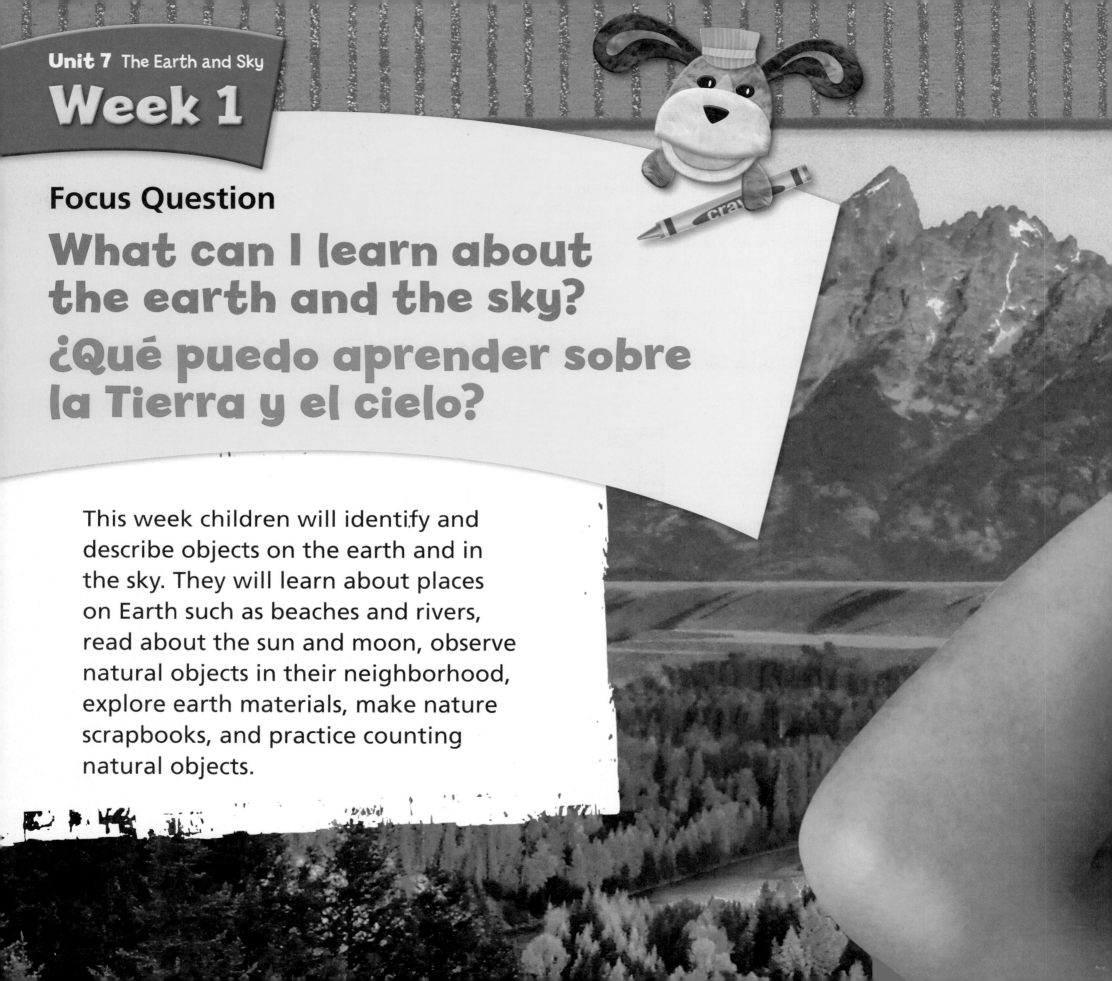

# Week 1

## Focus Question

# What can I learn about the earth and the sky?

# ¿Qué puedo aprender sobre la Tierra y el cielo?

This week children will identify and describe objects on the earth and in the sky. They will learn about places on Earth such as beaches and rivers, read about the sun and moon, observe natural objects in their neighborhood, explore earth materials, make nature scrapbooks, and practice counting natural objects.

# Week 1 — Learning Goals

| Social and Emotional Development | DAY 1 | 2 | 3 | 4 | 5 |
|---|---|---|---|---|---|
| Child maintains concentration/attention skills until a task is complete. | ✓ | ✓ | ✓ | ✓ | ✓ |
| Child shows eagerness, curiosity, and confidence while learning new concepts and trying new things. | ✓ | ✓ | | | |

| Language and Communication | 1 | 2 | 3 | 4 | 5 |
|---|---|---|---|---|---|
| Child demonstrates an understanding of oral language by responding appropriately. | | | ✓ | ✓ | |
| Child follows two- and three-step oral directions. | | ✓ | | ✓ | |
| Child follows basic rules for conversations (taking turns, staying on topic, listening actively). | | | | ✓ | |
| Child names and describes actual or pictured people, places, things, actions, attributes, and events. | ✓ | ✓ | ✓ | ✓ | ✓ |
| Child uses newly learned vocabulary daily in multiple contexts. | ✓ | ✓ | ✓ | ✓ | ✓ |

| Emergent Literacy: Reading | 1 | 2 | 3 | 4 | 5 |
|---|---|---|---|---|---|
| Child enjoys and chooses reading-related activities. | ✓ | ✓ | ✓ | ✓ | ✓ |
| Child names most upper- and lowercase letters of the alphabet. | ✓ | ✓ | ✓ | ✓ | ✓ |
| Child identifies the letter that stands for a given sound. | ✓ | ✓ | ✓ | ✓ | ✓ |
| Child describes, relates to, and uses details and information from books read aloud. | ✓ | ✓ | | | |
| Child asks and answers questions about books read aloud (such as "Who?" "What?" "Where?"). | | | | | ✓ |

| Emergent Literacy: Writing | 1 | 2 | 3 | 4 | 5 |
|---|---|---|---|---|---|
| Child participates in free drawing and writing activities to deliver information. | | | ✓ | | |
| Child uses scribbles, shapes, pictures, symbols, and letters to represent language. | | | ✓ | | ✓ |
| Child writes own name or a reasonable approximation of it. | | | | | ✓ |

| Mathematics | 1 | 2 | 3 | 4 | 5 |
|---|---|---|---|---|---|
| Child recites number words in sequence from one to thirty. | ✓ | ✓ | | ✓ | |
| Child counts 1–10 concrete objects correctly. | ✓ | | | | |
| Child demonstrates that the numerical counting sequence is always the same. | | | | ✓ | ✓ |
| Child demonstrates that, when counting, the last number indicates how many objects were counted. | | ✓ | | | |
| Child uses concrete objects or makes a verbal word problem to add up to 5 objects. | | | ✓ | | |

| Science | DAY 1 | 2 | 3 | 4 | 5 |
|---|---|---|---|---|---|
| Child investigates and describes energy sources (light, heat, electricity). | ✓ | ✓ | ✓ | | ✓ |
| Child observes, identifies, explores, describes, and compares earth materials (such as rocks, soil, sand, water) and their uses. | ✓ | ✓ | ✓ | | ✓ |
| Child observes, identifies, compares, and discusses objects in the sky (such as clouds, sun, moon, stars). | ✓ | ✓ | ✓ | ✓ | ✓ |
| Child describes the effects of natural forces (such as wind, gravity). | ✓ | | | | |
| Child follows basic health and safety rules. | ✓ | | ✓ | | ✓ |

| Social Studies | 1 | 2 | 3 | 4 | 5 |
|---|---|---|---|---|---|
| Child identifies common areas and features of home, school, and community. | | | ✓ | | |

| Fine Arts | 1 | 2 | 3 | 4 | 5 |
|---|---|---|---|---|---|
| Child uses and experiments with a variety of art materials and tools in various art activities. | | ✓ | | | |
| Child expresses emotions or ideas through art. | | ✓ | | | ✓ |
| Child shares opinions about artwork and artistic experiences. | | | | | ✓ |
| Child expresses ideas, emotions, and moods through individual and collaborative dramatic play. | | | | ✓ | |

| Physical Development | 1 | 2 | 3 | 4 | 5 |
|---|---|---|---|---|---|
| Child develops small-muscle strength and control. | | ✓ | | | |
| Child completes tasks that require eye-hand coordination and control. | | ✓ | ✓ | | |

| Technology Applications | 1 | 2 | 3 | 4 | 5 |
|---|---|---|---|---|---|
| Child opens and correctly uses age-appropriate software programs. | | ✓ | ✓ | | |
| Child names and uses various computer parts (such as mouse, keyboard, CD-ROM, microphone, touch screen). | | | | ✓ | |
| Child uses computer software or technology to express original ideas. | | | | ✓ | |

# Materials and Resources

| DAY 1 | DAY 2 | DAY 3 | DAY 4 | DAY 5 |
|-------|-------|-------|-------|-------|

## Program Materials

| DAY 1 | DAY 2 | DAY 3 | DAY 4 | DAY 5 |
|-------|-------|-------|-------|-------|
| • ABC Big Book<br>• ABC Take-Home Book<br>• Building Blocks Online Math Activities<br>• Concept Big Book 4: *The Earth and Sky*<br>• Connecting Cubes<br>• Hand Lenses<br>• Home Connections Resource Guide<br>• Oral Language Development Card 61<br>• Making Good Choices Flip Chart<br>• Math and Science Flip Chart<br>• Primary Balance Scale<br>• Rhymes and Chants Flip Chart<br>• Teacher's Treasure Book | • ABC Big Book<br>• ABC Take-Home Book<br>• Alphabet/Letter Tiles<br>• Building Blocks Online Math Activities<br>• Concept Big Book 4: *The Earth and Sky*<br>• Dog Puppets<br>• Making Good Choices Flip Chart<br>• Math and Science Flip Chart<br>• Photo Library CD-ROM<br>• Teacher's Treasure Book | • ABC Big Book<br>• ABC Take-Home Book<br>• Building Blocks Online Math Activities<br>• Dog Puppets<br>• Flannel Board Patterns for "The Sun and the Moon"<br>• Making Good Choices Flip Chart<br>• Oral Language Development Card 62<br>• Rhymes and Chants Flip Chart<br>• Teacher's Treasure Book | • ABC Picture Cards<br>• Building Blocks Online Math Activities<br>• Counting Cards 1–10 (Teacher's Treasure Book, pp. 506–507)<br>• Dog Puppets<br>• Farm Animal Counters<br>• Flannel Board Patterns for "The Sun and the Moon" and "Henny-Penny"<br>• Math and Science Flip Chart<br>• Step-by-Step Number Line<br>• Teacher's Treasure Book | • Alphabet/Letter Tiles<br>• Building Blocks Online Math Activities<br>• Concept Big Book 4: *The Earth and Sky*<br>• Counting Cards 1–10<br>• Making Good Choices Flip Chart<br>• Oral Language Development Card 63<br>• Rhymes and Chants Flip Chart<br>• Teacher's Treasure Book |

## Other Materials

| DAY 1 | DAY 2 | DAY 3 | DAY 4 | DAY 5 |
|-------|-------|-------|-------|-------|
| • crayons<br>• cups<br>• buckets<br>• beach toys<br>• nature books<br>• paper<br>• potting soil<br>• sand, small rocks, shells<br>• sieve<br>• sunglasses<br>• water | • construction paper (large)<br>• crayons<br>• cups<br>• paint and paintbrushes<br>• paper plates<br>• pictures of landforms (mountains, forests)<br>• pictures of rivers and ocean beaches<br>• ruler<br>• sand, potting soil, twigs, leaves, pebbles, shells<br>• smocks | • blocks<br>• circle pattern<br>• construction paper<br>• crayons<br>• miniature neighborhood toys (cars, homes, trees)<br>• paper<br>• sand, potting soil, rocks<br>• tape<br>• water<br>• yarn | • building blocks<br>• empty egg cartons<br>• fabric paint<br>• recordings of nature-related and counting songs<br>• sand<br>• socks<br>• spoons | • blocks<br>• cardstock and construction paper<br>• cotton balls<br>• crayons<br>• glue<br>• letter cards<br>• nature magazines<br>• nature objects (dried flowers, twigs, leaves, pebbles, shells)<br>• nature toys (miniature trees, animals)<br>• paint and paintbrushes<br>• yarn |

## Home Connection

| DAY 1 | DAY 2 | DAY 3 | DAY 4 | DAY 5 |
|-------|-------|-------|-------|-------|
| Remind children to tell families what they learned about Earth. Send home the Weekly Parent Letter, Home Connections Resource Guide, pp. 61–62; ABC Take-Home Book for *Qq,* (English) p. 23 or (Spanish) p. 54. | Encourage children to discuss with their families what things they can see in the sky. Send home the ABC Take-Home Book for *Ww,* (English) p. 29 or (Spanish) p. 60. | Remind children to tell their families what they learned about their neighborhood. Send home the ABC Take-Home Book for *Zz,* (English) p. 32 or (Spanish) p. 63. | Encourage children to tell their families the story of Henny-Penny and why she thought the sky was falling. | Remind children to tell their families what they learned this week about the earth and the sky. |

## Assessment

As you observe children throughout the week, you may fill out an Anecdotal Observational Record Form to document an individual's progress toward a goal or signs indicating the need for developmental or medical evaluation. You may also choose to select work for each child's portfolio. The Anecdotal Observational Record Form and Weekly Assessment rubrics are available in the assessment section of DLMExpressOnline.com.

## More Literature Suggestions

- **The Earth and I** by Frank Asch
- **Into the Sky** by Ryan Ann Hunter
- **Geography from A to Z: A Picture Glossary** by Jack Knowlton
- **Earth Day – Hooray!** by Stuart J. Murphy

- **Oye al desierto** por Pat Mora
- **El libro de las nubes** por Tomie dePaola
- **En casa antes de anochecer** por Ian Beck
- **Teo en avión** por Violeta Denou

| | **DAY 1** | **DAY 2** |
|---|---|---|
| **Let's Start the Day**<br>**Language Time**  large group | **Opening Routines** p. 26<br>**Morning Read Aloud** p. 26<br>**Oral Language and Vocabulary** p. 26 Places on Earth<br>**Phonological Awareness** p. 26 Segmenting Phonemes  | **Opening Routines** p. 32<br>**Morning Read Aloud** p. 32<br>**Oral Language and Vocabulary** p. 32 Place Names and Characteristics<br>**Phonological Awareness** p. 32 Segmenting Phonemes |
| **Center Time**  small group | **Focus On:**<br>Library and Listening Center p. 27<br>Pretend and Learn Center p. 27 | **Focus On:**<br>ABC Center p. 33<br>Creativity Center p. 33 |
| **Circle Time**<br>**Literacy Time**  large group | **Read Aloud**<br>*Concept Big Book 4: The Earth and Sky/ La Tierra y el cielo* p. 28<br>**Learn About Letters and Sounds:** *Qq* p. 28  | **Read Aloud**<br>*Concept Big Book 4: The Earth and Sky/ La Tierra y el cielo* p. 34<br>**Learn About Letters and Sounds:** *Ww* p. 34 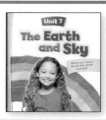 |
| **Math Time**  large group | **I'm Thinking of a Number (Length)** p. 29  | **I'm Thinking of a Number (Ruler)** p. 35 |
| **Social and Emotional Development**  large group | **Completing Tasks** p. 29  | **Completing Tasks** p. 35  |
| **Content Connection** large group | **Science:**<br>**Oral Language and Academic Vocabulary** p. 30 What's Outside?<br>**Observe and Investigate** p. 30 Nature Walk  | **Math:**<br>**Count on It** p. 36 Counting to 10<br>**X-Ray Vision 2** p. 36 Counting Forward and Back  |
| **Center Time** small group | **Focus On:**<br>Math and Science Center p. 31<br>Purposeful Play p. 31 | **Focus On:**<br>Math and Science Center p. 37<br>Purposeful Play p. 37 |
| **Let's Say Good-Bye**  large group | **Read Aloud** p. 31<br>**Writing** p. 31<br>**Home Connection** p. 31 | **Read Aloud** p. 37<br>**Writing** p. 37<br>**Home Connection** p. 37 |

# DAY 3

**Opening Routines** p. 38
**Morning Read Aloud** p. 38
**Oral Language and Vocabulary**
p. 38 Place Names and Characteristics
**Phonological Awareness** p. 38 Segmenting Phonemes

**Focus On:**
**Writer's Center** p. 39
**Creativity Center** p. 39

**Read Aloud**
"The Sun and the Moon"/
"El Sol y la Luna" p. 40
**Learn About Letters and Sounds:** *Zz* p. 40

**Finger Word Problems** p. 41

**Completing Tasks** p. 41

**Social Studies:**
**Oral Language and Academic Vocabulary**
p. 42 Talking About School and Home
**Understand and Participate**
p. 42 Looking at Our Neighborhood

**Focus On:**
**Construction Center** p. 43
**Purposeful Play** p. 43

**Read Aloud** p. 43
**Writing** p. 43
**Home Connection** p. 43

# DAY 4

**Opening Routines** p. 44
**Morning Read Aloud** p. 44
**Oral Language and Vocabulary**
p. 44 Storybook Characters
**Phonological Awareness**
p. 44 Segmenting Phonemes

**Focus On:**
**Library and Listening Center** p. 45
**Pretend and Learn Center** p. 45

**Read Aloud**
"Henny-Penny"/
"Gallinita-Nita" p. 46
**Learn About Letters and Sounds:**
Review *Qq, Ww, Zz*
p. 46

**I'm Thinking of a Number** p. 47

**Completing Tasks** p. 47

**Math:**
**Count on It**
p. 48 Counting to 10
**X-Ray Vision 2**
p. 48 Counting Forward and Back

**Focus On:**
**Math and Science Center** p. 49
**Purposeful Play** p. 49

**Read Aloud** p. 49
**Writing** p. 49
**Home Connection** p. 49

# DAY 5

**Opening Routines** p. 50
**Morning Read Aloud** p. 50
**Oral Language and Vocabulary**
p. 50 Place Names and Characteristics
**Phonological Awareness**
p. 50 Segmenting Phonemes

**Focus On:**
**Writer's Center** p. 51
**ABC Center** p. 51

**Read Aloud**
*Concept Big Book 4: The Earth and Sky/*
*La Tierra y el cielo* p. 52
**Learn About Letters and Sounds:**
Review *Qq, Ww, Zz* p. 52

**I'm Thinking of a Number (Clues)** p. 53

**Completing Tasks** p. 53

**Art:**
**Oral Language and Academic Vocabulary**
p. 54 Our Earth and Sky
**Explore and Express**
p. 54 Earth/Sky Collage

**Focus On:**
**Construction Center** p. 55
**Purposeful Play** p. 55

**Read Aloud** p. 55
**Writing** p. 55
**Home Connection** p. 55

# Week 1

**My World**

# Learning Centers

## Math and Science Center

### Exploring Earth
Children feel, experiment with, and describe the properties of natural materials. See p. 31.

### Make a Landform
Children use natural materials to make landform models and label them in drawings or photos. See p. 37.

### How Many Eggs?
Children fill egg cartons with sand and count the 10 sand compartments. See p. 49.

### Count Sky Objects
Children draw sky objects (such as clouds, stars, and airplanes) in a picture. They count the objects and write the number on the picture.

## ABC Center

### Letter Concentration
Children use Alphabet/Letter Tiles to identify upper and lower case letters and sounds and match them. See p. 33.

### Matching Letters
Children discuss how upper and lower case forms of this week's letters are written. Then they form the letters out of yarn and draw an item that begins with the letter sound. See p. 51.

### Classroom Letters
Give partners sticky notes. Ask them to search the classroom to find letters they learned this week. Have them put sticky notes under letters they find.

## Creativity Center

### River and Ocean Water
Children paint a river and beach scene. They mix colors and discuss the tint and shade of the paints they use to depict the water in different locations. See p. 33.

### Wiggle Worms
Children use paper circles to create worms. They describe where real worms live and the properties of natural materials around them. See p. 39.

### My Home
Children draw a picture of the building in which they live. Pictures should include depictions of the earth and sky around the building.

## Library and Listening Center

**Browsing Nature Books**

Children find a favorite natural setting in a book and draw it. They describe its features. See p. 27.

**Nature Songs**

Children sing songs related to counting and the earth and sky. They explain which items in the songs are found in the sky or on the earth. See p. 45.

**Real and Make-Believe Settings**

Children browse through books with forest settings, such as "Hansel and Gretel" and "Little Red Riding Hood." Children draw the characters in the forest setting, including details such as leaves and tree trunks. Children then tell what parts of the picture could be real and what parts cannot.

## Construction Center

**Neighborhood Model**

Children pair up and use blocks and small toys to make a model of their neighborhood. They describe buildings and other features in the neighborhood. See p. 43.

**Build a Mountain Scene**

Children work in pairs and use blocks, art supplies, and natural materials to make a model of a mountain. They discuss how they will work together and describe their finished mountain. See p. 55.

**Make a Tiny Beach**

Children use sand in tubs or trays, small toys (such as people and boats), and natural materials (such as shells and rocks) to build a model of a beach. They describe activities people can do at the beach.

**Friendly Skies**

Children use blocks and toys, such as airplanes and helicopters, to show things in flight. They discuss what natural and human-made objects they see in the sky.

## Writer's Center

**Wally Worm's Adventure**

Children make up and write a story about Wally Worm. They draw Wally in the story setting and describe what he's doing. See p. 39.

**Nature Scrapbook**

Children clip nature pictures from magazines and attach them and natural objects to scrapbook pages. They dictate where the place is and where the objects may be found. See p. 51.

**Beach Diagram**

Children draw beach scenes and label the sun, sky, water, and sand. Then they describe their drawing to a partner.

## Pretend and Learn Center

**A Day at the Beach**

Children use natural materials to pretend they are playing on a beach. They describe the scene and their activities. See p. 27.

**Retell and Act Out Stories**

Children use the flannel board patterns to retell "The Sun and the Moon" and make stick or sock puppets to retell "Henny-Penny." See p. 45.

**Earth Scenes Pantomime**

Children refer to picture cards of different natural settings, such as a beach, mountain, desert, or forest. They take turns showing an activity they would do in one of the places. A partner guesses the activity and setting.

# DAY 1

**Focus Question**

## What can I learn about the earth and the sky?
## ¿Qué puedo aprender sobre la Tierra y el cielo?

 **Learning Goals**

**Social and Emotional Development**
• Child maintains concentration/attention skills until a task is complete.

**Language and Communication**
• Child uses newly learned vocabulary daily in multiple contexts.

## Vocabulary

| | | | |
|---|---|---|---|
| beach | playa | clouds | nubes |
| ocean | océano | sand | arena |
| starfish | estrella marina | sunny | soleado |

## Differentiated Instruction

 **Extra Support**

**Phonological Awareness**
**If...**children have difficulty segmenting a word by onset and rime, **then...**focus on segmenting just the first sound (onset). Also focus on words that begin with continuous sounds, which are easier to segment, such as words beginning with the /f/, /l/, /m/, /n/, /r/, /s/, /v/, or /z/ sounds.

⭐ **Enrichment**

**Phonological Awareness**
Challenge children to segment the words *sun* and *can* from the *Rhymes and Chants Flip Chart* sound by sound.

## Accommodations for 3's

**Phonological Awareness**
**If...**children have difficulty segmenting a word, **then...**show three picture cards and the Letter Tiles for the initial letters of those items' names. Have children point to and say the letter for the beginning sound of each pictured item.

# Let's Start the Day

▶ **Opening Routines and Transition Tips**
For **Opening Routines** and **Transition Tips** turn to pages 178–181 and visit DLMExpressOnline.com for more ideas.

📖 Read **"The Wind and the Sun"/**"El viento y el sol" from the *Teacher's Treasure Book*, page 185, for your morning Read Aloud.

## Language Time

 large group 15 minutes

👤👤👤 **Social and Emotional Development** Provide three-step directions for children to follow, such as "Put your toys away, find your place on the mat, and sit quietly." Ask children to tell how well they followed directions as a group.

## Oral Language and Vocabulary

✓ **Can children use a large vocabulary and new words to tell about a place?**

**Places on Earth** Tell children that Earth has many different places. One kind of place is a beach. Ask: *Have you ever been to a beach? If so, what did you see? Was it sunny? Were there clouds?* ¿Han ido a la playa alguna vez? ¿Qué vieron allí? ¿Era un día soleado? ¿Había nubes? Encourage children to use many different descriptive words.

• Display *Oral Language Development Card 61.* Name the place and some of the things found there, including the ocean, sand, and starfish. Follow the suggestions on the back of the card.

*Oral Language Development Card 61*

## Phonological Awareness

✓ **Can children segment a word by onset and rime?**

**Segmenting Phonemes** Display *Rhymes and Chants Flip Chart,* page 29. Explain that words are made of sounds. You can break a word into its separate sounds. For example, *fun* is made up of the first sound /f/ and the remaining sounds -*un.* Say: **Listen. /f/ -un, fun.** Escuchen. /f/ -un, fun. Read "Sun, Earth, Moon." Guide children to segment *sun* and *moon* by stating the onset and then the rest of the word.

**ELL** Use the *Rhymes and Chants Flip Chart* to revisit the word *round.* Hold a ball in your hand. Say: **This ball is round.** Let children hold the ball and turn it in their hands as you repeat **This ball is round.** Then use a block to repeat the activity, saying **This block is not round.**

*Rhymes and Chants Flip Chart, page 29/ page 61*

# Center Time

▶ **Center Rotation** Center Time includes teacher-guided activities and independent activities. Refer to the **Learning Centers** on pages 24–25 for activities in additional centers.

small group  60–90 minutes

## Library and Listening Center

| | Center Tip |
|---|---|
| ✓ Track the use of new nature words as children share drawings of a natural setting.<br><br>**Materials** nature books, paper, crayons<br><br>**Browsing Nature Books** Remind children that there are different kinds of places on Earth. Have them browse through nature books and choose a favorite place. Help them name and describe the place.<br><br>● Have children draw their favorite place and share their drawings.<br><br>● Ask: *What can you find in this place? ¿Qué pueden ver en este lugar?* | **If...**children have difficulty recalling a nature word or a new vocabulary word, **then...**give them a clue by offering the first sound of the word. |

## Pretend and Learn Center

| | Center Tip |
|---|---|
| ✓ Look for examples of children continuing with planned activities until they are completed.<br><br>**Materials** sand, small rocks, shells buckets, tubs of water, beach toys (such as plastic shovels), sunglasses<br><br>**A Day at the Beach** Tell children that they will explore earth materials as they play "A Day at the Beach."<br><br>● Place containers of sand, small rocks, shells, water, and beach toys at the center. Have children use the materials to pretend they are at the beach. For example, children might build a sandcastle.<br><br>● As children role play, ask questions to spark discussion: *What is the weather like on your beach today? Is it sunny? What will you do at the beach today? What does this shell feel like? ¿Cómo está el tiempo hoy? ¿Es un día soleado? ¿Qué harán hoy en la playa?* | **If...**children have difficulty using the materials, **then...**model using the tools to dig, or add a little water to the sand to make it easier to work with. |

 **Learning Goals**

**Social and Emotional Development**
• Child maintains concentration/attention skills until a task is complete.

**Language and Communication**
• Child uses newly learned vocabulary daily in multiple contexts.

## Differentiated Instruction

 **Extra Support**
**Pretend and Learn Center**
**If...**children have difficulty making or following a plan for their play, **then...**offer them a concrete suggestion with clear steps, such as *You can build a sandcastle. First, make a pile of sand.* *Pueden construir un castillo de arena. Primero, hagan una montaña de arena.*

 **Enrichment**
**Library and Listening Center**
Challenge children to label items in their picture, writing the letters they know.

 **Special Needs**
**Cognitive Challenges**
**If...**children have difficulty naming items in the nature scene, **then...**point to items, name them, and have children repeat with you before you ask: *What is this called? ¿Qué es esto?*

## What can I learn about the earth and the sky? ¿Qué puedo aprender sobre la Tierra y el cielo?

### Learning Goals

**Emergent Literacy: Reading**
- Child names most upper- and lowercase letters of the alphabet.
- Child identifies the letter that stands for a given sound.
- Child describes, relates to, and uses details and information from books read aloud.

**Science**
- Child investigates and describes energy sources (light, heat, electricity).
- Child observes, identifies, explores, describes, and compares earth materials (such as rocks, soil, sand, water) and their uses.
- Child observes, identifies, compares, and discusses objects in the sky (such as clouds, sun, moon, stars).

### Vocabulary

| | | | |
|---|---|---|---|
| earth | Tierra | energy | energía |
| moon | Luna | rock | rocas |
| sand | arena | sky | cielo |
| soil | tierra | | |

### Differentiated Instruction

#### ✋ Extra Support

**Learn About Letters and Sounds**
**If...**children have difficulty writing the letter *Qq*, **then...**have them trace circles and add lines, or make the letter out of clay.

#### ⭐ Enrichment

**Learn About Letters and Sounds**
Challenge children to find words that begin with *Qq* in classroom alphabet books, and then make the words using the Alphabet/Letter Tiles. Read the words children make aloud to the class.

## Literacy Time

large group  15 minutes

### 📖 Read Aloud

✓ **Can children use information learned from the book to describe items found on the earth and in the sky?**

**Build Background** Tell children that you will read a book about things found on the earth and in the sky. Ask: **What do you see when you look up at the sky?** *¿Qué ven cuando miran al cielo?*

**Listen for Enjoyment** Display *Concept Big Book 4: The Earth and Sky*, and read the title.

- Conduct a picture walk through the book. Ask: **Where can you find water? Rocks? Sand? Soil? The sun? When have you seen them?** *¿Dónde pueden encontrar agua? ¿Y piedras? ¿Y arena? ¿Y tierra? ¿Y el sol? ¿Dónde han visto estas cosas?*

- Name and describe the items pictured as you read pages 5–9 aloud.

**Respond to the Book** Have children name the items you pointed out. Ask: **What did the photos show us about the things found on the earth and in the sky? How are they the same? How are they different?** *¿Qué nos muestran las fotos acerca de las cosas que se encuentran en la Tierra y en el cielo? ¿En qué se parecen? ¿En qué se diferencian?*

💡 TIP Encourage children to use photo details to describe and compare items found on the earth and in the sky.

ELL Point to specific places in the photos as you say the names and place details in the book. Encourage children to point to the photos and name things they know. For additional suggestions on how to meet the needs of children at the Beginning, Intermediate, Advanced, and Advanced-High levels of English proficiency, see pages 184–187.

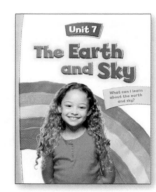

*The Earth and Sky*
*La Tierra y el cielo*

### Learn About Letters and Sounds

✓ **Can children identify the /kw/ sound?**

**Learn About the Letter *Qq*** Sing the "ABC Song" with children as you page through the *ABC Big Book*, stopping when you get to *Qq* on page 36. Point to the "queen" photo on page 37. Explain that the letter *Qq* makes the /kw/ sound. Have children stand and chant "/kw/ /kw/ /kw/, the queen sits quickly and quietly," and then sit quickly and quietly.

- Model how to write upper case *Q* on chart paper or an interactive whiteboard. Have children trace *Q* in the air with their fingers, saying the sound each time they trace the letter.

- Repeat for lower case *q*.

*ABC Big Book, page 36*
*Superlibro abecé*

# Math Time

## Observe and Investigate

☑ **Can children count to 10?**

**I'm Thinking of a Number (Length)** Make a Connecting Cube step between 1 and 10, and hide it. Show a complete Connecting Cube stairs you made from 1 to 10. Ask: **How many steps are there?** *¿Cuántos escalones hay?* Chorally count each step with children.

● Tell children a secret step is hidden that is the same length as one of the steps in the stairs, and ask them to guess its number. For incorrect guesses, say: **The secret step is more (or less) than your guess.** *El escalón escondido tiene más (o menos) cubos que el que ustedes dijeron.*

● When a child guesses the secret number, excitedly reveal the step and count its cubes with children. Show how it matches the corresponding step in the complete set. Allow children to feel the lengths of the steps.

● Ask children to tell why they made their guess. Encourage answers such as "Three was too little and nine was too much so I guessed in between."

**ELL** Focus on *more* and *less*. Show 10 Connecting Cube stairs. Count the steps Then show 6 Connecting Cube stairs. Count the steps. Give the 10 stairs to a child. Say: **You have more steps than I do. Who has more?** Continue with *less*.

### Building Blocks

**Online Math Activity**

Introduce Off the Tree: Add Apples, where children add two dot amounts to find the sum and move forward that many. Each child should complete the activity this week.

# 👬 Social and Emotional Development

## Making Good Choices

☑ **Can children sustain attention and contribute ideas during discussion?**

**Completing Tasks** Discuss children's recent art projects. Ask children what they did to start and finish the projects. After they finished, did they put their materials away? Display the *Making Good Choices Flip Chart,* page 29.

● Ask: **What do the girls need to do next? How can they help each other?** *¿Qué deben hacer las niñas ahora? ¿Cómo pueden ayudarse unas a otras?*

● Discuss the importance of finishing projects. Explain that it is fine to take breaks from projects day to day, but any time children use art or other materials they should clean up and put materials away when they are finished using the materials. Invite children to give examples of when they have done and should do this.

*Making Good Choices Flip Chart, page 29*

---

## Learning Goals

**Social and Emotional Development**
● Child shows eagerness, curiosity, and confidence while learning new concepts and trying new things.

**Mathematics**
● Child recites number words in sequence from one to thirty.
● Child counts 1–10 concrete objects correctly.

## Vocabulary

| count | contar | length | largo |
|-------|--------|--------|-------|
| less | menos | more | más |
| number | número | | |

## Differentiated Instruction

### ✋ Extra Support
**Observe and Investigate**
**If...**children struggle comparing lengths, **then...** hold each object side by side for them to visually compare. Then break apart the stairs into individual steps. Place each step in a cup. Ask: **Which cup has more?** *¿Qué vaso tiene más?*

### 💫⭐ Enrichment
**Observe and Investigate**
Challenge children to create and compare Connecting Cube stairs of up to 30 steps.

### 💜 Special Needs
**Vision Loss**
Allow children to feel the Connecting Cubes stairs you assembled before the activity begins. Help them use their fingers to count the grooves in order to know where cubes begin and end.

**Focus Question**

## What can I learn about the earth and the sky?
## ¿Qué puedo aprender sobre la Tierra y el cielo?

 **Learning Goals**

**Social and Emotional Development**
• Child maintains concentration/attention skills until a task is complete.

**Language and Communication**
• Child names and describes actual or pictured people, places, things, actions, attributes, and events.

**Science**
• Child observes, identifies, explores, describes, and compares earth materials (such as rocks, soil, sand, water) and their uses.
• Child follows basic health and safety rules.

### Vocabulary

| river | río | rough | áspero |
|-------|-------|--------|--------|
| sand | arena | smooth | liso |
| soil | tierra | water | agua |

## Differentiated Instruction

 **Extra Support**
*Observe and Investigate*
**If...**children have difficulty focusing on the characteristics of the natural object,
**then...**suggest specific things for them to look at or descriptive words to use: *Look at the different colors on the rock. Feel the rock. Is it smooth? Miren los diferentes colores de la piedra. Toquen la piedra. ¿Es lisa?*

 **Enrichment**
*Observe and Investigate*
Challenge children to use robust vocabulary on the walk: *nature, observe, compare.*

# Science Time

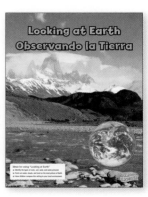
large group · 20 minutes

**Personal Safety Skills** Model how to hold the Hand Lens properly during the science activity.

## Oral Language and Academic Vocabulary

✓ **Can children identify and compare earth materials and their uses?**

**What's Outside?** Display *Math and Science Flip Chart* page 53. Say: *This is a river. A river is a body of water on Earth. There is land around the river. This is the riverbank. Éste es un río. Los ríos los masas de agua de la Tierra. Hay arena a los costados del río. Ésa es la costa o ribera del río.* Explain that just as an ocean has a beach, a river has a riverbank.

● Say: *The water in this river flows near the mountains. I see large rocks in the river. I also see smaller rocks. El agua de este río corre a través de las montañas. Veo grandes rocas en el río. También veo piedras más pequeñas.* Discuss other things in the picture, such as where the trees are growing.

● Ask: *What do we use water for? What can we build with rocks? Do we use them in the same way or for the same things? ¿Para qué usamos el agua? ¿Qué podemos construir con las rocas? ¿Usamos el agua y las rocas de la misma manera o para hacer lo mismo?* Encourage children to consider that they drink water and use it for washing.

## Observe and Investigate

✓ **Can children describe characteristics of rocks, sand, water, and soil?**

**Nature Walk** Take children on a nature walk. Tell them that you will look for examples of rocks, sand, water, and soil around the playground.

● Hold up a Hand Lens. Remind children that the Hand Lens enables you to look closely at rocks and other items you see. Model how to use the lens. Make comments as you observe, such as: *I see different colors on this smooth rock. I see rocks being used to make a wall around flowers. Veo diferentes colores en esta piedra lisa. Vi que las rocas se usan para hacer canteros alrededor de las flores.*

● Let children take turns using the lens as you find natural items. Ask: *What details can you see through the lens? How does this feel—rough or smooth? ¿Qué detalles pueden ver a través de la lupa? ¿Cómo se siente esto: áspero o liso?*

**TIP** Tell children that they will have more opportunities to explore rocks, sand, soil, and water at the Math and Science Center.

**ELL** To help children use descriptive words, place assorted soft, rough, heavy, and smooth objects on a table. Model using words to describe and compare the objects: *The cotton ball is soft. Is the rock soft?* Hold up two objects and prompt a child to use a comparison.

*Math and Science Flip Chart, page 53*

Looking at Earth
Observando la Tierra

# Center Time

▶ **Center Rotation** Center Time includes teacher-guided activities and independent activities. Refer to the **Learning Centers** on pages 24–25 for activities in additional centers.

  small group · 30 minutes

## Math and Science Center

☑ **Look for examples of descriptive words children use to tell about rocks, sand, water, and soil.**

**Materials** sand, rocks, water, soil, cups, paper, crayons, sieve, Hand Lenses, Primary Balance Scale

**Exploring Earth** Explain that Earth is made of different materials.

- Place bowls filled with sand, small rocks, water, and soil on the table. Add the tools. Allow children to explore and talk about what each material feels like, how heavy it is, whether it fits through the sieve, what it can be balanced with, and what it is used for.

- Help children fold a sheet of paper into four squares. Have them draw and label each material in one of the squares. Have them draw themselves using the sieve or balance in their pictures.

### Center Tip

**If...**children have difficulty describing the materials, **then...** offer language such as *soft, rough, smooth, or heavy.*

## Purposeful Play

☑ **Observe children completing a task with a classmate.**

Children choose an open center for free playtime. Encourage children to play going on a nature walk with a friend. Prompt children to continue their planned activity until it is finished.

## Let's Say Good-Bye

 large group · 15 minutes

 **Read Aloud** Revisit "The Wind and the Sun"/"El viento y el sol" for your afternoon Read Aloud. Remind children to listen for names of things that can be found on the earth or in the sky.

 **Home Connection** Refer to the Home Connection activities listed in the Materials and Resources chart on page 21. Remind children to tell their families what they learned about places and things found on Earth. Sing the "Good-bye Song"/"Hora de ir a casa" as children prepare to leave.

---

 **Learning Goals**

**Social and Emotional Development**
- Child maintains concentration/attention skills until a task is complete.

**Language and Communication**
- Child names and describes actual or pictured people, places, things, actions, attributes, and events.

**Science**
- Child uses basic measuring tools to learn about objects.
- Child observes, identifies, explores, describes, and compares earth materials (such as rocks, soil, sand, water) and their uses.

### Writing

Recap the day. Have children name things found on the earth that they observed or learned about. Ask: **What did you learn about the earth? About earth materials?** *¿Qué aprendieron sobre la Tierra? ¿Y sobre los materiales de la Tierra?* Record their answers. Read them back as you track the print. Emphasize that you read left to right and top to bottom.

# DAY 2

## Focus Question

**What can I learn about the earth and the sky?**

**¿Qué puedo aprender sobre la Tierra y el cielo?**

▶ **Opening Routines and Transition Tips**
For **Opening Routines** and **Transition Tips** turn to pages 178–181 and visit
DLMExpressOnline.com for more ideas.

 Read **"Summer at the Beach"/**"Verano en la playa" from the
*Teacher's Treasure Book,* page 221, for your morning Read Aloud.

---

 **Learning Goals**

### Social and Emotional Development
• Child maintains concentration/attention skills until a task is complete.

### Language and Communication
• Child names and describes actual or pictured people, places, things, actions, attributes, and events.

### Science
• Child observes, identifies, explores, describes, and compares earth materials (such as rocks, soil, sand, water) and their uses.

## Vocabulary

| Earth | Tierra | energy | energía |
|-------|--------|--------|---------|
| moon | Luna | rock | roca |
| sand | arena | sky | cielo |
| soil | tierra | | |

---

## Differentiated Instruction

 **Extra Support**
**Oral Language and Vocabulary**
**If...**children have difficulty describing sand, rock, or water, **then...**display examples that they can touch and observe.

**Enrichment**
**Oral Language and Vocabulary**
Expand children's vocabularies by adding words such as *materials, sunlight,* or *waves.*

 **Special Needs**
**Hearing Impairment**
Have hearing-impaired children sit closest to the Dog Puppets. Instruct them to watch your lips as the puppets talk. If children sign, ask them to sign each word as the group segments it.

---

# Language Time

 large group / 15 minutes

**Social and Emotional Development** Acknowledge children's efforts to follow directions and complete tasks by specifically calling out what you see them attempting or doing well.

## Oral Language and Vocabulary

✓ **Can children use descriptive words to tell about a place?**

**Place Names and Characteristics** Display page 7 of *Concept Big Book 4: The Earth and Sky.* Talk about things found in natural places. Focus on places pictured. Ask: **What do you see in the river? Where else do you see water?** *¿Qué vieron en el río? ¿En qué otro lugar vieron agua?*

● Have children describe in detail the characteristics of sand, water, and rocks. Ask: **What color is sand? What color are the rocks? What does sand feel like? How does sand feel different from soil? How does water feel?** *¿De qué color es la arena? ¿Cómo se siente la arena? ¿En qué se diferencian cómo se siente al tocar la arena y al tocar la tierra?*

● Encourage children to describe other places pictured and what earth materials are found there, inside or out. For each earth material children mention, ask: **What do people use that for?** *¿Para qué se usa?*

**ELL** Place assorted soft, rough, heavy, and smooth objects on the table. Model describing and comparing the objects: **The sandpaper is rough. Is the rock rough?** Hold up two objects and prompt a child to give a descriptive word.

## Phonological Awareness

✓ **Can children segment words by onset and rime?**

**Segmenting Phonemes** Display the Dog Puppets. Tell children that one puppet will say a word. The other will break apart the word into its smaller sounds. If the second dog correctly segments the word, the children should clap. If the dog cannot correctly segment the word, the children should help by finishing the word. Have the puppet correctly segment one or two words, but require the children to segment the rest: *sun, rock, moon, sand (/s/ -un; /r/ -ock; /m/ -oon; /s/ -and).*

# Center Time

**▶ Center Rotation** Center Time includes teacher-guided activities and independent activities. Refer to the **Learning Centers** on pages 24–25 for activities in additional centers.

small group  60–90 minutes

## ABC Center

### Center Tip

  Track the letter sounds children are beginning to master.

**Materials** Alphabet/Letter Tiles

**Letter Concentration** Place upper case and lower case tiles for *Qq* and two other letters previously learned facedown on a table.

- Have children turn over two tiles, and name the letters and sounds. Ask: *What is the sound of each letter? Do these letters match? ¿Cuál es el sonido de cada letra? ¿Son iguales estas letras?*

- If the letters match, children keep the tiles. If they do not match, children turn them over and try again.

- Add the tiles for *Ww* and *Zz* as they are introduced this week. Have children play concentration with the new letters.

**If...**children have difficulty remembering the sound for one of the week's letters, **then...**tell them to listen for the first sound as you say a word beginning with that letter.

## Creativity Center

### Center Tip

  Listen for words children use to compare rivers and oceans.

**Materials** paper plates, paint, paintbrushes, cups of water, plastic cups for mixing, smocks, pictures of rivers and ocean beaches

**River and Ocean Water** Tell children that they will make paintings of two types of water found on Earth: rivers and oceans.

- Ask: *What colors do you see in the river water? How does the sky look at the beach? What color is sand? Rock? ¿Qué colores ven en el agua del río? ¿Cómo se ve el cielo en la playa? ¿De qué color es la arena? ¿Y las rocas?*

- Have children mix white paint with different colors, then black paint with different colors. Ask: *How do the colors change? ¿Se ponen más claros u oscuros los colores?*

- Have children use the mixed paints to paint a river on one paper plate and an ocean beach scene on the other. Encourage them to paint clouds in the scenes. Have children label their pictures.

**If...**children have difficulty deciding which colors to mix, **then...**give them hints. Ask: *Is this water almost green? What colors can you mix to paint water that looks both blue and green? ¿Es el agua casi verde? ¿Qué colores pueden mezclar para pintar el agua y que se vea azul y verde?*

### Learning Goals

**Emergent Literacy: Reading**
- Child names most upper- and lowercase letters of the alphabet.
- Child identifies the letter that stands for a given sound.

**Science**
- Child observes, identifies, compares, and discusses objects in the sky (such as clouds, sun, moon, stars).

### Differentiated Instruction

**✋ Extra Support**
**ABC Center**
**If...**children have difficulty remembering the sound of a letter, **then...**have them trace or write the letter in sand as they say the sound.

**★ Enrichment**
**ABC Center**
Challenge children to find words that begin with this week's letters in classroom books and make the words using Alphabet/Letter Tiles or magnetic letters. Read aloud the words formed.

**Accommodations for 3's**
**ABC Center**
**If...**children have difficulty finding and identifying matching letters from a 6-tile set, **then...**reduce the number of tiles used. State the name of the letter and its sound as children turn over each tile. Have them repeat.

## Focus Question
**What can I learn about the earth and the sky?**
**¿Qué puedo aprender sobre la Tierra y el cielo?**

## Learning Goals

**Emergent Literacy: Reading**
• Child names most upper- and lowercase letters of the alphabet.
• Child identifies the letter that stands for a given sound.
• Child describes, relates to, and uses details and information from books read aloud.

**Science**
• Child investigates and describes energy sources (light, heat, electricity).
• Child observes, identifies, compares, and discusses objects in the sky (such as clouds, sun, moon, stars).
• Child observes, identifies, explores, describes, and compares earth materials (such as rocks, soil, sand, water) and their uses.

### Vocabulary

| Earth | Tierra | energy | energía |
|-------|--------|--------|---------|
| moon  | Luna   | rock   | roca    |
| sand  | arena  | sky    | cielo   |
| soil  | tierra |        |         |

## Differentiated Instruction

### Extra Support
**Learn About Letters and Sounds**
**If...**children have difficulty writing the letter *Ww*, **then...**help them form the letter using small sticks and then trace it with their fingers as they say "/w/ /w/ wiggle worms."

### Enrichment
**Learn About Letters and Sounds**
Teach children how to read and write the word *will*. Write the phrase **I will** _____ for children to copy and complete on their own papers. Children can illustrate their sentences.

---

## Literacy Time

large group · 15 minutes

### Read Aloud

☑ **Can children use information learned from the book to describe and compare objects found on the earth and in the sky?**

**Build Background** Tell children that you will read about things found on the earth and in the sky.

● Ask: ***What can you find on the earth outside of our school? Are there things you play with outdoors? What do we see when we look at the sky?*** *¿Qué podrían encontrar en la tierra que rodea nuestra escuela? ¿Hay cosas con las que juegan cuando están al aire libre? ¿Qué vemos cuando miramos al cielo?*

**Listen for Understanding** Display *Concept Big Book 4: The Earth and Sky*.

● Read pages 6–9. Point to and read the labels on the photographs after reading the main text. Encourage children to ask you to reread parts.

● Ask: ***What do you learn about the earth from the book? The sky?*** *¿Qué aprendieron sobre la Tierra en este libro? ¿Y sobre el cielo?*

**Respond to the Book** Have children name the items found on the earth and in the sky. Ask: ***How are the things in the sky different during the day and at night? What gives us heat in the day? What gives us light at night?*** *¿En qué se diferencian las cosas en el cielo de día y de noche? ¿Qué nos da calor de día? ¿Qué nos alumbra de noche?*

**TIP** Help children see how electricity makes the indoors bright by turning the classroom lights on and off.

**ELL** As you read, point to specific places in the photos as you say the names and place details. Ask follow-up questions with simple answers, such as: ***Is the moon in the night sky? Is this sand or rock? Does the sun give light?***

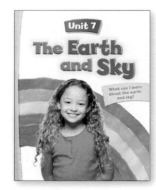

*The Earth and Sky*
*La Tierra y el cielo*

### Learn About Letters and Sounds

☑ **Can children identify the /w/ sound?**

**Learn About the Letter *Ww*** Sing the "ABC Song" with children as you page through the *ABC Big Book,* stopping when you get to the letter *Ww* on page 48. Point to the "worm" photo on page 49. Tell children that *worm* begins with the /w/ sound. Have them chant "/w/ /w/ /w/ wiggle worms" as they pretend to wiggle like worms.

● Model how to write uppercase *W*. Have children trace *W* in the air with their fingers, saying /w/ each time they trace the letter.

● Repeat for lowercase *w*. Point out the similarities in upper- and lowercase *Ww*.

*ABC Big Book, page 48*
*Superlibro abecé*

large group 15 minutes

# Math Time

## Observe and Investigate

**Can children count to 10 and beyond?**

**I'm Thinking of a Number (Ruler)** Chorally count to 30 with children. Then chorally count to 12 as you show a ruler. Review that it measures how long something is. Tell children that you are thinking of a secret number for a length, and ask them to guess what it is.

- When a child guesses correctly, say yes and show the length on the ruler, moving your hand from 0 to the number. Tell whether an incorrect guess is longer or shorter than the secret length.
- As children become familiar with the activity, ask them why or how they made their guesses. For example, a child might say, "I knew four was more than the secret number and two was less than it, so I guessed three."
- As you introduce Dinosaur Shop 3: Add Dinosaurs, ask children to show you how to open the program. After you model navigating it, have a volunteer show the group what you did and how.

**Building Blocks**

**Online Math Activity**

Introduce Dinosaur Shop 3: Add Dinosaurs (1–10), in which a child hears two number orders and has to click the sum that tells how many will be in a customer's box. Each child should complete the activity this week.

large group 15 minutes

# Social and Emotional Development

## Making Good Choices

**Do children understand the importance of completing tasks?**

**Completing Tasks** Revisit *Making Good Choices Flip Chart* page 29.

- Display a Dog Puppet. Say: ***Who would like to tell the puppet what the girls need to do to finish their project? Who would like to tell the puppet what the girls should do after they finish?*** *¿Quién puede explicarle al perrito qué deben hacer las niñas para terminar su proyecto? ¿Quién quiere decirle al perrito que deberían hacer las niñas después de terminar?*
- Provide each child a turn to tell the puppet about the girls properly completing their work and cleaning up. Ask children why they should finish projects started during Center Time before moving on to something new.

**ELL** Provide a sentence frame to help during the conversation with the Dog Puppet: **The girls must ________ because ________.** Model using the frame. Have children repeat, then apply their own words. Some children may feel more comfortable just repeating the completed frame you provide.

*Making Good Choices Flip Chart, page 29*

### Learning Goals

**Social and Emotional Development**

- Child maintains concentration/attention skills until a task is complete.

**Mathematics**

- Child recites number words in sequence from one to thirty.

**Technology Applications**

- Child opens and correctly uses age-appropriate software programs.

### Vocabulary

| | | | |
|---|---|---|---|
| count | contar | length | largo |
| longer | más largo | measure | medir |
| number | número | ruler | regla |
| shorter | más corto | | |

### Differentiated Instruction

**Extra Support**

**Observe and Investigate**

**If...**children struggle with the instructional terms *longer* and *shorter*, **then...**use gestures to distinguish them. Move your hands far apart as you pronounce *longer* and move your hands close together as you say *shorter.*

**Enrichment**

**Observe and Investigate**

Have children measure the lengths of classroom objects using a stick ruler or an earth material, such as a twig.

Focus Question
**What can I learn about the earth and the sky?**
**¿Qué puedo aprender sobre la Tierra y el cielo?**

## Learning Goals

**Social and Emotional Development**
• Child shows eagerness, curiosity, and confidence while learning new concepts and trying new things.

**Language and Communication**
• Child follows two- and three-step oral directions.

**Mathematics**
• Child demonstrates that, when counting, the last number indicates how many objects were counted.

### Vocabulary

| | | | |
|---|---|---|---|
| back | hacia atrás | count | contar |
| forward | hacia delante | number | número |
| row | fila | | |

## Differentiated Instruction

 **Extra Support**

Math Time

**If...**children have difficulty counting without seeing the numbers, **then...**chorally count out loud as you point to the facedown cards. Stop on the answer. Ask: *What number is this? ¿Qué número es éste?*

 **Enrichment**

Math Time

Challenge children to count to 20 or higher by counting more than one row on the flip chart.

# Math Time

 large group 20 minutes

**Language and Communication Skills** State two- and three-step oral directions for children to follow during the lesson. Have them repeat the sequence as and after they complete each step of the directions.

 **Can children count to 10?**

**Count on It** Begin a math warm-up by chorally chanting numbers 1 to 30 with children. Then have children count forward and back to 10.

● Display *Math and Science Flip Chart* page 54, "Count to 10". Discuss the number of earth materials in each row. Have children chorally count the items in each row.

● Select a rock in the first row. Say: ***Let's count to rock number 4.*** *Vamos a contar hasta que lleguemos a la roca número 4.* Count with children. Ask: ***Which rock is 2 more than 4? Let's count together.*** *¿Qué roca está a 2 espacios después de la número 4? Vamos a contar juntos.* Continue with other numbers and the other rows.

 **Can children count forward and back?**

**X-Ray Vision 2** Show Counting Cards from 1–10 (*Teacher's Treasure Book,* pages 506–507) in order, and count them with children. Then place the cards facedown in order. Tell children that this is a new way to play X-Ray Vision, keeping cards face up after they are guessed.

● Point to any card. Say: ***Use your X-ray vision to figure out which card it is.*** *Usen su visión de rayos X para adivinar qué tarjeta es.* Review counting from 1 if needed. Flip the card to show whether children are correct and, if so, keep the card face up, reviewing that you are doing so on purpose.

● Point to the card that is two cards from the card facing up. Ask children to use their X-ray vision again to determine which card it is and how they figured it out. Discuss how to count forward from the card facing up.

● Now with both cards facing up, repeat with another card that is two away. Repeat with several cards, sometimes choosing one or three from the nearest card facing up.

TIP Remind children that the cards are in the same order as the objects on the *Math and Science Flip Chart.*

ELL Focus on the meaning of *face* as the side of an object or card that has an image. Use picture cards with blank backs to reinforce this. Place cards randomly face up or down. Have children pick cards with the faces showing. Have them draw faces on one side of an index card and repeat the game with those.

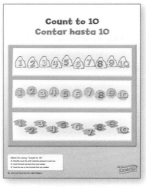

*Math and Science Flip Chart, page 54*

# Center Time

▶ **Center Rotation** Center Time includes teacher-guided activities and independent activities. Refer to the **Learning Centers** on pages 24–25 for activities in additional centers.

   small group   30 minutes

## Math and Science Center

✓ **Observe children as they make landforms with earth materials.**

**Materials** large sheets of construction paper, sand, dirt, twigs, leaves, pebbles, crayons, shells, landform pictures

**Make a Landform** Display pictures of landforms such as mountains, forests, or dunes. Discuss what might be found in each natural setting. Ask, for example: *What do you see on the mountain? ¿Qué podrían encontrar en una montaña?*

- Have children use the natural materials to create temporary landforms on large sheets of paper. Prompt them to add details. Ask: *Will there be rocks on your mountain? What else? ¿Pondrán piedras en su montañas? ¿Y qué más?*

- Children can draw pictures of their completed landforms, or take photos to paste on a sheet of paper and label. Then they should take apart their landforms so others can use the materials.

### Center Tip

**If**...children need help selecting materials for their landforms, **then**...have them refer to the landform pictures. Ask questions about picture details, for example: *What can we use to make trees on our mountainside? ¿Qué podemos usar para hacer árboles en la ladera de nuestra montaña?*

## Learning Goals

**Social and Emotional Development**
- Child maintains concentration/attention skills until a task is complete.

**Language and Communication**
- Child names and describes actual or pictured people, places, things, actions, attributes, and events.

**Science**
- Child observes, identifies, explores, describes, and compares earth materials (such as rocks, soil, sand, water) and their uses.
- Child observes, identifies, compares, and discusses objects in the sky (such as clouds, sun, moon, stars).

### Writing

Recap the day. Have children name objects on the earth and in the sky. Ask: *What did you learn about the sky today? ¿Qué aprendieron hoy sobre el cielo?* Ask them to draw a picture showing an example of something in the sky and label it.

## Purposeful Play

✓ **Observe children as they sustain attention until center tasks are completed.**

Children choose an open center for free playtime. Encourage children to work together on a project, such as in the Creativity Center. Encourage children to continue their planned activity until it is finished.

## Let's Say Good-Bye

 large group   15 minutes

 **Read Aloud** Revisit "Summer at the Beach"/"Verano en la playa" from the *Teacher's Treasure Book,* page 221, for your afternoon Read Aloud. Remind children to listen for things found on the beach.

 **Home Connection** Refer to the Home Connection activities listed on page 21. Remind children to tell families about objects in the sky. Sing the "Good-bye Song"/"Hora de ir a casa" as children prepare to leave.

# DAY 3

**Focus Question**

## What can I learn about the earth and the sky?
## ¿Qué puedo aprender sobre la Tierra y el cielo?

### Learning Goals

**Social and Emotional Development**
• Child maintains concentration/attention skills until a task is complete.

**Language and Communication**
• Child uses newly learned vocabulary daily in multiple contexts.

## Vocabulary

| | | | |
|---|---|---|---|
| autumn | otoño | branches | ramas |
| colors | colores | fall | otoño |
| leaves | hojas | pile | pila |
| trunk | tronco | | |

### Differentiated Instruction

 **Extra Support**
*Phonological Awareness*

**If...**children have difficulty segmenting the first or last sound in a word, **then...**focus on segmenting words that begin with continuous sounds as they will be easier to segment. Stretch the target sound of the word, as in *ssssand* or *sunnnn*.

**Enrichment**
*Phonological Awareness*

Challenge children to segment earth-related words such as *rock, road, sun,* and *sea*.

### Accommodations for 3's
*Phonological Awareness*

**If...**children have difficulty segmenting a word, **then...**show picture cards and Alphabet/Letter Tiles for the initial letters of the pictures' names. Have children point to and say the letter for the beginning sound of the picture card.

# Let's Start the Day

▶ **Opening Routines and Transition Tips**

For **Opening Routines** and **Transition Tips** turn to pages 178–181 and visit **DLMExpressOnline.com** for more ideas.

📖 Read **"Wally Worm's World"/***"El mundo del gusano Wally"* from the *Teacher's Treasure Book*, page 212, for your morning Read Aloud.

# Language Time

large group  15 minutes

👧👦 **Social and Emotional Development** Encourage children to complete assigned tasks and listen carefully to each step in multi-step directions.

## Oral Language and Vocabulary

✓ **Can children use a large speaking vocabulary to tell about a place?**

**Place Names and Characteristics** Remind children that Earth is made up of many different kinds of places. Share that places can change, such as during changes in seasons, when new plants and flowers can appear or disappear. Talk about places near children's school and homes, such as a playground or park. Ask: **What can you do on a playground? What can you find in a park?** *¿Qué pueden hacer en un patio de recreo? ¿Qué podrían encontrar en parque?*

● Display *Oral Language Development Card 62*. Name the place and some of the things found there. Follow the suggestions on the back of the card.

*Oral Language Development Card 62*

## Phonological Awareness

✓ **Can children segment words by the first or last sound?**

**Segmenting Phonemes** Revisit *Rhymes and Chants Flip Chart* page 29.

● Remind children that words are made up of smaller sounds. For example, the word *sand* starts with the /s/ sound and ends with the /d/ sound.

● Have children join in as you read "Sun, Earth, Moon." Add motions to help them anticipate the upcoming words, such as circling your arms for *round*.

● Then say several words from the poem, such as *sun, dark,* and *light*. Ask: **What is the first sound you hear in** sun? **What is the last sound you hear in** sun? *¿Cuál es el primer sonido que escuchan en* sun? *¿Cuál es el último sonido que escuchan en* sun? Model as needed by stretching or emphasizing the target sound.

**ELL** Revisit the words *peeking*, and *shining*. Use actions and objects to teach the words, such as peeking around your hands or shining a flashlight.

*Rhymes and Chants Flip Chart, page 29/ page 61*

# Center Time

▶ **Center Rotation** Center Time includes teacher-guided activities and independent activities. Refer to the **Learning Centers** on pages 24–25 for activities in additional centers.

small group | 60–90 minutes

## Writer's Center

 Monitor children's ability to create and tell a unique story using words or scribbles.

**Materials**  paper, crayons

**Wally Worm's Adventure**  Tell children that you want them to create a new adventure for Wally Worm.

● Have children draw Wally Worm in a setting of their choice. Ask: *Where will Wally go? What will he do there? ¿A dónde irá Wally? ¿Qué hará allí?*

● Have children write about Wally's adventure. Have them write their stories on their own using letters, words, symbols, or scribbles, and then dictate it to you. Record their story in your own print underneath theirs. Read back the story.

### Center Tip

**If**...children have difficulty thinking of an adventure, **then**...suggest a place Wally Worm could go, or ask: *What will Wally Worm do next? What will happen in this place? ¿Qué hará Wally después? ¿Qué sucederá en ese lugar?*

## Creativity Center

 Listen for words children use to describe the characteristics of sand, water, soil, and rock.

**Materials**  construction paper, circle pattern, tape, yarn, crayons; containers of sand, water, soil, rocks

**Wiggle Worms**  Tell children they will make pretend wiggle worms.

● Have children trace and cut out construction paper circles. Help them attach the circles using yarn and tape to make long wiggle worms. Children can decorate their worms with crayons.

● Ask: *Where can your worm go? Can it wiggle in the sand? In the soil? In the water? Through a rock? ¿A dónde podría ir su gusano? ¿Puede deslizarse por la arena? ¿Por la tierra? ¿Por el agua? ¿Por una piedra?*

● Have children explore the earth materials with their fingers to determine what their worm could move through and explain why.

### Center Tip

**If**...children have difficulty taping the yarn to attach their worms' body parts, **then**...provide pre-cut tape pieces or hold the yarn in place while they tape it.

### Learning Goals

**Emergent Literacy: Writing**
● Child participates in free drawing and writing activities to deliver information.
● Child uses scribbles, shapes, pictures, symbols, and letters to represent language.

**Science**
● Child observes, identifies, explores, describes, and compares earth materials (such as rocks, soil, sand, water) and their uses.

**Fine Arts**
● Child uses and experiments with a variety of art materials and tools in various art activities.
● Child expresses emotions or ideas through art.

### Differentiated Instruction

**Extra Support**
**Creativity Center**
**If**...children have difficulty understanding how worms behave in nature, **then**...place some worms in a clear container with soil and a few pebbles. Have children observe the worms.

**Enrichment**
**Creativity Center**
Challenge children to role play a day in the life of their wiggly worm. They can discuss what they see and do as they travel on and through the earth.

**Special Needs**
**Delayed Motor Development**
**If**...children have difficulty cutting circles for the worm's body parts, **then**...hold the paper while they cut around the marked edges or guide them by cutting with your hand over theirs.

## Focus Question
**What can I learn about the earth and the sky?**
**¿Qué puedo aprender sobre la Tierra y el cielo?**

## Learning Goals

**Language and Communication**
• Child demonstrates an understanding of oral language by responding appropriately.

**Emergent Literacy: Reading**
• Child names most upper- and lowercase letters of the alphabet.

• Child identifies the letter that stands for a given sound.

**Science**
• Child investigates and describes energy sources (light, heat, electricity).

• Child observes, identifies, compares, and discusses objects in the sky (such as clouds, sun, moon, stars).

### Vocabulary

| cave | cueva | clouds | nubes |
|------|-------|--------|-------|
| light | luz | lonely | solo |
| moon | Luna | sky | cielo |
| sun | Sol | | |

## Differentiated Instruction

### ✋ Extra Support
**Read Aloud**
**If...**children have difficulty recalling how the sun benefitted the earth, **then...**reread the paragraph explaining the benefits (sent wonderful light, warmed Earth, plants began to grow, people danced and played). List them on a chart and have children illustrate one.

### ⭐ Enrichment
**Read Aloud**
Challenge children to create sun and moon puppets using construction paper and craft sticks. Have them create a dialogue between the sun and moon explaining what each does now.

## Literacy Time

**large group** 🕐 15 minutes

### 📖 Read Aloud

☑ Can children respond appropriately by recalling story details about the sun and the moon?

**Build Background** Tell children that you will be reading a story about two objects in the sky.

● Ask: *What do you see in the sky during the day? What do you see at night?* *¿Qué ven en el cielo de día? ¿Qué ven de noche?*

**Listen for Understanding** Read aloud "The Sun and the Moon," from the *Teacher's Treasure Book*, page 241. Use the flannel board patterns as you read the story to help children connect the text to its meaning.

● Ask: *Where did the sun and moon live at first? Where did they go after leaving the cave? How did the sun affect the earth?* *¿Dónde vivían la Luna y el Sol primero? ¿A dónde fueron después de irse de la cueva? ¿Qué ocurrió en la Tierra cuando el Sol y la Luna se fueron al cielo?*

**Respond to the Story** Have children tell why the sun wanted to find the moon. Ask: *Why did the sun go looking for the moon? What did the moon do? Where is the moon now?* *¿Por qué fue el Sol a buscar a la Luna? ¿Qué hizo la Luna? ¿Dónde está la Luna ahora?*

💡 **TIP** Emphasize to children that although the story is make-believe, the real sun does give the earth heat and light.

*Teacher's Treasure Book, page 241*

### Learn About Letters and Sounds

☑ Can children identify the /z/ sound?

**Learn About the Letter Zz** Sing the "ABC Song" with children as you page through the *ABC Big Book*, stopping at *Zz* on page 54. Point to the "zipper" photo. Tell children that the word *zipper* begins with the /z/ sound. Have them chant "/z/ /z/ /z/ zip that zipper" as they pretend to zip a zipper.

● Model how to write upper case *Z* on chart paper or an interactive whiteboard. Have children trace the letter *Z* on their desks with their fingers.

● Have them make the /z/ sound each time they trace the letter.

● Repeat for lower case *z*. Point out the similarities in upper and lower case *Zz*.

**ELL** Show the photos for "zebra" and "zig-zag" from the *ABC Big Book*. Read each word as you point to the picture. Have children state the colors of the zebra using the frame **A zebra is _____ and _____.** Have children draw a zigzag line as they say "zigzag." For additional suggestions on how to meet the needs of children at varying levels of English proficiency, see pages 184–187.

*ABC Big Book, page 54*
*Superlibro abecé*

# Math Time

## Observe and Investigate

 **Can children use models to add up to 5?**

**Finger Word Problems** Tell children to solve simple addition problems with their fingers. They should place their hands in their laps between problems.

- Tell children that you want to buy three star stickers and two star stickers. Ask: *How many star stickers is that altogether? ¿Cuántas pegatinas de estrellas son en total?* Guide children in showing three fingers on one hand and two fingers on the other, and reiterate: *How many is that altogether? ¿Cuántas pegatinas de estrellas son en total?*

- Ask children how they got their answer, and repeat with other problems.

- During computer time, ask children to show you how they can open and navigate through the online math activities.

##  Social and Emotional Development

### Making Good Choices

 **Do children understand the importance of completing tasks?**

**Completing Tasks** Display *Making Good Choices Flip Chart* page 29, "What Do I Do Next?" Ask children to tell you what the girls should do to finish their paintings and clean up.

- With a Dog Puppet, role play other situations to model properly completing tasks and the rules of task completion in general. (For example, always clean up before leaving an area.) Explain that the puppet is building a block tower and decides he wants to do something else before finishing. Model what you would say and do to help the puppet complete his project.

- After the role play, ask: *How did I help the puppet finish the project? What should happen next? ¿Cómo ayudé al títere a terminar su proyecto? ¿Qué debería suceder ahora?*

**ELL** Act out your role-playing dialogue. Pause to ask simple questions to check children's comprehension. For example: *Am I playing with blocks or cars? Should I stop or finish my block tower?* Encourage children to use complete sentences to answer. For additional suggestions on how to meet the needs of children at varying levels of English proficiency, see pages 184–187.

---

### Building Blocks

**Online Math Activity**

Children can complete Off the Tree and Dinosaur Shop 3 during computer time or Center Time.

*Making Good Choices Flip Chart, page 29*

---

 **Learning Goals**

**Social and Emotional Development**
- Child maintains concentration/attention skills until a task is complete.

**Mathematics**
- Child uses concrete objects or makes a verbal word problem to add up to 5 objects.

**Technology Applications**
- Child opens and correctly uses age-appropriate software programs.

### Vocabulary

| | | | |
|---|---|---|---|
| add | sumar | altogether | total |
| complete | completo | count | contar |
| how many | cuántos | | |

---

## Differentiated Instruction

### ✋ Extra Support
**Observe and Investigate**
**If**...children struggle during Finger Word Problems, **then**...use only small numbers and/or help children show their fingers pressed against a table.

### ★ Enrichment
**Observe and Investigate**
Use larger numbers during Finger Word Problems. For numbers more than 5, encourage children to put one number "in their heads" while using their fingers to "hold" the other number, and then add them for the answer.

### 💜 Special Needs
**Behavioral/Social/Emotional**
**If**...children struggle and become frustrated during Math Time, **then**...redirect them to focus on adding only one at a time. Praise their efforts to try the complex problem. Allow them to take a time out in a calming area.

## Learning Goals

**Social and Emotional Development**
• Child maintains concentration/attention skills until a task is complete.

**Language and Communication**
• Child names and describes actual or pictured people, places, things, actions, attributes, and events.

**Science**
• Child follows basic health and safety rules.

**Social Studies**
• Child identifies common areas and features of home, school, and community.

### Vocabulary

| home | casa | nearby | cerca |
|------|------|--------|-------|
| neighborhood | vecindario | | |
| school | escuela | | |
| street | calle | | |

## Differentiated Instruction

 **Extra Support**

Oral Language and Academic Vocabulary
**If...**children have difficulty identifying key features of a school or home, **then...**display pictures of different types of local homes and of school. Ask: *What is this? What can you do in this room? ¿Qué es esto? ¿Qué pueden hacer en esta habitación?*

 **Enrichment**

Oral Language and Academic Vocabulary
Challenge children to create a map of their neighborhood using construction paper and crayons. Children can cut out homes, trees, and other features to glue onto the map.

---

# Social Studies Time

large group   20 minutes

**Personal Safety Skills** During the walk around the neighborhood, reinforce safety habits such as the proper way to cross a street.

## Oral Language and Academic Vocabulary

✓ **Can children identify common features at school and home?**

**Talking About School and Home** Explain to children that all over Earth are different kinds of homes and schools. Ask children to describe the things they see at their school. Ask: *Where is the library? What does it have in it? What is on the playground? ¿Dónde está la biblioteca? ¿Qué hay allí? ¿Qué hay en el patio de recreo?*

● Repeat by having children describe their homes.

● Ask: *What are things that we have both at home and at school? Do you have a sink at home? Books? Trees nearby? ¿Qué cosas hay en casa y en la escuela? ¿Tienen un lavamanos en casa? ¿Y libros? ¿Hay árboles cerca?*

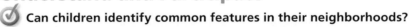 Use pictures to teach children words associated with schools and homes, such as *lunchroom, library, basement, bathroom*, and *living room*. Have children draw a picture of their school or home, or use play objects to recreate it. Help them identify the key features of the place.

## Understand and Participate

✓ **Can children identify common features in their neighborhoods?**

**Looking at Our Neighborhood** Ask children what they learned about things found on the earth from the *Concept Big Book* and their nature walk. Remind them that rocks, sand, water, and soil can be found in many places.

● Take children on a brief walk around the immediate neighborhood. Point out any rocks, soil, sand, or water nearby. Focus also on streets, buildings, and key landmarks.

● Ask: *How many houses do you see? Are there big buildings? What are they used for? What is the name of this street? ¿Cuántas casas ven? ¿Hay edificios grandes? ¿Para qué se usan? ¿Cuál es el nombre de esta calle?*

● Use direction and size words as you discuss what you see. Say, for example: *This house is near to the school. What do you see far away from the school? Is that rock big or small? Esta casa está cerca de la escuela. ¿Qué cosas están lejos de la escuela? ¿Esta roca es grande o pequeña?*

**TIP** Bring paper and crayons so children can draw pictures of the neighborhood before you return to school.

# Center Time

**Center Rotation** Center Time includes teacher-guided activities and independent activities. Refer to the **Learning Centers** on pages 24–25 for activities in additional centers.

small group · 30 minutes

## Construction Center

| | Center Tip |
|---|---|

✓ **Monitor children as they make and describe a model of their neighborhood.**

**Materials** blocks, miniature neighborhood toys (cars, homes, trees)

**Neighborhood Model** Tell children that they will use blocks and miniature toys to build a model of their neighborhood with a classmate.

- Create a road by placing tape down the middle of an area in the center. Have children use blocks and toys to create the buildings on either side of the street. Ask: *What buildings do you see on the street near our school? Is there anything else you see?* *¿Qué edificios ven en la calle cerca de nuestra escuela? ¿Ven alguna otra cosa?*

- Have children describe their finished neighborhoods.

**Center Tip**

**If...** children need help sharing the blocks and working together, **then...** suggest roles for each child in the building of the neighborhood. For example, each child can build one side of the street.

## Learning Goals

**Social and Emotional Development**
- Child maintains concentration/attention skills until a task is complete.

**Language and Communication**
- Child names and describes actual or pictured people, places, things, actions, attributes, and events.

**Emergent Literacy: Writing**
- Child participates in free drawing and writing activities to deliver information.

**Social Studies**
- Child identifies common areas and features of home, school, and community.

**Physical Development**
- Child develops small-muscle strength and control.
- Child completes tasks that require eye-hand coordination and control.

## Purposeful Play

✓ **Observe children as they work in pairs to complete a project.**

Children choose an open center for free playtime. Encourage cooperation skills by suggesting that they work together to create another model, such as of the school.

### Writing

Recap the day. Have children name things found in their neighborhood. Ask: *What did we find on the earth near our school? What was in the sky?* *¿Qué pueden encontrar en la tierra que rodea nuestra escuela?* Record their answers on chart paper or an interactive board. Share the pen by having children write letters and words they know. Ask children to draw a picture to illustrate each sentence.

## Let's Say Good-Bye

large group · 15 minutes

 **Read Aloud** Revisit "Wally Worm's World"/"*El mundo del gusano Wally*" from the *Teacher's Treasure Book,* page 212, for your afternoon Read Aloud. Remind children to listen for where Wally Worm lives.

 **Home Connection** Refer to the Home Connection activities listed in the Materials and Resources chart on page 21. Remind children to tell their families about the nature walk they took today. Sing the "Good-bye Song"/"*Hora de ir a casa*" as children prepare to leave.

# DAY 4

## Let's Start the Day

**Focus Question**

**What can I learn about the earth and the sky?**

*¿Qué puedo aprender sobre la Tierra y el cielo?*

### Learning Goals

**Social and Emotional Development**
• Child maintains concentration/attention skills until a task is complete.

**Language and Communication**
• Child follows basic rules for conversations (taking turns, staying on topic, listening actively).

### Vocabulary

| characters | personajes | friends | amigos |
|---|---|---|---|
| mean | cruel | moon | Luna |
| sun | Sol | | |

### Differentiated Instruction

 **Extra Support**

**Oral Language and Vocabulary**

**If**...children have difficulty describing characters, **then**...name a character's actions. Ask: *Is this a nice thing to do? Would this character make a good friend? ¿Ésta es una buena forma buena de comportarse? ¿Es este personaje un buen amigo?*

**Enrichment**

**Oral Language and Vocabulary**

Challenge children to create dialogues between story characters during Center Time. You might wish to provide props, such as stick puppets.

**Special Needs**

**Speech and Language Delays**

**If**...children have difficulty understanding what others say to the puppets, **then**...repeat the word yourself. Keep your sentences short and simple. Ask questions to be sure children understand and can repeat the word as clearly as they are able.

---

 **Opening Routines and Transition Tips**

For **Opening Routines** and **Transition Tips** turn to pages 178–181 and visit DLMExpressOnline.com for more ideas.

Read **"In the Woods"/**"Allí en el bosque florido" from the *Teacher's Treasure Book*, page 90, for your morning Read Aloud.

## Language Time

 large group — 15 minutes

**Social and Emotional Development** Provide encouragement that will help children complete tasks during lessons and Center Time. Ask: *After you finish this part, what else might you do? ¿Qué pueden hacer después de terminar esta parte?*

### Oral Language and Vocabulary

☑ **Can children identify and describe story characters?**

☑ **Can children follow verbal conversation rules during discussion?**

**Storybook Characters** Remind children that the characters in a story are who the story is about. Ask: *Who were the characters in the story "The Sun and the Moon" that we read together yesterday? ¿Quiénes son los personajes del cuento "El Sol y la Luna"?*

● Discuss how each character is different. For example, Sun is lonely without Moon. Moon is afraid of Sun.

● Point out that some story characters are friendly, while others might even be mean. Prompt children to listen for characters' names and the details describing them in upcoming stories. For example, children can compare and contrast Henny-Penny and Foxy-Loxy in today's flannel board story.

### Phonological Awareness

☑ **Can children segment words by stating the first or last sound?**

**Segmenting Phonemes** Display the Dog Puppets. Have pairs of children hold the puppets. Whisper a word, such as *zoo,* in one child's ear. Have the child say the word to his or her puppet. Ask the other child holding a puppet: *What is the first sound you hear in the word* zoo? *¿Cuál es el primer sonido que escuchan en la palabra* zoo? Repeat with the ending sound. Ask: *What is the last sound you hear in the word* zoo? *¿Cuál es el último sonido que escuchan en la palabra* zoo? Provide modeling and corrective feedback as needed.

**ELL** Work with initial and final sounds children have difficulty pronouncing. Show children the proper position of the mouth (lips, teeth, tongue) when making specific sounds. Use hand mirrors if available. Then say words with the target sound and have children repeat.

# Center Time

**Center Rotation** Center Time includes teacher-guided activities and independent activities. Refer to the **Learning Centers** on pages 24–25 for activities in additional centers.

small group · 60–90 minutes

## Library and Listening Center

**Center Tip**

 Track children's ability to listen and recall song words.

**Materials** recordings of nature-related and counting songs

**Nature Songs** Use recordings of songs related to this week's content, such as "Twinkle, Twinkle, Little Star" or "1, 2, Buckle My Shoe." Have children listen to the songs several times.

- Say, for example: *Listen to this song about the sky. What words do you hear that name things you can see in the night sky?* *Escuchen esta canción sobre el cielo. ¿Qué palabras nombran cosas que se ven en el cielo?*

- Sing the songs with children during transition times.

**If**...children have difficulty remembering the songs, **then**...teach movements that correspond to the lyrics.

## Pretend and Learn Center

**Center Tip**

 Track how well children can retell stories read aloud to them.

**Materials** flannel board patterns for this week's stories (*Teacher's Treasure Book* pages 424–425 and 369–370); clean socks, fabric paint

**Retell and Act Out Stories** Explain to children that they will retell the stories you read aloud this week.

- Display the flannel board patterns for "The Sun and the Moon." Have children use the patterns as they retell or act out yesterday's story. Encourage them to focus on the characters' moods.

- Continue with today's story, "Henny-Penny," after it is read. Children can make and use sock or stick puppets for their retellings.

**If**...children have difficulty retelling one of the stories, **then**... ask leading questions and provide clues about story details, such as: *What did Henny-Penny think fell on her? Look up!* *¿Qué creyó Gallinita-Nita que le había caído encima?*

## Learning Goals

**Social and Emotional Development**
- Child maintains concentration/attention skills until a task is complete.

**Language and Communication**
- Child uses newly learned vocabulary daily in multiple contexts.

**Emergent Literacy: Reading**
- Child enjoys and chooses reading-related activities.

**Fine Arts**
- Child expresses ideas, emotions, and moods through individual and collaborative dramatic play.

## Differentiated Instruction

### ✋ Extra Support
**Pretend and Learn Center**
**If**...children have difficulty retelling one of the stories, **then**...place the flannel patterns in the sequence in which they appear in the story. Prompt children to tell about each picture in order.

### ⭐ Enrichment
**Pretend and Learn Center**
Challenge children to make up additional dialogue between story characters to extend the story. Ask: *What did Foxy-Loxy say to Henny-Penny and her friends in the den?* *¿Qué les dijo Zorro-Gorro a Gallinita-Nita y sus amigos?*

### Accommodations for 3's
**Pretend and Learn Center**
**If**...children have difficulty retelling the story, **then**...narrate the story as they act it out.

# Circle Time

**Focus Question**

**What can I learn about the earth and the sky?**

**¿Qué puedo aprender sobre la Tierra y el cielo?**

## Literacy Time

### Read Aloud

 **Can children identify and describe story characters?**

**Build Background** Tell children that you will be reading a story about a hen named Henny-Penny who is hit on the head by something falling from above.

- Ask: *What can you find in the sky? What could fall from above? What can't fall from the sky? Why? ¿Qué hay en el cielo? ¿Qué podría caerse del cielo? ¿Por qué?*

**Listen for Enjoyment** Read aloud "Henny-Penny" from the *Teacher's Treasure Book*, page 302. Display the flannel board patterns as you read the story to help children connect the text to its meaning.

- Ask: *Who are Henny-Penny's friends? How do they help her? Where are they all going? ¿Quiénes son los amigos de Gallinita-Nita? ¿Cómo la ayudan? ¿A dónde van todos?*

**Respond to the Story** Have children tell what happened to Henny-Penny and her friends. Ask: *Why were Henny-Penny and her friends going to see the king? Where did Foxy-Loxy take them? Do you think Foxy-Loxy is a good character or a bad one? Why? ¿Por qué iban Gallinita-Nita y sus amigos a ver al rey? ¿A dónde los llevó Zorro-Gorro? ¿Es Zorro-Gorro un personaje bueno o malo? ¿Por qué?*

**TIP** Help children use the flannel board patterns to recall story details.

**ELL** Point to each flannel board pattern during the Read Aloud and name the animal: Duck, Goose, Turkey, Hen, Fox. Have children tell what they know about the animal. Provide additional detail and ask questions about them. For example: *The fox has red fur. What does the fox have?*

### Learn About Letters and Sounds

 **Can children identify *Qq, Ww, Zz,* and sounds /kw/, /w/, /z/?**

**Review Letters *Qq, Ww, Zz*** Place *ABC Picture Cards Qq, Ww,* and *Zz* on three different chairs. Play musical chairs with a small group of children. When the music stops, each child states the sound of the letter on his or her chair. Continue with other groups of children.

- Then display photos of words beginning with *Qq, Ww,* or *Zz,* such as *queen, quilt, wagon, walrus, watermelon, winter, zebra,* and *zipper.*

- Say a picture name. Have children match the beginning sound of the picture name to a letter. Ask: *Does zebra begin with the letter Z? Listen, /z/ /z/ zebra. ¿Comienza la palabra zebra con Z? Escuchen: /z/ /z/ zebra.*

*Teacher's Treasure Book, page 302*

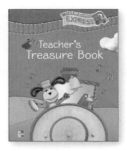

*ABC Picture Cards*
*Tarjetas abecé de imágenes*

**large group** — 15 minutes

---

## Learning Goals

**Language and Communication**
- Child demonstrates an understanding of oral language by responding appropriately.

**Emergent Literacy: Reading**
- Child names most upper- and lowercase letters of the alphabet.
- Child identifies the letter that stands for a given sound.

**Science**
- Child observes, identifies, compares, and discusses objects in the sky (such as clouds, sun, moon, stars).

### Vocabulary

| | | | |
|---|---|---|---|
| character | personaje | den | guarida |
| fell | caer | friends | amigos |
| head | cabeza | journey | viaje |
| king | rey | | |

## Differentiated Instruction

### Extra Support
**Learn About Letters and Sounds**
**If...**children have difficulty remembering the letter sounds, **then...**show them the corresponding *ABC Big Book* page. Ask: *What is this picture?* (zipper) *What sound do you hear at the beginning of the picture name?* (/z/) *¿Qué hay en esta fotografía? ¿Cón qué sonido comienza esa palabra?*

### Enrichment
**Learn About Letters and Sounds**
Give children a set of Alphabet/Letter Tiles or place up to 10 magnetic letters on a table. Call out a letter name or sound. Challenge children to find the corresponding letter quickly.

**Online Math Activity**

Children can complete Off the Tree and Dinosaur Shop 3 during computer time or Center Time.

# Math Time

## Observe and Investigate

☑ **Can children count to 10?**

**I'm Thinking of a Number** Choose and hide a Counting Card from 1–10 (*Teacher's Treasure Book,* pages 506–507).

- Tell children what you did. Ask: **What is the number?** *¿Cuál es el número?* When a child guesses correctly, excitedly reveal the card. Until then, provide hints, telling children whether a guess is more or less than the secret number.

- As children become familiar with the game, ask them to explain their guesses. For example, a child might say: "I knew four was more than the secret number and two was less than it so I said three."

- Use the Step-by-Step Number Line for an active variation. Have children indicate their guesses by stepping to the particular number. For hints after incorrect guesses, tell children whether they should step forward or backward.

# ✸✸✸ Social and Emotional Development

## Making Good Choices

☑ **Do children understand how and why to complete tasks?**

**Completing Tasks** Display the Dog Puppets and a set of building blocks. Tell children that the puppets are in the middle of building a town, but one wants to stop before it is completed. Model a dialogue between the puppets that ends in them deciding how to complete the project and clean up.

- After the role play, ask: **What problem did the puppets have? How well did they do at finishing their block town?** *¿Qué problema tenían los títeres? ¿Cómo hicieron para terminar su ciudad de bloques?*

- Remind children that it is important to finish one project before starting a new one. Ask: **How is working together to use and clean-up center materials a way to be helpful to others?** *¿Por qué es considerado con los otros trabajar en grupo para ordenar los materiales del centro?*

Some children may have difficulties following the conversation between the Dog Puppets. While role playing, act out the dogs' actions. Use simple phrases such as **I want to stop** or **Let's work together. Let's pick up the blocks.**

---

### ✓ Learning Goals

**Social and Emotional Development**
- Child maintains concentration/attention skills until a task is complete.

**Mathematics**
- Child recites number words in sequence from one to thirty.

### Vocabulary

| | | | |
|---|---|---|---|
| count | contar | guess | adivinar |
| less | menos | more | más |
| number | número | secret | secreto |

---

### Differentiated Instruction

 **Extra Support**

*Observe and Investigate*

**If...**children struggle with the concepts of *more* and *less*, **then...**use manipulatives to demonstrate a number, then show *more* by placing additional manipulatives in the pile. Repeat for *less*.

 **Enrichment**

*Observe and Investigate*

Play "I'm Thinking of a Number" with numbers larger than 10. Begin by having children count as high as they can go up to 30. Then select a secret number for them to guess.

 **Special Needs**

*Cognitive Challenges*

**If...**children struggle with the concepts of *more* and *less*, **then...**use manipulatives and focus on only one concept. Say, for example: *I'm thinking of a number. It is one more than two. What is my number? Estoy pensando en un número. Es uno más (o menos) que 2. ¿Cuál es mi número?*

## Learning Goals

**Social and Emotional Development**
• Child maintains concentration/attention skills until a task is complete.

**Language and Communication**
• Child follows two- and three-step oral directions.

**Mathematics**
• Child recites number words in sequence from one to thirty.

• Child demonstrates that the numerical counting sequence is always the same.

### Vocabulary

| | | | |
|---|---|---|---|
| back | hacia atrás | count | contar |
| forward | hacia adelante | number | número |
| row | fila | | |

## Differentiated Instruction

 **Extra Support**

**Math Time**

**If...**children have difficulty counting without seeing the numbers, **then...**chorally count out loud as you point to the facedown cards. Stop on the answer. Ask: **What number is this?** *¿Qué número es éste?*

**Enrichment**

**Math Time**

Challenge children to count out 20 Vehicle Counters in any one color.

---

# Math Time

**Language and Communication Skills** State two- and three-step oral directions for children to follow during X-Ray Vision 2. Engage the children in helping to construct the steps as you go.

 **Can children count to 10?**

**Count on It** This lesson repeats the activities introduced on Day 2. Have children count forward and back to 10.

● Display *Math and Science Flip Chart* page 54, "Count to 10". Discuss the number of earth materials in each row.

● Have children chorally count the items in each row.

● Point to the shells in the second row. Say: **Let's count until we get to shell number 6.** *Vamos a contar hasta que lleguemos a la roca número 6.* Count with children. **What shell is two more than 6? Let's count together.** *¿Qué roca es dos más que 6? Vamos a contar juntos.*

● Continue with other numbers and the other rows.

 **Can children count forward and back?**

**X-Ray Vision 2** Guide children as they work in pairs, making sure they count forward and back.

● Instruct pairs of children to put Counting Cards 1–10 in order, count them to check, and then place them facedown still in order.

● Children should take turns pointing to any card. One child points to a card, and the other uses his or her "X-ray vision" to tell which it is. The child who pointed flips the card to show whether the other is correct and, if so, keeps the card face up. Children switch roles until all cards are facing up.

● As you interact with children, emphasize instances of *right after, right before, in between,* and *one (or two) more* or *less than* numbers.

**TIP** Tell children that the cards are in the same order as the objects on the *Math and Science Flip Chart.*

**ELL** Focus on the concepts *in between, before,* and *after*. Display three different Farm Animal Counters. Say: **I see three counters. The duck is in between the horse and pig.** Point to the middle counter. Ask: **Which counter is in between the horse and pig?** Repeat with other counters. Continue with *before* and *after*.

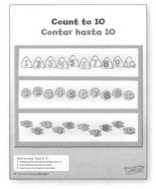

*Math and Science Flip Chart, page 54*

# Center Time

▶ **Center Rotation** Center Time includes teacher-guided activities and independent activities. Refer to the **Learning Centers** on pages 24–25 for activities in additional centers.

 small group  30 minutes

## Math and Science Center

☑ **Track children's ability to count to 10.**

**Materials** egg cartons, sand, plastic spoons

**How Many Eggs?** Tell children that they will fill ten slots in an egg carton with sand as they count the "eggs."

- Give children an empty egg carton, sand, and a spoon. Ask: *How many eggs are in your carton now?* (0) *¿Cuántos huevos hay en la caja?*

- Once children fill the slots in their egg carton, have them ask a classmate to count to confirm. There should be two empty slots.

### Center Tip

**If...**children need help counting, **then...**give them Farm Animal Counters and have them match one manipulative to each slot filled. Then help them count the animals as you point to the Counting Cards in order.

## Purposeful Play

☑ **Observe children selecting and completing tasks.**

Children choose an open center for free playtime. For example, children can retell another flannel board story with a friend. Encourage children to complete a task fully before moving on.

## Let's Say Good-Bye

 large group  15 minutes

 **Read Aloud** Revisit the poem, "In the Woods"/"Allí en el bosque florido" for your afternoon Read Aloud. Tell children to listen for the names of things found in the woods, such as rocks, streams, and trees.

 **Home Connection** Refer to the Home Connection activities listed in the Materials and Resources chart on page 21. Remind children to tell families about Henny-Penny and why she thought the sky was falling. Sing the "Good-bye Song"/"Hora de ir a casa" as children prepare to leave.

### ✓ Learning Goals

**Social and Emotional Development**
- Child maintains concentration/attention skills until a task is complete.

**Language and Communication**
- Child names and describes actual or pictured people, places, things, actions, attributes, and events.

**Mathematics**
- Child demonstrates that the numerical counting sequence is always the same.

**Physical Development**
- Child completes tasks that require eye-hand coordination and control.

**Technology Applications**
- Child names and uses various computer parts (such as mouse, keyboard, CD-ROM, microphone, touch screen).
- Child uses computer software or technology to express original ideas.

### Writing

Recap the day. Say: *Let's pretend to write an e-mail to Henny-Penny. Imaginemos que le escribimos un correo electrónico a Gallinita-Nita.* Ask: *What should we say? What can we tell her about the sky? About Foxy-Loxy? ¿Qué deberíamos decirle? ¿Qué podemos contarle acerca del cielo? ¿Y sobre Zorro-Gorro?* Record their answers in a word processing document or using an interactive board. Let volunteers type certain letters. Emphasize that letters form words and words are separated by spaces. Have children name the input devices that they use during the activity.

# Let's Start the Day

**Focus Question**

**What can I learn about the earth and the sky?**

**¿Qué puedo aprender sobre la Tierra y el cielo?**

## Learning Goals

**Language and Communication**
• Child uses newly learned vocabulary daily in multiple contexts.

**Science**
• Child observes, identifies, compares, and discusses objects in the sky (such as clouds, sun, moon, stars).

## Vocabulary

| | | | |
|---|---|---|---|
| climb | escalar | equipment | equipo |
| helmet | casco | mountain | montaña |
| rock | roca | rope | cuerda |

## Differentiated Instruction

 **Extra Support**

Oral Language and Vocabulary
**If...**children have difficulty describing the mountain scene, **then...**point to and name discrete aspects of the photo, such as snow and hills. Then ask questions such as: *Are there many mountains in the picture? What color is the sky behind the climber? ¿Hay muchas montañas en la foto? ¿De qué color es el cielo detrás del escalador?*

**Enrichment**

Oral Language and Vocabulary
Use photos to teach the names and characteristics of less familiar natural places, such as a rainforest, volcano, or desert.

 **Opening Routines and Transition Tips**
For **Opening Routines** and **Transition Tips** turn to pages 178–181 and visit **DLMExpressOnline.com** for more ideas.

Read **"Cloud"/"Nube"** from the *Teacher's Treasure Book,* page 122, for your morning Read Aloud. Read the poem twice through.

## Language Time

large group    15 minutes

 **Social and Emotional Development** Remind children to take turns during discussion. Ask them what they should do when you give instructions that have more than one part. Ask how many parts they need to follow.

### Oral Language and Vocabulary

**Can children share what they know about the earth and sky?**

**Place Names and Characteristics** Talk about the many places on the earth and in the sky that children have seen or learned about this week. Ask: **What can you find on the earth? What can you see in the sky?** *¿Qué pueden encontrar en la Tierra? ¿Qué pueden ver en el cielo?*

● Display *Oral Language Development Card 63.* Name the place and some things in the background, such as the snowy mountaintops. Follow the suggestions on the back of the card.

**ELL** Ask simple one-word answer questions about objects found on Earth or in the sky, such as: **Are clouds white? Are clouds in the sky or on the earth?** Focus on objects occurring in your local environment.

### Phonological Awareness

**Can children segment words?**

**Segmenting Phonemes** Reread "Sun, Earth, Moon" from the *Rhymes and Chants Flip Chart,* page 29. Remind children that words are made of different sounds. Point to the sun in the picture. Ask: **What is the first sound in the word** sun? **What is the last sound?** *¿Cuál es el primer sonido de la palabra* sun? *¿Cuál es el último sonido?* Repeat using the words *moon* and *round.*

*Oral Language Development Card 63*

*Rhymes and Chants Flip Chart, page 29/ page 61*

# Center Time

▶ **Center Rotation** Center Time includes teacher-guided activities and independent activities. Refer to the **Learning Centers** on pages 24–25 for activities in additional centers.

  small group  60–90 minutes

## Writer's Center

**Center Tip**

 Track the use of descriptive words as children tell about things found on the earth and in the sky.

**Materials** magazines, glue, paper, crayons, nature objects

**Nature Scrapbook** Have children create a nature scrapbook using nature pictures from magazines and objects such as twigs, leaves, and pebbles.

- Have children cut out and glue a nature picture or object to a sheet of paper.

- Ask: *Where is this place? ¿Dónde está este lugar?* or *Where can you find this object? ¿Dónde podrían encontrar este objeto?* Have children write on another sheet of paper what they know. Ask them to dictate their comments for you to record under their writings.

- Continue with at least one more picture or object. Bind the pages to create a class scrapbook.

**If...**children have difficulty recalling nature details, **then...**ask them questions about their pictures, such as: *Where is this found? What color is it? Is it soft or rough?* *¿Dónde se puede encontrar esto? ¿De qué color es? ¿Es liso o áspero?*

## ABC Center

**Center Tip**

 Track children's ability to match upper and lower case letters.

**Materials** letter cards, Alphabet/Letter Tiles, paper, glue, yarn

**Matching Letters** Explain to children that they will match the upper and lower case forms of this week's letters. Reinforce each letter's sound as children work.

- As children match the letter forms, ask: *How is upper case W like lower case w? How is it different? ¿En qué se parecen la W mayúscula y la w minúscula? ¿En qué se diferencian?*

- Have children write each letter with glue on paper, then add yarn. They can add a drawing of an animal whose name begins with that letter sound.

**If...**children have difficulty recalling the letter sound, **then...**have them trace the letter with a finger and repeat the sound you say before continuing with the activity.

---

## ✓ Learning Goals

**Language and Communication**
- Child names and describes actual or pictured people, places, things, actions, attributes, and events.

**Emergent Literacy: Reading**
- Child names most upper- and lowercase letters of the alphabet.
- Child identifies the letter that stands for a given sound.

**Emergent Literacy: Writing**
- Child uses scribbles, shapes, pictures, symbols, and letters to represent language.

## Differentiated Instruction

✋ **Extra Support**
**Writer's Center**
**If...**children have difficulty deciding what to write about their item, **then...**give them sentence stems to finish, such as, **This is _____ . It is the color_____ . I like the way it _____ .**

⭐ **Enrichment**
**Writer's Center**
Challenge children to make additional pages for their Nature Scrapbook. Children might divide the book into two sections: (1) Earth and (2) Sky.

💜 **Special Needs**
**Vision Loss**
Provide children with all objects that they can touch, such as pebbles, twigs, and shells; and smell, such as leaves (free of mold) and dried flowers. Allow them to work with a partner to help glue the items. Provide voice recorders at the center so they can dictate their writing.

### Focus Question
**What can I learn about the earth and the sky?**
*¿Qué puedo aprender sobre la Tierra y el cielo?*

## Literacy Time

### 📖 Read Aloud

☑ Can children use information learned from the book to describe objects on the earth and in the sky?

**Build Background** Tell children that you will be rereading the selection from *Concept Big Book 4: The Earth and Sky*.

● Ask: **What did we learn about things found on the earth? In the sky?** *¿Qué aprendimos sobre las cosas que se encuentran en la Tierra? ¿Y en el cielo?*

**Listen for Understanding** Display *Concept Big Book 4: The Earth and Sky*. Reread the title and pages 6–9. Pause and have children name and describe the pictures of objects found on the earth and in the sky. Help children compare the properties of the objects they know.

● Ask: **How does sand feel? How is it different from rock? Does it smell different than soil? When do you see the sun? The moon?** *¿Cómo es la arena? ¿En qué se diferencia de las rocas? ¿Y de la tierra? ¿Cuándo ves el sol? ¿Y la luna?*

**Respond and Connect** Help children connect their learning to their daily lives. Ask: **What do you see when you look up into the night sky? What makes lights come on in your home? Do you live near a rocky hillside? A river?** *¿Qué ven en el cielo de noche? ¿Y cuándo encienden las luces en su casa? ¿Viven cerca de una colina rocosa? ¿O de un río?*

**TIP** Remind children that heat and light can come from objects outside, like the sun, and inside, like lamps and heaters.

**ELL** Provide sentence frames to help children talk about the *Concept Big Book*. Use frames such as **I see _____** and **It is _____**. Model using each frame, then have children repeat and apply their own words.

*The Earth and Sky*
*La Tierra y el cielo*

### Learn About Letters and Sounds

☑ Can children identify letters and their sounds?

**Review Letters Qq, Ww, Zz** Create and display upper- and lowercase letter cards for *Qq*, *Ww*, and *Zz*. Review the name and sound of each letter.

● Place the cards facedown for a matching game. Each child turns over two cards and states whether or not the two cards match.

● When a match is found, ask: **What letter is this? What sound does it make? Can you think of any words that begin with this sound?** *¿Qué letra es ésta? ¿Qué sonido tiene? ¿Pueden pensar palabras que empiecen con ese sonido?*

*ABC Picture Cards*
*Tarjetas abecé de imágenes*

---

# Math Time

## Observe and Investigate

 **Can children count to 10?**

**I'm Thinking of a Number (Clues)** Choose and hide a Counting Card from 1–10 (*Teacher's Treasure Book*, pages 506–507). Tell children you hid a card, and explain that they will guess the number after you give them clues.

- Based on the card you hid, the first clue should share the number that is one more and the number that is one less than your secret number. For example, if you hid 7, say: *It is more than 6 but less than 8* *Es más que 6 pero menos que 8.* Give other clues as needed, such as **Less than 9,** *Es menos que 9* or **More than 5 but less than 10.** *Es más que 5 pero menos que 10.*

- When a child guesses the correct number, excitedly reveal the card. Until then, provide hints, telling children whether a guess is more or less than the secret number.

# ☆☆☆ Social and Emotional Development

## Making Good Choices

 **Do children understand how and why to complete tasks?**

**Completing Tasks** Display *Making Good Choices Flip Chart* page 29, "What Do I Do Next?"

- Ask: *What did we learn about finishing the projects we start?* *¿Qué aprendimos sobre completar los proyectos que empezamos?*

- Check for understanding by asking children to brainstorm possible tasks or projects they could do, and then explain to you what steps they would need to take in order to complete the tasks. Chart the steps children provide and review them for accuracy as a group.

- Say: *Draw a picture of the two girls finishing their project or cleaning up after it. Hagan un dibujo de dos niñas terminando su proyecto u ordenando después de terminar.* Ask: *Why is it important to finish a project and clean up after it? ¿Por qué es importante terminar un proyecto y luego ordenar?*

- Make sure children complete their drawings. Offer them a chance to explain what they drew and why it is important.

**ELL** Provide one direction at a time and model it. Have children repeat. Then say the full multi-step direction. Narrate as children complete the actions.

---

**Building Blocks**

**Online Math Activity**

Children can complete Off the Tree and Dinosaur Shop 3 during computer time or Center Time.

*Making Good Choices Flip Chart, page 29*

---

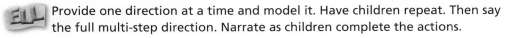

Focus Question
**What can I learn about the earth and the sky?**
**¿Qué puedo aprender sobre la Tierra y el cielo?**

## Learning Goals

**Social and Emotional Development**
• Child maintains concentration/attention skills until a task is complete.

**Science**
• Child observes, identifies, explores, describes, and compares earth materials (such as rocks, soil, sand, water) and their uses.
• Child observes, identifies, compares, and discusses objects in the sky (such as clouds, sun, moon, stars).
• Child follows basic health and safety rules.

**Fine Arts**
• Child shares opinions about artwork and artistic experiences.

### Vocabulary

| | | | |
|---|---|---|---|
| clouds | nubes | earth | Tierra |
| energy | energía | rocks | rocas |
| sand | arena | sky | cielo |
| water | agua | | |

## Differentiated Instruction

 **Extra Support**
**Explore and Express**
**If...**children have difficulty remembering details about natural environments, **then...**display *Concept Big Book 4* pages 6–9 for children to refer to while creating their collages.

★ **Enrichment**
**Explore and Express**
Have children add labels to their collages. Encourage them to write the letters they know.

# Art Time

large group  20 minutes

**Personal Safety Skills** Model how to use, clean, carry, and store art tools, scissors, and supplies properly.

## Oral Language and Academic Vocabulary

✓ **Can children describe objects found on the earth and in the sky?**

**Our Earth and Sky** Remind children what they have learned about objects found on the earth and in the sky. Prompt them to tell what favorite things they observed or discussed this week, and to use descriptive words when telling about objects found on the earth and in the sky.

● Ask: *What can you find on the earth? What does a rock look and feel like? What color is sand? Water? Soil? ¿Qué pueden encontrar en la Tierra? ¿Cómo son las rocas? ¿Y la arena? ¿Y el agua? ¿Y la tierra?*

● Ask: *What can you see in the sky during the day? At night? What does the moon look like? How does the sun feel? ¿Qué pueden ver en el cielo de día? ¿De noche? ¿Cómo es la Luna? ¿Cómo es el Sol?*

## Explore and Express

✓ **Can children create a collage using items from nature?**

**Earth/Sky Collage** Tell children that they will work with a partner but each create a collage of objects found either on the earth or in the sky. Show a sample collage and explain how it differs from a regular (single) picture.

● Distribute heavy stock paper, art materials, and objects such as leaves, twigs, pebbles, dried flowers, cotton balls, and magazine pictures to pairs of children. Children should share materials with their partners but make individual collages of either the earth or the sky.

● As children work and after they finish, encourage them to discuss their work with each other. Say: *Tell me about your partner's collage. What materials do you see? What is your favorite part? Describan el collage de su compañero. ¿Qué materiales ven? ¿Cuál es tu parte favorita?*

TIP Display children's creations for all to see. Have children tell others about their work. Prompt children to tell what they like about each other's artwork and to respond to classmates' comments nicely.

ELL Display *Oral Language Development Card* or Photo Library CD-ROM photos to provide children with examples for their art. When asking children to consider adding a detail (such as clouds to the sky), point to the detail in one of the photos and state the direction simply: *Add a cloud like this.* Have children repeat you and demonstrate the action to confirm understanding.

# Center Time

▶ **Center Rotation** Center Time includes teacher-guided activities and independent activities. Refer to the **Learning Centers** on pages 24–25 for activities in additional centers.

small group · 30 minutes

## Construction Center

| | Center Tip |
|---|---|

✓ **Monitor children as they make and describe a mountain setting.**

**Materials** blocks, sticks, construction paper, nature toys (miniature trees, animals)

**Build a Mountain Scene** Tell children that they will use blocks and other art materials to make a mountain setting. They should include mountains, roads, trees, rivers, and anything else they want.

- Have children work with a partner. Ask: *What will you make? How will you share the job?* *¿Qué harán? ¿Cómo compartirán el trabajo?*

- Have children describe their finished mountain scenes. Ask: *What can be found on or near your mountain? What does it look and feel like?* *¿Qué hay cerca de su montaña? ¿Cómo es y cómo se siente?*

**Center Tip**

**If...**children need help sharing the materials and working together, **then...**suggest roles for each child in the building of the mountain setting.

## Purposeful Play

✓ **Observe children sustaining their attention to complete a project.**

Children choose an open center for free playtime. Encourage cooperation skills by offering support as children work together. Prompt children to complete their chosen tasks before moving on to something new.

# Let's Say Good-Bye

large group · 15 minutes

 **Read Aloud** Revisit "Cloud"/"Nube" from the *Teacher's Treasure Book,* page 122, for your afternoon Read Aloud. Tell children to imagine things they have seen in the sky as they listen.

 **Home Connection** Refer to the Home Connection activities listed in the Materials and Resources chart on page 21. Remind children to tell their families what they learned this week about the earth and sky. Sing the "Good-bye Song"/"Hora de ir a casa" as children prepare to leave.

---

 **Learning Goals**

**Social and Emotional Development**
- Child maintains concentration/attention skills until a task is complete.

**Language and Communication**
- Child names and describes actual or pictured people, places, things, actions, attributes, and events.

**Emergent Literacy: Writing**
- Child writes own name or a reasonable approximation of it.

**Science**
- Child observes, identifies, explores, describes, and compares earth materials (such as rocks, soil, sand, water) and their uses.

### Writing

Recap the day and week. Say: *Tell me one thing you learned about the earth or the sky this week. Cuéntenme algo que hayan aprendido sobre la Tierra y el cielo esta semana.* Record answers on chart paper. Share the pen with children as you write. Have each child write his or her name on the paper.

# Week 2

## Focus Question

## What weather can I observe each day?

## ¿Qué tiempo puedo observar todos los días?

This week children will learn about different types of weather and how people dress for them. They will record weather observations, identify what causes weather changes, discuss characteristics of the seasons, describe precipitation, and identify solid shapes.

# Week 2 ✓ Learning Goals

| Social and Emotional Development | 1 | 2 | 3 | 4 | 5 |
|---|---|---|---|---|---|
| Child recognizes and manages feelings and impulses; increasingly maintains self-control in difficult situations (can increase or decrease intensity of emotions with guidance). | | | | | ✓ |
| Child maintains concentration/attention skills until a task is complete. | | | | ✓ | |
| Child participates in a variety of individual, small- and large-group activities. | ✓ | ✓ | ✓ | ✓ | ✓ |
| Child initiates play scenarios with peers that share a common plan and goal. | ✓ | ✓ | ✓ | | ✓ |
| Child understands and respects the different ideas, feelings, perspectives, and behaviors of others. | ✓ | ✓ | ✓ | ✓ | |

| Language and Communication | 1 | 2 | 3 | 4 | 5 |
|---|---|---|---|---|---|
| Child demonstrates some understanding of English spoken by teachers and peers. (ELL) | | | ✓ | | |
| Child uses oral language for a variety of purposes. | | ✓ | | ✓ | |
| Child experiments with and produces a growing number of sounds in English words. (ELL) | | | ✓ | ✓ | |
| Child names and describes actual or pictured people, places, things, actions, attributes, and events. | ✓ | ✓ | | ✓ | |
| Child exhibits an understanding of instructional terms used in the classroom. | | ✓ | ✓ | ✓ | |
| Child speaks in complete sentences of four or more words including a subject, verb, and object. | ✓ | | ✓ | | |
| Child understands and uses regular and irregular plural nouns, regular past tense verbs, personal and possessive pronouns, and subject-verb agreement. | ✓ | | ✓ | | ✓ |
| Child understands and uses sentences having two or more phrases or concepts. | ✓ | | ✓ | | |
| Child understands and uses sentences of increasing length and complexity. | ✓ | | ✓ | | |
| Child uses complex sentences that include many details, tell about one topic, and communicate meaning clearly. | ✓ | | ✓ | ✓ | |
| Child uses nonverbal cues to communicate with others who do not speak his or her home language. (ELL) | | ✓ | | | ✓ |
| Child uses individual words and short phrases to communicate. (ELL) | | ✓ | | | ✓ |
| Child tries to use newly learned vocabulary and grammar. (ELL) | ✓ | | ✓ | ✓ | |

| Emergent Literacy: Reading | 1 | 2 | 3 | 4 | 5 |
|---|---|---|---|---|---|
| Child independently engages in pre-reading behaviors and activities (such as, pretending to read, turning one page at a time). | ✓ | | | ✓ | |
| Child explores books and other texts to answer questions. | | ✓ | ✓ | | |
| Child deletes syllables from a word. | | | | | ✓ |
| Child names most upper- and lowercase letters of the alphabet. | ✓ | ✓ | ✓ | ✓ | ✓ |
| Child asks and answers questions about books read aloud (such as "Who?" "What?" "Where?"). | ✓ | ✓ | ✓ | | ✓ |

| Emergent Literacy: Writing | 1 | 2 | 3 | 4 | 5 |
|---|---|---|---|---|---|
| Child uses scribbles, shapes, pictures, symbols, and letters to represent language. | | | | ✓ | |
| Child writes own name or a reasonable approximation of it. | | ✓ | ✓ | | ✓ |
| Child writes some letters or reasonable approximations of letters upon request. | | | | ✓ | ✓ |

| Mathematics | 1 | 2 | 3 | 4 | 5 |
|---|---|---|---|---|---|
| Child recognizes, names, describes, matches, compares, sorts common two-dimensional shapes (such as circle, square, rectangle, triangle, rhombus). | ✓ | ✓ | ✓ | ✓ | ✓ |

| Science | 1 | 2 | 3 | 4 | 5 |
|---|---|---|---|---|---|
| Child uses senses to observe, classify, investigate, and collect data. | | ✓ | | ✓ | |
| Child observes, identifies, compares, and discusses objects in the sky (such as clouds, sun, moon, stars). | | ✓ | ✓ | ✓ | |
| Child describes the effects of natural forces (such as wind, gravity). | ✓ | ✓ | ✓ | ✓ | ✓ |

| Social Studies | 1 | 2 | 3 | 4 | 5 |
|---|---|---|---|---|---|
| Child identifies common events and routines. | | ✓ | | | |
| Child understands basic human needs for food, clothing, shelter. | ✓ | ✓ | ✓ | | ✓ |

| Fine Arts | 1 | 2 | 3 | 4 | 5 |
|---|---|---|---|---|---|
| Child uses and experiments with a variety of art materials and tools in various art activities. | | | ✓ | ✓ | ✓ |
| Child expresses emotions or ideas through art. | | ✓ | | ✓ | |
| Child expresses thoughts, feelings, and energy through music and creative movement. | | | | | ✓ |

| Physical Development | 1 | 2 | 3 | 4 | 5 |
|---|---|---|---|---|---|
| Child coordinates body movements in a variety of locomotive activities (such as walking, jumping, running, hopping, skipping, climbing). | | | | | ✓ |

| Technology Applications | 1 | 2 | 3 | 4 | 5 |
|---|---|---|---|---|---|
| Child opens and correctly uses age-appropriate software programs. | | ✓ | ✓ | | |
| Child names and uses various computer parts (such as mouse, keyboard, CD-ROM, microphone, touch screen). | | ✓ | | ✓ | |
| Child knows some ways that technology affects people's lives. | ✓ | | | ✓ | |

# Materials and Resources

| DAY 1 | DAY 2 | DAY 3 | DAY 4 | DAY 5 |
|---|---|---|---|---|

## Program Materials

| DAY 1 | DAY 2 | DAY 3 | DAY 4 | DAY 5 |
|---|---|---|---|---|
| • ABC Picture Cards *Qq* and *Ww*<br>• Building Blocks Online Math Activities<br>• Home Connections Resource Guide<br>• Making Good Choices Flip Chart<br>• Math and Science Flip Chart<br>• Oral Language Development Card 64<br>• Rhymes and Chants Flip Chart<br>• Teacher's Treasure Book<br>• *Who Likes Rain?* Big Book | • ABC Picture Cards<br>• Building Blocks Online Math Activities<br>• Dog Puppets<br>• Making Good Choices Flip Chart<br>• Math and Science Flip Chart<br>• Pattern Blocks<br>• Teacher's Treasure Book<br>• *Who Likes Rain?* Big Book | • ABC Big Book<br>• ABC Picture Cards<br>• Alphabet/Letter Tiles<br>• Concept Big Book 4: *The Earth and Sky*<br>• Dog Puppets<br>• Oral Language Development Card 65<br>• Making Good Choices Flip Chart<br>• Pattern Blocks<br>• Photo Library CD-ROM<br>• Rhymes and Chants Flip Chart<br>• Teacher's Treasure Book | • Alphabet/Letter Tiles<br>• Dog Puppets<br>• Flannel Board Patterns for "The Stonecutter"<br>• Home Connections Resource Guide<br>• Math and Science Flip Chart<br>• Pattern Blocks<br>• Teacher's Treasure Book | • ABC Picture Cards *Ww* and *Qq*<br>• Flannel Board Patterns for "The Stonecutter"<br>• Home Connections Resource Guide<br>• Making Good Choices Flip Chart<br>• Rhymes and Chants Flip Chart<br>• Pattern Blocks<br>• Photo Library CD-ROM<br>• Teacher's Treasure Book<br>• *Who Likes Rain?* Big Book |

## Other Materials

| DAY 1 | DAY 2 | DAY 3 | DAY 4 | DAY 5 |
|---|---|---|---|---|
| • blue butcher paper (large sheets)<br>• brass brad<br>• colored tape, masking tape, or sidewalk chalk<br>• goggles<br>• paper towel rolls (bare)<br>• paint<br>• picture books about weather and seasons (see p. 65)<br>• pool toys<br>• poster board<br>• raincoat and rain hat<br>• scissors<br>• stapler<br>• sticky notes<br>• crepe paper<br>• umbrella | • bag or box for Feely Box<br>• crayons, markers<br>• cube, cylinder, and sphere blocks<br>• objects in cube, cylinder, and sphere shapes (balls, cans, fuzzy dice)<br>• glue, play clay<br>• index cards (large)<br>• objects that float and sink (three each); water<br>• paper plates<br>• postcards<br>• ruler, scissors<br>• sparkles or glitter<br>• stapler or tape<br>• two-column chart labeled *float* and *sink,* laminated (see p. 71)<br>• yarn | • calendar<br>• crayons<br>• finger paint<br>• paper<br>• pencil<br>• pictures of rainbows<br>• play clay | • bag or box for Feely Box<br>• brown paper lunch bags<br>• cone, cube, cylinder, and sphere blocks<br>• construction paper, scissors<br>• crayons<br>• glue<br>• objects for art (beads, shells, cotton balls)<br>• paint and paintbrushes<br>• picture books about each season<br>• poster board<br>• popular classroom board game<br>• sun and cloud stick puppets<br>• sticky notes | • construction paper<br>• crayons<br>• dress up clothes for kings and queens<br>• elastic headbands<br>• objects related to *Q* words (quilts, quarters, toy ducks)<br>• paper<br>• pictures of stormy weather<br>• recording of Tchaikovsky's "The Storm" Overture Op. 76<br>• recordings of music about various types of weather<br>• scissors |

## Home Connection

| DAY 1 | DAY 2 | DAY 3 | DAY 4 | DAY 5 |
|---|---|---|---|---|
| Remind children to tell families about the weather. Send home the Weekly Family Letter, Home Connections Resource Guide, pp. 63–64. | Encourage children to play "I Spy" with their families, spying the shapes they learned about in Math Time. | Encourage children to discuss their daily routines at home with their families. | Send home Take-Home Storybook 19, Home Connections Resource Guide, pp. 153–156. Remind children to read the storybook with their families. | Encourage children to play "What Weather Am I?" with families, where one person provides clues about a type of weather for others to guess. |

## Assessment

As you observe children throughout the week, you may fill out an Anecdotal Observational Record Form to document an individual's progress toward a goal or signs indicating the need for developmental or medical evaluation. You may also choose to select work for each child's portfolio. The Anecdotal Observational Record Form and Weekly Assessment rubrics are available in the assessment section of DLMExpressOnline.com.

## More Literature Suggestions

- **The Snowy Day** by Ezra Jack Keats
- **Tracks in the Snow** by Wong Herbert Yee
- **Feel the Wind** by Arthur Dorros
- **Clouds** by Anne Rockwell
- **Captain Invincible and the Space Shapes** by Stuart J. Murphy

- **Las cuatro estaciones: el otoño** por Maria Rius
- **Un día con viento** por Robin Nelson
- **Elmer y el tiempo** por David McKee
- **El tiempo** por Pascale de Bourgoing y Gallimard Jeunesse
- **Jugamos bajo la lluvia** por Angela Shelf Medearis

| | DAY 1 | DAY 2 |
|---|---|---|
| **Let's Start the Day**<br>**Language Time** `large group` | **Opening Routines** p. 64<br>**Morning Read Aloud** p. 64<br>**Oral Language and Vocabulary**<br>p. 64 A Hot Summer Day<br>**Phonological Awareness**<br>p. 64 Segmenting Phonemes | **Opening Routines** p. 70<br>**Morning Read Aloud** p. 70<br>**Oral Language and Vocabulary**<br>p. 70 A Rainy Day<br>**Phonological Awareness**<br>p. 70 Segmenting Phonemes |
| **Center Time** `small group` | **Focus On:**<br>**Pretend and Learn Center** p. 65<br>**Library and Listening Center** p. 65 | **Focus On:**<br>**Writer's Center** p. 71<br>**Math and Science Center** p. 71 |
| **Circle Time**<br>**Literacy Time** `large group` | **Read Aloud**<br>*Who Likes Rain?/*<br>*¿A quién le gusta la*<br>*lluvia?* p. 66<br>**Learn About Letters**<br>**and Sounds:**<br>*Qq* and *Ww* p. 66 | **Read Aloud**<br>*Who Likes Rain?/*<br>*¿A quién le gusta la*<br>*lluvia?* p. 72<br>**Learn About Letters**<br>**and Sounds:**<br>*Qq* and *Ww* p. 72 |
| **Math Time** `large group` | **Shape Step (Properties)** p. 67 | **Feely Box (Describe)** p. 73 |
| **Social and**<br>**Emotional**<br>**Development** `large group` | **Classroom Helpers** p. 67 | **Being Helpful** p. 73 |
| **Content**<br>**Connection** `large group` | **Science:**<br>**Oral Language and Academic Vocabulary**<br>p. 68 Talking About Weather<br>**Observe and Investigate**<br>p. 68 Weather Chart | **Math:**<br>**Geometric Solids**<br>p. 74 Naming Solid Figures<br>**Solids**<br>p. 74 Making Solid Shapes |
| **Center Time** `small group` | **Focus On:**<br>**Math and Science Center** p. 69<br>**Purposeful Play** p. 69 | **Focus On:**<br>**Construction Center** p. 75<br>**Purposeful Play** p. 75 |
| **Let's Say**<br>**Good-Bye** `large group` | **Read Aloud** p. 69<br>**Writing** p. 69<br>**Home Connection** p. 69 | **Read Aloud** p. 75<br>**Writing** p. 75<br>**Home Connection** p. 75 |

**Focus Question**

What weather can I observe each day?
¿Qué tiempo puedo observar todos los días?

# DAY 3

**Opening Routines** p. 76
**Morning Read Aloud** p. 76
**Oral Language and Vocabulary**
p. 76  Snowy Weather
**Phonological Awareness**
p. 76  Segmenting Phonemes

**Focus On:**
**Creativity Center** p. 77
**ABC Center** p. 77

**Read Aloud**
*Concept Big Book 4:*
*The Earth and Sky/*
*La Tierra y el cielo* p. 78
**Learn About Letters and Sounds:** *Qq* and *Ww*
p. 78

**Mr. Mixup** p. 79

**Classroom Helpers** p. 79

**Social Studies:**
**Oral Language and Academic Vocabulary**
p. 80  Daily Schedule
**Understand and Participate**
p. 80  Daily Comparisons

**Focus On:**
**Writer's Center** p. 81
**Purposeful Play** p. 81

**Read Aloud** p. 81
**Writing** p. 81
**Home Connection** p. 81

# DAY 4

**Opening Routines** p. 82
**Morning Read Aloud** p. 82
**Oral Language and Vocabulary**
p. 82  Weather Changes
**Phonological Awareness**
p. 82  Segmenting Phonemes

**Focus On:**
**Library and Listening Center** p. 83
**Creativity Center** p. 83

**Read Aloud**
"The Stonecutter"/"El picapedrero" p. 84
**Learn About Letters and Sounds:**
*Qq* and *Ww* p. 84

**Shape Parts (Triangle)** p. 85

**Classroom Helpers** p. 85

**Math:**
**Identify Solid Shapes**
p. 86 Describing Solid Shapes
**Feely Box**
p. 86 Naming Solid Shapes

**Focus On:**
**Construction Center** p. 87
**Purposeful Play** p. 87

**Read Aloud** p. 87
**Writing** p. 87
**Home Connection** p. 87

# DAY 5

**Opening Routines** p. 88
**Morning Read Aloud** p. 88
**Oral Language and Vocabulary**
p. 88  Relate to Weather
**Phonological Awareness**
p. 88  Segmenting Phonemes

**Focus On:**
**ABC Center** p. 89
**Creativity Center** p. 89

**Read Aloud**
*Who Likes Rain?/*
*¿A quién le gusta la lluvia?* p. 90
**Learn About Letters and Sounds:**
*Qq* and *Ww* p. 90

**I Spy (Properties)** p. 91

**Classroom Helpers** p. 91

**Music and Movement:**
**Oral Language and Academic Vocabulary**
p. 92  Stormy Weather
**Explore and Express**
p. 92  The Storm

**Focus On:**
**Pretend and Learn Center** p. 93
**Purposeful Play** p. 93

**Read Aloud** p. 93
**Writing** p. 93
**Home Connection** p. 93

# Week 2

**Outside My Window**

# Learning Centers

## Math and Science Center

### Observe the Wind
Children make Wind Detectors and observe how the wind blows. See p. 69.

### Do They Float?
Children test whether objects float or sink and create a chart to show results. See p. 71.

### Signs of Rain
Children discuss the things they see outside when it is raining that are not there when it is sunny.

### Cloud Count
Children pick up a handful of cotton balls and count the "clouds."

## ABC Center

### Review Letter *Ss*
Children form the letter *Ss* using clay, trace it, and write it. They convert the tracing into a snake drawing and segment the word *snake* by onset and rime. See p. 77.

### Kings and Queens
Children make *Q or QK* crowns and identify things that begin with the /kw/ sound. See p. 89.

### Sand Tracing
Children trace the letter *Qq* on sandpaper or in a sandbox while making the /kw/ sound.

### *Ww* Detectives
Child pairs search for the letter *Ww* in environmental print. They use a rubber band to put a ring around the letter when they find it.

## Creativity Center

### Rainbows
Children finger paint rainbows and identify the colors in them. See p. 77.

### Weather Puppets
Children make weather symbol paper bag puppets and use the puppets to discuss different types of weather. See p. 83.

### Art Inspired by Music
Children draw pictures to show what they visualized while listening to music about weather. See p. 89.

### Weather in Art
Show children pictures of landscape paintings such as Monet's "La Promenade" or Bruegel's "Winter Landscape with a Bird Trap" and discuss the type of weather that is depicted. Children make their own landscape pictures inspired by the art.

### Snowflakes
Fold square white or silver tissue paper into eighths and have children cut or rip between the folds to make snowflakes.

## Library and Listening Center

**My Favorite Weather**
Children find their favorite type of weather as shown in books, and explain why they like it. See p. 65.

**Season Hunt**
Children find pictures of their favorite season in books and discuss with a small group why they like that season. See p. 83.

**Sing About Rain**
Children listen to and sing "The Itsy Bitsy Spider" and draw a picture of the rainy portion of the song.

## Construction Center

**Another Solid: Cone**
Children make and decorate cone shapes from paper plates. See p. 75.

**3-D Object Mural**
Children make a mural with objects in solid shapes such as spheres, cubes, cylinders, and cones. See p. 87.

**Weather Picture**
Children construct a weather picture using solids such as cotton balls, drinking straws, noodles, and sugar cubes.

**Give Me Shelter**
Children use blocks to create shelters. They pretend it rains or snows, and toy people or animals use the shelters.

## Writer's Center

**Make a Postcard**
Children draw and sign postcards showing favorite types of weather. See p. 71.

**Fun Activity**
Children draw summer activities they enjoy doing and dictate sentences about them. See p. 81.

**Make a Stamp**
Children create postage stamps to depict types of weather. They dictate labels for the stamps.

## Pretend and Learn Center

**Going Swimming**
Children pretend to swim on a hot day. They describe what they wear and do. See p. 65.

**The Stonecutter**
Children act out the mood and sequence of events in the story "The Stonecutter." See p. 93.

**Falling Leaves**
Children pretend they are leaves falling on a windy day and then mimic raking leaves.

# Let's Start the Day

**Focus Question**

## What weather can I observe each day?
## ¿Qué tiempo puedo observar todos los días?

▶ **Opening Routines and Transition Tips**
For **Opening Routines** and **Transition Tips** turn to pages 178–181 and visit
DLMExpressOnline.com for more ideas.

 Read **"Sing Me a Rainbow"/**"Cántame un arco iris" from the
*Teacher's Treasure Book,* page 165, for your morning Read Aloud.

### ✓ Learning Goals

**Social and Emotional Development**
• Child shows eagerness, curiosity, and confidence while learning new concepts and trying new things.

**Language and Communication**
• Child uses newly learned vocabulary daily in multiple contexts.

### Vocabulary

| | | | |
|---|---|---|---|
| goggles | antiparras | pool | piscina |
| splash | chapotear | summer | verano |
| swim | nadar | weather | tiempo |

## Differentiated Instruction

###  Extra Support
**Phonological Awareness**
**If...**children have difficulty segmenting words, **then...**say the word *rain* and have them make the sound of an engine (/r/). Then have them say the word ending (*-ain*). Repeat with other familiar /r/ words like *race, ran, ring, red.*

###  Enrichment
**Phonological Awareness**
Challenge children to take turns choosing a word from "Raindrops" and segmenting it.

###  Special Needs
**Cognitive Challenges**
**If...**children have difficulty with vocabulary words, **then...**offer them multi-sensory ways to remember the words. Have them move their arms in swimming motions and say "I can swim" and use their fingers to make circles around their eyes as they say "I wear goggles."

# Language Time

 large group · 15 minutes

👫👫 **Social and Emotional Development** If children become distracted during discussion, ask them how they have promised to be during discussion time.

## Oral Language and Vocabulary

✓ **Can children add new words to their daily vocabularies?**

**A Hot Summer Day** Explain to children that weather can be hot or cold, wet or dry. Talk about a hot, summer day. Ask: *What do you like to do on a hot day? What kinds of things do you do outside when it is hot?* ¿Qué les gusta hacer en un día caluroso? ¿Qué tipo de cosas hacen afuera cuando hace calor?

● Display *Oral Language Development Card 64.* Name the swimming pool and what the children are doing. Follow the suggestions on the back of the card.

## Phonological Awareness

✓ **Can children segment words?**

**Segmenting Phonemes** Display *Rhymes and Chants Flip Chart* page 30. Read "Raindrops" aloud to children. Point to the word *rain.* Explain that *rain* is made up of beginning sounds and ending sounds: /r/ /ā/ /n/. Have children echo the segmenting and blend the words back together. If necessary, segment only two sounds at a time: (first /r/ /ā/, then *ray* /n/.) Repeat for *sun* (/s/ /u/ /n/) and *fall* (/f/ /a/ /l/).

**ELL** Revisit *clouds* and *rainbow.* Point to the *Rhymes and Chants Flip Chart* picture. Say: *I see clouds.* Have children repeat as they point to the dark clouds at the top of the image. Ask: *What do you see?* Have children respond: *I see clouds.* Repeat with *rainbow.*

*Oral Language Development Card 64*

*Rhymes and Chants Flip Chart, page 30/ page 62*

# Center Time

▶ **Center Rotation** Center Time includes teacher-guided activities and independent activities. Refer to the **Learning Centers** on pages 62–63 for activities in additional centers.

## Pretend and Learn Center

✓ **Track children's use of new vocabulary words and grammar.**

**Materials** blue butcher paper, goggles, pool toys

**Going Swimming** Tape large sheets of blue butcher paper to the floor to represent a swimming pool.

- Let children pretend that they are playing in a swimming pool on a hot day. Tell them the pool rules are no running or pushing around the pool.

- Ask: *How do you play in the pool? What do you wear? Do you splash and swim? How is the weather at the pool? ¿Cómo juegan en la piscina? ¿Qué ropa usan? ¿Chapotean y nadan? ¿Cómo es el tiempo en la piscina?*

### Center Tip

**If...**children are not following the pool rules, **then...**assign one child to be lifeguard to remind children to play safely.

## Library and Listening Center

✓ **Observe children identifying and describing a kind of weather.**

✓ **Listen for children combining ideas into complete sentences.**

**Materials** picture books about weather and seasons such as *A Tree for All Seasons* by Robin Bernard; the Four Seasons series by Nuria Roca; the Celebrate the Seasons series by Linda Glaser; sticky notes

**My Favorite Weather** Have children browse the books to observe different kinds of weather.

- Say: *Look at the pictures. Turn the pages slowly. What kinds of weather do you see?* *Miren las imágenes. Hojeen lentamente las páginas. ¿Qué climas ven?*

- Prompt children to choose a kind of weather that they like best. Have them find a picture that shows it and place a sticky-note flag on it.

- Let children show the picture they flagged and tell the group why they like this kind of weather.

### Center Tip

**If...**children have difficulty choosing just one picture, **then...**allow them to flag two pictures. Then sit with the child and review the two pictures in order to pick the best one.

## Learning Goals

**Social and Emotional Development**
- Child participates in a variety of individual, small- and large-group activities.
- Child understands and respects the different ideas, feelings, perspectives, and behaviors of others.

**Language and Communication**
- Child understands and uses sentences of increasing length and complexity.
- Child tries to use newly learned vocabulary and grammar. (ELL)

**Emergent Literacy: Reading**
- Child independently engages in pre-reading behaviors and activities (such as, pretending to read, turning one page at a time).

## Differentiated Instruction

✋ **Extra Support**
**Library and Listening Center**
**If...**children have difficulty talking about their weather choice, **then...**have them draw a picture of themselves outside in their favorite weather and display it for others to see.

⭐ **Enrichment**
**Library and Listening Center**
Challenge children to tell activities they like to do in their favorite kind of weather.

**Accommodations for 3's**
**Pretend and Learn Center**
**If...**children have difficulty understanding what a pool is, **then...**remind them of water experiences in a bathtub or water play at school.

## ✓ Learning Goals

**Social and Emotional Development**
• Child understands and respects the different ideas, feelings, perspectives, and behaviors of others.

**Emergent Literacy: Reading**
• Child names most upper- and lowercase letters of the alphabet.
• Child identifies the letter that stands for a given sound.
• Child asks and answers questions about books read aloud (such as "Who?" "What?" "Where?").

**Social Studies**
• Child understands basic human needs for food, clothing, shelter.

### Vocabulary

| | | | |
|---|---|---|---|
| puddle | charco | rain | lluvia |
| raincoat | impermeable | | |
| raindrops | gotas de lluvia | | |
| shelter | refugiarse | showers | aguaceros |
| umbrella | paraguas | weather | tiempo |

## Differentiated Instruction

### ✋ Extra Support

**Learn About Letters and Sounds**
**If...**children have difficulty making the letter *W*, **then...**have them use beverage stirrers placed on diagonals to form *W*. Then have them trace the letter.

### ★ Enrichment

**Learn About Letters and Sounds**
Have children find classroom objects with names that begin with *Ww*.

## Literacy Time

### 📖 Read Aloud

🗸 **Can children form an opinion and answer appropriately about a book?**

**Build Background** Tell children that you will be reading a book about a certain kind of weather. Remind them that weather changes. Explain that all people need things to protect them from weather, like clothing and shelter, or buildings like homes. Share that some weather is gentle and clothing protects people from it so they can go outside, but in other weather we need to stay inside.

● Ask: *What do you like to do when it rains? Do you go outside or stay in? Do you like a rainy day? Why or why not?* ¿Qué les gusta hacer cuando llueve? ¿Les gusta quedarse adentro o salir? ¿Les gustan los días lluviosos? ¿Por qué?

**Listen for Enjoyment** Display the Big Book *Who Likes Rain?* and read the title and author's name.

● Read the story aloud. Emphasize the rhythm and rhyme of the text.

**Respond to the Story** Have children tell which part of the story they liked best. Review the pages to help children make choices. Ask: *What part made you laugh? What is something you'd like to try?* ¿Qué parte los hizo reír? ¿Hay algo de lo que pasa en el cuento que les gustaría probar?

**TIP** Provide children with a raincoat, rain hat, and umbrella to help them have concrete understandings of the vocabulary words.

### Learn About Letters and Sounds

🗸 **Can children make *Qq* and *Ww* and recognize the letters' sounds?**

**Learn About the Letters *Qq* and *Ww*** Review the /kw/ sound for *Qq* and the /w/ sound for *Ww*.

● Display *ABC Picture Card Qq*. Say: **Queen begins with /kw/, Q. Trace the upper case letter Q on your desk with your finger. Say the sound and the word: /kw/, queen.** Queen empieza con /kw/, Q. Tracen con el dedo la letra mayúscula Q sobre su escritorio. Digan el sonido y luego la palabra: /kw/, queen.

● Repeat for uppercase *W* and *worm* with the *ABC Picture Card Ww*.

● Repeat for lowercase *q* and lowercase *w*.

**ELL** To give children practice making the /w/ sound, isolate and repeat the sound before words that begin with it. Have children repeat after you. Say, for example, /w/ /w/ /w/ *worm;* /w/ /w/ /w/ *water;* /w/ /w/ /w/ *wind;* /w/ /w/ /w/ *wagon.* Instruct children to round their lips like making a kiss for each /w/ sound. For additional suggestions on how to meet the needs of children at varying levels of English proficiency, see pages 184–187.

*Who Likes Rain?*
*¿A quién le gusta la lluvia?*

*ABC Picture Cards*
*Tarjetas abecé de imágenes*

# Math Time

## Observe and Investigate

☑ **Can children identify common shapes?**

**Shape Step (Properties)** Make large shapes on which children can step: use colored or masking tape to form shapes, make chalk shapes outside, or enlarge and laminate printed shapes.

- Have a group of four children step only on the shape you describe, such as trapezoids (only one pair of parallel sides). Ask all other children to make sure group members step on all examples of the correct shape. Afterward, ask group members to explain how they knew the shapes they stepped on were correct.

- Repeat with different properties and groups of children, focusing on shapes of your choice. For example, rhombuses: four sides all the same; squares: four sides all the same with all right angles; and parallelograms: two pairs of equal sides.

# ✗✗✗ Social and Emotional Development

## Making Good Choices

☑ **Do children assume responsibilities in the classroom?**

**Classroom Helpers** Play the song "Everybody Needs Help Sometimes"/"Todos necesitan ayuda alguna vez" from the Making Good Choices Audio CD. Ask children what they think the song is telling them about why we should help others. Then, ask children how they help in the classroom.

- Explain the difference between helping in the classroom and helping another person directly. Display the Making Good Choices Flip Chart, page 30. Point to each pictured child and have children identify what job that child is doing.

- Discuss how the Job Chart in the picture shows the children what to do. Ask which jobs in the picture are like those on your classroom Job Chart.

**ELL** Have each child act out each chore and complete the sentence pattern **I can _____ the _____.** For example, **I can hold the door; I can water the plant; I can set the table.** For additional suggestions on how to meet the needs of children at the Beginning, Intermediate, Advanced, and Advanced-High levels of English proficiency, see pages 184–187.

### Building Blocks

**Online Math Activity**

Introduce Piece Puzzler 2: Assemble Pieces, in which children drag and sometimes flip shapes into place. Shapes touch at their sides, encouraging children to see how shapes combine to fill regions. Each child should complete the activity this week.

*Making Good Choices Flip Chart, page 30*

### ☑ Learning Goals

**Social and Emotional Development**
- Child participates in a variety of individual, small- and large-group activities.

**Language and Communication**
- Child tries to use newly learned vocabulary and grammar. (ELL)

**Mathematics**
- Child recognizes, names, describes, matches, compares, sorts common two-dimensional shapes (such as circle, square, rectangle, triangle, rhombus).

### Vocabulary

| | |
|---|---|
| equal | igual |
| opposite | opuesto |
| parallelogram | paralelogramo |
| rhombus | rombo |
| square | cuadrado |
| trapezoid | trapecio |

### Differentiated Instruction

✋ **Extra Support**

**Observe and Investigate**
**If**...children struggle identifying shapes, **then**... emphasize the parts of a shape by having children trace its outline, count the shape's sides, and, when applicable, its corners.

⭐ **Enrichment**

**Observe and Investigate**
Let a child call out a shape and describe it.

**Accommodations for 3's**

**Observe and Investigate**
**If**...children struggle differentiating shape properties, **then**...focus on two simple shapes such as triangle and square, noting their differences by counting sides.

## What weather can I observe each day?
## ¿Qué tiempo puedo observar todos los días?

### Learning Goals

**Social and Emotional Development**
• Child demonstrates appropriate conflict-resolution strategies, requesting help when needed.

**Language and Communication**
• Child names and describes actual or pictured people, places, things, actions, attributes, and events.

**Science**
• Child describes the effects of natural forces (such as wind, gravity).

**Technology Applications**
• Child knows some ways that technology affects people's lives.

### Vocabulary

| | | | |
|---|---|---|---|
| cloudy | nublado | rainy | lluvioso |
| snowy | nevoso | sunny | soleado |
| windy | ventoso | | |

### Differentiated Instruction

 **Extra Support**

**Oral Language and Academic Vocabulary**
**If...**children have difficulty telling the difference between sunny and cloudy, **then...**show them pictures of a sunny day and point out the sun and blue skies. Have them chant, "It's a sunny day" several times. Show them pictures of a cloudy day and point out that they can't see the sun and the sky is not blue. Have them chant, "It's a cloudy day."

 **Enrichment**

**Oral Language and Academic Vocabulary**
Challenge children to add robust vocabulary to their spoken language repertoire: *stormy, foggy, drizzly, sleet.*

# Science Time

  large group 20 minutes

**Social and Emotional Development** Model how to ask for assistance politely when putting on boots, jackets, and other outdoor gear.

## Oral Language and Academic Vocabulary

✓ Can children describe weather and what to wear when weather changes?

**Talking About Weather** Display the *Math and Science Flip Chart* page 55. Say: *These pictures show four kinds of weather. Estas imágenes muestran cuatro estados del tiempo.*

● Help children identify the four kinds of weather pictured (rainy, windy, snowy, sunny). Ask: **What special clothing is each child wearing? Why?** *¿Qué ropa especial usan los niños cuando llueve? ¿Por qué?*

● Invite volunteers to tell what kinds of clothes they put on to keep them warm, cool, or dry in different types of weather.

## Observe and Investigate

✓ Can children observe and record weather?

✓ Do children recognize that information is available through technology?

**Weather Chart** Divide a poster board into four sections. In each, draw a symbol for a kind of weather children might observe during the current season. For example, *sunny, windy, rainy, cloudy*. Use a brad to attach an arrow to the center of the sections. Explain the symbols on the chart.

● Have children look out the window. Ask: **What is the weather outside?** *¿Cómo está el tiempo?* Prompt discussion by asking questions such as, **Are the leaves moving?** *¿Se mueven las hojas de los árboles?* Have a volunteer move the arrow to the correct weather for today.

● Draw a 5-column chart on the poster board. Track all symbols that apply to the day's weather, such as *sunny* and *windy*.

● Then ask: **If we couldn't see outside, how could we find out the weather? How can we learn about tomorrow's weather?** *Si no vemos el exterior, ¿cómo sabremos cómo está el tiempo? ¿Cómo podemos saber qué tiempo hará mañana?* Prompt children to think of using technology such as TV, radio, and internet for weather information.

**TIP** The Weather Chart activity can become a part of a daily routine. Add symbols each time the weather changes in a day.

**ELL** Point to the flip chart and have children repeat these descriptive sentences employing various verbs: **The boy stands in rain. It is rainy. The kite blows in the wind. It is windy. The girl is holding snow. It is snowy.**

*Math and Science Flip Chart, page 55*

# Center Time

## Center Rotation
Center Time includes teacher-guided activities and independent activities. Refer to the **Learning Centers** on pages 62–63 for activities in additional centers.

## Math and Science Center

| | Center Tip |

✓ **Observe as children describe what happens when wind blows.**

**Materials** paper towel rolls, crepe paper, paint, scissors, stapler

**Observe the Wind** Tell children that they will make Wind Detectors and watch the wind blow.

- Have children paint the paper towel rolls and cut the paper into strips. Help children staple the strips to the ends of their rolls.

- Take children outside on a windy day and have them hold the Wind Detectors over their heads. Or, set up a table fan to be the wind. Discuss what happens to the paper. Ask: **Does the Wind Detector tell you which way the wind is blowing?** *¿Les dice el detector de viento en qué dirección sopla el viento?* Prompt children to give detailed descriptions of how the wind blows the paper.

- Take children somewhere blocking the wind (or turn off the fan) to observe the Wind Detectors again. Save them for other windy days.

### Center Tip
**If...**children have trouble describing what happens when the wind blows, **then...**help them think of ways to describe the movement, such as, **The paper moves like the flag flaps in the wind. How does it move?** *El papel se mueve como una bandera que ondea con el viento. ¿De qué manera se mueve?*

## Purposeful Play

✓ **Listen for children speaking in complex sentences with subject-verb agreement.**

Children choose an open center for free playtime. Encourage cooperation by suggesting they pretend to play in the snow. Partway through playtime, tell them the weather changed to rain, and ask how they would play now. Change the weather several times.

## Let's Say Good-Bye

large group 15 minutes

 **Read Aloud** Revisit "Sing Me a Rainbow"/"Cántame un arco iris" from the *Teacher's Treasure Book,* page 165, for your afternoon Read Aloud. Ask children what words make up the word *rainbow.*

 **Home Connection** Refer to the Home Connection activities listed in the chart on page 59. Remind children to tell families about the weather chart they made. Sing the "Good-bye Song" as children prepare to leave.

### ✓ Learning Goals

**Social and Emotional Development**
- Child initiates play scenarios with peers that share a common plan and goal.

**Language and Communication**
- Child names and describes actual or pictured people, places, things, actions, attributes, and events.

- Child speaks in complete sentences of four or more words including a subject, verb, and object.

- Child understands and uses regular and irregular plural nouns, regular past tense verbs, personal and possessive pronouns, and subject-verb agreement.

- Child understands and uses sentences having two or more phrases or concepts.

- Child understands and uses sentences of increasing length and complexity.

- Child uses complex sentences that include many details, tell about one topic, and communicate meaning clearly.

**Science**
- Child describes the effects of natural forces (such as wind, gravity).

### Writing

Recap the day. Review the weather the class observed. Ask: **Has the weather changed? What is it like now?** *¿Ha cambiado el tiempo? ¿Cómo está tiempo ahora?* Encourage children to answer in complete sentences. Model combining their ideas as you record their answers. Track the print, emphasizing correspondence between speech and print.

## DAY 2

**Focus Question**

## What weather can I observe each day?
## ¿Qué tiempo puedo observar todos los días?

 **Learning Goals**

**Social and Emotional Development**
• Child participates in a variety of individual, small- and large-group activities.

**Language and Communication**
• Child names and describes actual or pictured people, places, things, actions, attributes, and events.
• Child uses words to identify and understand categories.

**Social Studies**
• Child understands basic human needs for food, clothing, shelter.

### Vocabulary

| | | | |
|---|---|---|---|
| boots | botas | hat | sombrero |
| raincoat | impermeable | | |
| rain gear | ropa de lluvia | | |
| weather | tiempo | | |

### Differentiated Instruction

 **Extra Support**

**Phonological Awareness**
**If...**children have difficulty segmenting words, **then...**hold a rubber band and say the word slowly, stretching the sounds as you stretch the rubber band. Let children try stretching the rubber band as they say /f/ /u/ /n/, *fun.*

 **Enrichment**

**Oral Language and Vocabulary**
Have children tell other kinds of weather where they might want to wear boots. Repeat for a hat and then a coat.

# Let's Start the Day

 **Opening Routines and Transition Tips**
For **Opening Routines** and **Transition Tips** turn to pages 178–181 and visit **DLMExpressOnline.com** for more ideas.

 Read **"Dress-Me-Bears for School"/"¡A vestirse para la escuela!"**, *Teacher's Treasure Book* page 233, for your morning Read Aloud.

# Language Time

**large group**   **15 minutes**

**Social and Emotional Development** Ask children to brainstorm ways they can help you during reading time. Make a list and rotate the responsibilities during the week.

## Oral Language and Vocabulary

✓ **Can children categorize and label special clothing needed for rainy weather?**

**A Rainy Day** Display the Big Book *Who Likes Rain?* and read the title. Then turn to page 4 and ask: **What is the girl wearing? Why do you think all people need clothing?** *¿Qué tiene puesto la niña? ¿Por qué creen que todos necesitamos ropa?*

• Have children close their eyes and imagine that it is raining. Tell them they are going to pretend to go outside. Ask: **What rain gear will you put on?** *¿Qué ropa de lluvia van a ponerse?*

• Show page 8 of the *Big Book.* Have children point to and name the clothes the girl is about to put on. Have them check their answers against page 11.

• Display pages 30–31 and ask what clothes the girl took off.

## Phonological Awareness

✓ **Can children segment words into phonemes?**

**Segmenting Phonemes** Display the Dog Puppets. Tell children that you will say a word, one puppet will say the beginning sound, and the other will say the middle and the ending sounds.

• Say *fun.* Have one puppet say /f/ and the other say /u/ /n/.

• Ask children to help the first puppet. Say *rain.* Have the first puppet turn to children for help. If needed, repeat the word, emphasizing the /r/ sound. Have children and the puppet say /r/ and the second puppet say /ā/ /n/. Repeat with the words *mud, melt,* and *fog.*

**ELL** Display a child's rain hat, coat, and boots. Have a child put on the hat and say, **This is a rain hat.** Continue with each piece of clothing. If something doesn't fit, have the child point to the item, say the sentence, and pantomime putting it on. Then ask: **What two words make the word** raincoat?

# Center Time

▶ **Center Rotation** Center Time includes teacher-guided activities and independent activities. Refer to the **Learning Centers** on pages 62–63 for activities in additional centers.

small group | 60–90 minutes

## Writer's Center

✓ Track children's abilities to identify one type of weather and a key element of it.

**Materials** sample postcards, large index cards, crayons, markers

**Make a Postcard** Show children postcards and explain what postcards are. Share that they will make weather postcards.

- Instruct children to draw a picture on one side of an index card. Tell them to show one kind of weather they like. Suggest they make the picture colorful.

- Have children sign their cards by writing their names on the back.

- Hang the cards from a mobile for classmates to enjoy and identify the kinds of weather depicted.

### Center Tip

**If...**children have difficulty knowing what to draw, **then...**provide pictures from the Photo Library CD-ROM of different kinds of weather to trigger their imaginations.

## Math and Science Center

✓ Observe children exploring whether objects sink or float.

**Materials** tub of water, three objects that float and three that sink; laminated two-column chart with one side labeled *float* (with picture of floating duck) and other side labeled *sink* (with picture of sunken rock)

**Do They Float?** Tell children to imagine that the tub of water is the puddle the girl jumped in. Demonstrate what floating and sinking means using two of the objects at the center.

- Instruct children to place each object in the water one at a time and watch what happens. If the object floats, they should place it in the *float* column. If it sinks, they should place it in the *sink* column.

- At the end of the activity, have children name the objects that floated and sank. Ask if they were surprised by any findings.

### Center Tip

**If...**children become more curious about floating and sinking, **then...**let them choose and experiment with other waterproof objects in the classroom.

## Learning Goals

**Emergent Literacy: Writing**
- Child writes own name or a reasonable approximation of it.

**Science**
- Child uses senses to observe, classify, investigate, and collect data.

- Child observes, identifies, explores, describes, and compares earth materials (such as rocks, soil, sand, water) and their uses.

**Fine Arts**
- Child expresses emotions or ideas through art.

## Differentiated Instruction

 **Extra Support**
**Writer's Center**
**If...**children have difficulty drawing a scene that depicts weather, **then...**have them draw one key element such as a sun, cloud, or raindrop.

 **Enrichment**
**Math and Science Center**
Challenge children to draw pictures of items that floated on one side of a paper and objects that sank on the other. Ask children to label their pictures. Prompt them to write the letters they know.

 **Special Needs**
**Behavorial/Social/Emotional**
**If...**children become frustrated sorting so many objects, **then...**provide one object that sinks and one that floats and have children work alone to try to find the one that floats. Praise children's efforts at the task.

**Focus Question**
## What weather can I observe each day?
## ¿Qué tiempo puedo observar todos los días?

---

## Literacy Time

 large group   15 minutes

### 📖 Read Aloud

✓ **Do children ask to be read to or ask the meaning of text?**

**Build Background** Tell children that you will reread the story about a rainy day.

● Ask: *What do you remember about this story? What did the girl do when it rained? What did she do after the rain?* *¿Qué recuerdan de este cuento? ¿Qué hizo la niña cuando llovió? ¿Qué hizo después de la lluvia?*

**Listen for Understanding** Display the cover of the Big Book *Who Likes Rain?*

● Track the print as you reread the title. Read the author's name and explain that he wrote the words in the story.

● Tell children to point out specific words that they do not know on the page as you read so you can tell them the meaning of written text.

**Respond to the Story** Have children tell what the girl did that shows she likes rain. Ask: *What did the girl do with her hat? What animals did she see in the rain? What was left after the rain? What did the girl do then?* *¿Qué hizo la niña con su sombrero? ¿Qué animales vio en la lluvia? ¿Qué quedó después de la lluvia? ¿Qué hizo la niña entonces?* Then have children share their own experiences with rain. Have them tell whether they like rain or not.

 **TIP** As you ask discussion questions, turn to key illustrations to aid children in responding.

### Learn About Letters and Sounds

✓ **Can children identify *Qq* and *Ww* and recognize the letters' sounds?**

**Learn About Letters *Qq* and *Ww*** Mix up the *ABC Picture Cards Hh, Jj, Qq, Ww,* and *Yy* and spread them face up in the center of a group of children.

● Call on a child to find the card for *Qq*. When the card is found, have the child say the letter and name the picture. Have all children repeat.

● Put the card back on the floor and mix them up again. Call on a child to find the card for *Ww* and repeat the game.

● If time allows, continue until each child has found *Qq* and *Ww*.

**ELL** Some English language learners may pronounce *Qq* with a /k/ sound. Provide fun alliterative sentences for children to practice the /kw/ sound, such as "The queen got quilts for a quarter."

---

*Who Likes Rain?*
*¿A quién le gusta la lluvia?*

*ABC Picture Cards*
*Tarjetas abecé de imágenes*

---

## Learning Goals

**Social and Emotional Development**
• Child understands and respects the different ideas, feelings, perspectives, and behaviors of others.

**Emergent Literacy: Reading**
• Child explores books and other texts to answer questions.

• Child names most upper- and lowercase letters of the alphabet.

• Child identifies the letter that stands for a given sound.

• Child asks and answers questions about books read aloud (such as "Who?" "What?" "Where?").

**Science**
• Child describes the effects of natural forces (such as wind, gravity).

### Vocabulary

| | | | |
|---|---|---|---|
| frog | rana | raindrops | gotas de lluvia |
| puddle | charco | rain gear | ropa de lluvia |
| worm | gusano | | |

---

## Differentiated Instruction

### 🖐 Extra Support

**Learn About Letters and Sounds**
**If...**children have difficulty finding a letter card, **then...**remove three cards so they choose from three. As they get to know letters, add more.

### ⭐ Enrichment

**Learn About Letters and Sounds**
When children find a card, have them say the letter, name the picture, and say an additional word that begins with the same sound.

### 💜 Special Needs

**Hearing Impairment**
Teach children the American Sign Language letters and allow them to show the group what letter they see when they turn a card. Encourage any interested children to learn the sign letters.

---

## Math Time

### Observe and Investigate

✓ Can children name and describe common shapes?

✓ Can children open and navigate through the online math activity?

**Feely Box (Describe)** Secretly hide a Pattern Block in the feely box. Have one child feel the shape and describe it well enough *without using its name* for the other children to name it. Ask children how they knew it was a certain shape. Repeat with several shapes, especially the trapezoid, hexagon, and rhombus.

- For a challenge, have a child name the shape and how he or she knows it *before* removing it from the box.

- As you introduce Shape Parts 1, ask children to show you how to open the program. After you model navigating it, have volunteers show the class what you did and how. Review with children the names of the computer input devices, such as the mouse and keyboard, as they use them.

### ᛱᛱᛱ Social and Emotional Development

### Making Good Choices

✓ Do children assume responsibilities in the classroom?

**Being Helpful** Again play the song "Everybody Needs Help Sometimes"/"Todos necesitan ayuda alguna vez" from the Making Good Choices Audio CD. Ask children what they recall from their discussion yesterday about helping others and helping in the classroom. Display *Making Good Choices Flip Chart* page 30.

- Display a Dog Puppet. Say: **Who would like to tell the puppet how each child in the picture is helping?** *¿Quién quiere contarle al títere cómo ayuda cada uno de los niños de la ilustración?*

- Provide each child a turn to tell the puppet how at least one child in the picture is helping. Then have children tell the puppet one thing they do or can do to help in their classroom.

  Pair English language learners with native speakers for a discussion of being helpful. Tell them to think of a skit to act out that shows how they can be helpful in class. Encourage native speakers to communicate simply and pay attention to the nonverbal communication of their English learning peers. Have pairs perform their skits and then describe the actions they performed in simple English.

large group 15 minutes

---

### Building Blocks

**Online Math Activity**

Introduce Shape Parts 1, in which children build shapes from their sides. Each child should complete the activity this week.

*Making Good Choices Flip Chart, page 30*

---

### ✓ Learning Goals

**Social and Emotional Development**
• Child participates in a variety of individual, small- and large-group activities.

**Language and Communication**
• Child uses nonverbal cues to communicate with others who do not speak his or her home language. (ELL)

• Child uses individual words and short phrases to communicate. (ELL)

**Mathematics**
• Child recognizes, names, describes, matches, compares, sorts common two-dimensional shapes (such as circle, square, rectangle, triangle, rhombus).

**Technology Applications**
• Child names and uses various computer parts (such as mouse, keyboard, CD-ROM, microphone, touch screen).

### Vocabulary

| | | | |
|---|---|---|---|
| corners | vértices | hexagon | hexágono |
| rhombus | rombo | round | redondo |
| sides | lados | trapezoid | trapecio |

### Differentiated Instruction

 **Extra Support**

*Observe and Investigate*
**If...**children have trouble describing a shape, **then...**prompt them with questions such as, *Is it round or does it have corners? ¿Es redonda o tiene vértices?*

 **Enrichment**

*Observe and Investigate*
Have children find objects in the room that are the same shape as the object they identified.

### Accommodations for 3's

*Observe and Investigate*
**If...**children struggle with complicated shapes, **then...**focus on circles, squares, and triangles until they are ready for more.

## Learning Goals

**Language and Communication**
• Child uses oral language for a variety of purposes.
• Child exhibits an understanding of instructional terms used in the classroom.

**Mathematics**
• Child recognizes, names, describes, matches, compares, sorts common two-dimensional shapes (such as circle, square, rectangle, triangle, rhombus).

### Vocabulary

| | | | |
|---|---|---|---|
| cube | cubo | cylinder | cilindro |
| shape | figura | solid | sólido |
| sphere | esfera | | |

## Differentiated Instruction

 **Extra Support**

**Math Time**

**If**...children need help remembering the names of the solid shapes, **then**...use *sphere, cube,* and *cylinder* when talking to children during block play and when referring to common objects in the classroom.

 **Enrichment**

**Math Time**

Challenge children to make all three solids out of play clay and match them to the ones pictured on the *Math and Science Flip Chart.*

# Math Time

 large group · 20 minutes

**Language and Communication Skills** Pause to check children's understanding of your instructional terms while you discuss each shape with them.

✓ **Can children name a solid figure?**

**Geometric Solids** Display a sphere, cube, and cylinder. For each solid, hand it to a child and say ***This is a (sphere). Say* sphere.** *Esta figura es (una esfera). Digan esfera.* Make sure each child holds each solid and repeats its name.

● Explain that all kinds of things are solids, or objects we can touch and feel. Share that many solids are spheres, cubes, and cylinders.

● Tell children that they can often see examples of spheres, such as basketballs and baseballs. Share that many natural things are like spheres, such as the planet Earth, the sun, and the moon. Provide examples of common objects that are cubes (boxes) and cylinders (rolls of paper towels).

● Display balls, cans, and fuzzy dice. Hold up the ball. Ask: ***Which of these is a sphere? Say* sphere.** *¿Cuál de estos sólidos es una esfera? Digan esfera.* Repeat for the cube and cylinder.

✓ **Can children name and make a solid shape?**

**Solids** Have children name and copy a solid shape.

● Display the *Math and Science Flip Chart* page 56, "Solids."

● Have children name and describe each solid.

● Assign children to work in groups. Assign each group one solid shape. Have children use modeling clay or play clay to make the shape.

**TIP** Allow children to have a solid shape model nearby to look at and feel as they make the shape.

**ELL** Explain to Spanish-speaking children that some English words are similar to Spanish words, such as *cubo* (cube), *esfera* (sphere), and *cilindro* (cylinder). Offer each cognate and repeat the three English shape words. Have children choose which word they think each cognate goes with. For additional suggestions on how to meet the needs of children at the Beginning, Intermediate, Advanced, and Advanced-High levels of English proficiency, see pages 184–187.

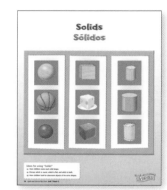

*Math and Science Flip Chart, page 56*

# Center Time

> **Center Rotation** Center Time includes teacher-guided activities and independent activities. Refer to the **Learning Centers** on pages 62–63 for activities in additional centers.

small group — 30 minutes

## Construction Center

✓ **Observe children as they make and decorate cones.**

**Materials** round paper plates, scissors, stapler or tape, glue, yarn, ruler, sparkles, paint

**Another Solid: Cone** Display a cone solid in the center and have children repeat the name after you.

- Put a dot in the center of each plate and draw a straight line using a ruler to show the radius of the circle.

- Model how to make a cone from a paper plate. First, cut the line on the plate. Then take the edges by the cut line and overlap them. The more the flaps overlap, the taller and narrower the cone will be. Staple or tape the cone together.

- Let children each make a cone and decorate the outside of it.

### Center Tip

**If**...children have difficulty cutting on the line, **then**...cut the radius lines for them and let children assemble the cones.

## Purposeful Play

✓ **Observe children taking care of classroom materials.**

Children choose an open center for free playtime. Encourage children to use dress-up rain gear in their imaginative play, and to ask other children what they would like to play before they begin. Remind children to share all materials.

### Learning Goals

**Social and Emotional Development**
- Child uses classroom materials carefully.
- Child initiates play scenarios with peers that share a common plan and goal.

**Emergent Literacy: Writing**
- Child participates in free drawing and writing activities to deliver information.

**Mathematics**
- Child recognizes, names, describes, matches, compares, sorts common two-dimensional shapes (such as circle, square, rectangle, triangle, rhombus).

**Fine Arts**
- Child expresses emotions or ideas through art.

**Physical Development**
- Child completes tasks that require eye-hand coordination and control.

### Writing

Recap the day. Ask children to draw a picture of what they like to do on a rainy day and label it. Allow children to use scribbles or letters to convey ideas.

## Let's Say Good-Bye

large group — 15 minutes

 **Read Aloud** Reread this morning's "Dress-Me-Bears for School/"¡A vestirse para la escuela!" story for your afternoon Read Aloud. Tell children to listen for what clothes the bears choose.

 **Home Connection** Refer to the Home Connection activities on page 59. Remind children to point out shapes that they see at home with their families. Sing the "Good-bye Song" as children prepare to leave.

# DAY 3

## Focus Question

**What weather can I observe each day?**

**¿Qué tiempo puedo observar todos los días?**

**Social and Emotional Development**
• Child shows eagerness, curiosity, and confidence while learning new concepts and trying new things.

**Language and Communication**
• Child demonstrates some understanding of English spoken by teachers and peers. (ELL)
• Child tries to use newly learned vocabulary and grammar. (ELL)

**Social Studies**
• Child understands basic human needs for food, clothing, shelter.

## Vocabulary

| | | | |
|---|---|---|---|
| boots | botas | coat | abrigo |
| gloves | guantes | hat | sombrero |
| snow | nieve | winter | invierno |

## Differentiated Instruction

 **Extra Support**

*Phonological Awareness*
**If...**children have difficulty segmenting words, **then...**say *splat* and have them make the sound of a snake (/s/), then add the word ending (-*plat*).

⭐ **Enrichment**

*Phonological Awareness*
Challenge children to say their own names and segment them.

**Accommodations for 3's**

*Oral Language and Vocabulary*
**If...**children have difficulty with vocabulary words, **then...**have them pantomime putting on boots, a coat, gloves, and a hat, naming each item of clothing as they do so.

# Let's Start the Day

 **Opening Routines and Transition Tips**

For **Opening Routines** and **Transition Tips** turn to pages 178–181 and visit **DLMExpressOnline.com** for more ideas.

📖 Read **"April Clouds"/"Nubes de abril"** from the *Teacher's Treasure Book*, page 134, for your morning Read Aloud.

## Language Time

👫 **Social and Emotional Development** Encourage children to participate as you teach them "Rain, Rain, Go Away." Ask them to brainstorm other types of weather words to fit into the rhyme.

## Oral Language and Vocabulary

✓ **Can children use new vocabulary to tell about snowy weather?**

**Snowy Weather** Review the kinds of weather, and the clothes for each, that children have learned about this week. Tell children that they will talk about cold, winter weather. Explain that winter weather is another reason all people need clothing and shelter. When it is cold out, people need a way to be warm.

● Display *Oral Language Development Card 65.* Have children share any experiences with snow or cold weather. Explain that there are many places in the world that almost never get snow, and other places that almost always have snow. Follow the suggestions on the back of the card.

*Oral Language Development Card 65*

## Phonological Awareness

✓ **Can children segment words into phonemes?**

**Segmenting Phonemes** Revisit *Rhymes and Chants Flip Chart* page 30. Remind children that they can break a word into its sounds.

Have children listen as you read the poem "Raindrops." Point to the word *rain*. Have children echo as you segment the word: /r/ *-ain.* Repeat with the words *sun* (/s/ *-un*) and *now* (/n/ *-ow*).

**ELL** Use the *Rhymes and Chants Flip Chart* to revisit the words *falling* and *ground.* Use actions and gestures to teach the words. Say: **This is falling!** as you drop a crayon to the ground. Then while touching the ground say: **This is the ground.** Have children repeat the movements and sentences. As children demonstrate understanding your language, use the sentence **This crayon is falling to the ground.**

*Rhymes and Chants Flip Chart, page 30/ page 62*

# Center Time

**Center Rotation** Center Time includes teacher-guided activities and independent activities. Refer to the **Learning Centers** on pages 62–63 for activities in additional centers.

small group · 60–90 minutes

## Creativity Center

### Center Tip

**If...**children complete the activity too quickly, **then...** encourage them to use cotton balls and glue to add clouds to their pictures.

☑ **Track what children know about rainbows.**

**Materials** pictures of rainbows, finger paint, paper

**Rainbows** Display pictures of rainbows so children can identify the colors: red, orange, yellow, green, blue, indigo, and violet. Ask children to compare the pictures. What do they notice about the colors in each rainbow? Set out small bowls of each paint color.

- Instruct children to dip one finger in a color. Show them how to make a curved line of color with their fingers.

- Have children wash the finger and change to the next color. Children should paint a rainbow with all the colors in it.

- Display the rainbows. Discuss when rainbows appear and why.

## ABC Center

### Center Tip

**If...**children have difficulty forming the clay into an *Ss* shape, **then...**lightly write an *S* in the center of the paper and have the child place the snake on it, and then continue the activity.

☑ **Track children's ability to make the letter *Ss*.**

**Materials** *ABC Picture Card Ss*, modeling clay or play clay, paper, crayons, pencil

**Review Letter *Ss*** Have children make the /s/ sound like a snake. Then have them segment *snake* into /s/ *-nake*.

- Tell children to make a snake out of clay and place it on the paper in the shape of an *Ss*.

- Instruct children to trace around the snake to make a large uppercase *S* on their papers.

- Have children remove the clay snake and color their traced *S*. Then have them write the letter *Ss* several times on the paper.

**Focus Question**

**What weather can I observe each day?**

**¿Qué tiempo puedo observar todos los días?**

## Learning Goals

**Social and Emotional Development**
• Child understands and respects the different ideas, feelings, perspectives, and behaviors of others.

**Language and Communication**
• Child experiments with and produces a growing number of sounds in English words. (ELL)

**Emergent Literacy: Reading**
• Child identifies the letter that stands for a given sound.
• Child asks and answers questions about books read aloud (such as "Who?" "What?" "Where?").

**Science**
• Child observes, understands, and discusses the relationship of plants and animals to their environments.
• Child describes the effects of natural forces (such as wind, gravity).

### Vocabulary

| cold | frío | cool | fresco |
|------|------|------|--------|
| hot | caluroso | seasons | estaciones |
| warm | tibio | weather | tiempo |

## Differentiated Instruction

 **Extra Support**

**Read Aloud**

**If...**the story is too long or has too many concepts for children to take in at once, **then...** only read pages 6, 7, 10, and 11 during this sitting.

 **Enrichment**

**Read Aloud**

Challenge children to predict what tomorrow's weather will be. Record their responses with words and symbols. In the morning, have children confirm if their predictions were correct.

## Literacy Time

 15 minutes

### 📖 Read Aloud

☑ **Can children tell how weather changes?**

**Build Background** Tell children that you will be rereading a story about the earth and sky. Ask what they recall having learned so far.

● Ask: *What kinds of things do you see in the sky? When do you see the sky change? ¿Qué cosas ven en la escuela? ¿Cuándo cambia el cielo?*

**Listen for Understanding** Display *Concept Big Book 4: The Earth and Sky* and read the title. Conduct a picture walk.

● Point to the kinds of weather depicted and identify each. Have children repeat the words after you.

● Read the text aloud, pausing to allow children to ask you to reread specific parts.

**Respond to the Book** Help children recall the kinds of weather they read about. Display page 10. Ask: *What kinds of weather do you see on this page? Which weather is most like our weather today? ¿Qué estados del tiempo ven en esta página? ¿Qué estado del tiempo se parece más al del día de hoy?* Display page 11. Ask: *Which picture shows autumn? winter? spring? summer? Which season do you like best? ¿Qué foto muestra el otoño? ¿Y el invierno? ¿Y primavera? ¿Y el verano? ¿Qué estación les gusta más?*

**TIP** Remind children that autumn is also called *fall*. Use the term children are most familiar with.

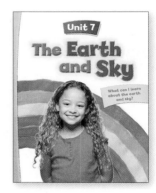

*The Earth and Sky*
*La Tierra y el cielo*

### Learn About Letters and Sounds

☑ **Can children identify the /kw/ sound spelled *Qq* and the /w/ sound spelled *Ww*?**

**Learn About the Letters *Qq* and *Ww*** Give each child an Alphabet/Letter Tile for *Qq* and *Ww*. Review the name of each letter and its sound.

● Display the *ABC Big Book* photo for *quilt,* page 36. Say: *Listen to the word* quilt. *Does* quilt *begin with the sound /kw/ or /s/? Escuchen la palabra* quilt. *¿Quilt comienza con /kw/ o con /s/?* Have children hold up the letter that matches the beginning sound. Continue, using the pictures for *quarter, question mark, wagon, watermelon,* and *walrus.*

**ELL** Explain to Spanish-speaking children that some English words are like Spanish words that they may already know, such as *cuarto* (quarter). Point out that the words sound similar, but in English the /kw/ sound is spelled *qu.*

*ABC Big Book, page 36*
*Superlibro abecé*

large group 15 minutes

# Math Time

## Observe and Investigate

☑ **Can children identify and describe shapes?**

**Mr. Mixup** Ask children whether or not they remember Mr. Mixup. Tell them Mr. Mixup has been confusing the names and parts of shapes and they need to correct him and explain how they know he has confused something (for example, by counting a shape's sides). Use drawings, Shape Sets, or Pattern Blocks to make his mistakes.

- Mr. Mixup may "confuse" categories such as these: rectangles versus rhombuses; rectangles versus squares; squares versus rhombuses; and hexagons versus octagons. Focus on any other shapes you would like to teach or children need to practice.

- Mr. Mixup should also incorrectly identify sides and corners, making sure children explain which is which. When possible, Mr. Mixup may point to call out his mistakes.

## Online Math Activity

Children can complete Piece Puzzler 2 and Shape Parts 1 during computer time or Center Time.

large group 15 minutes

# ⚔ Social and Emotional Development

## Making Good Choices

☑ **Do children assume responsibilities in the classroom?**

**Classroom Helpers** Display *Making Good Choices Flip Chart* page 30.

- Have children explain the Job Chart from the picture or your own classroom to one of the Dog Puppets. Have the puppet say silly statements such as, *If I have a door by my name, it is time for me to leave. Si hay una puerta al lado de mi nombre, me toca salir.* Have children correct the puppet (for example, "If you have a door by your name, it's your turn to hold the door open"). Give each child a turn.

**ELL** Point to each symbol on the Job Chart in the picture and give children a one-word cue to repeat such as *water, door,* and *cups.* Prompt children to use the word in a phrase such as, *water the plants, hold the door, place the cups.*

*Making Good Choices Flip Chart, page 30*

### Differentiated Instruction

✋ **Extra Support**
Observe and Investigate
**If...**children struggle during Mr. Mixup, **then...**have him make more obvious mistakes or make mistakes for the most common shapes.

⭐ **Enrichment**
Observe and Investigate
During Mr. Mixup, include "foolers" (shapes that closely resemble a target shape but are formed incorrectly, such as a circle with a gap or a square missing a right angle) with children's shape choices.

**Accommodations for 3's**
Observe and Investigate
**If...**children struggle during Mr. Mixup, **then...**play the game only using square, triangle, and circle.

### Focus Question

## What weather can I observe each day?
## ¿Qué tiempo puedo observar todos los días?

---

✔ **Learning Goals**

**Language and Communication**
• Child exhibits an understanding of instructional terms used in the classroom.

• Child understands and uses regular and irregular plural nouns, regular past tense verbs, personal and possessive pronouns, and subject-verb agreement.

• Child understands and uses sentences having two or more phrases or concepts.

• Child understands and uses sentences of increasing length and complexity.

**Science**
• Child practices personal hygiene skills independently (for example, washes hands, blows nose, covers mouth, brushes teeth).

**Social Studies**
• Child identifies common events and routines.

### Vocabulary

| | | | |
|---|---|---|---|
| different | diferente | routine | rutina |
| same | mismo | today | hoy |
| usual | usual | yesterday | ayer |

---

### Differentiated Instruction

 **Extra Support**
**Understand and Participate**
**If...**children have difficulty understanding the concept of *yesterday*, **then...**take photographs each day. Review details in the photos to trigger memories of the day before.

 **Enrichment**
**Understand and Participate**
Challenge children to look for schedule patterns between today and yesterday. Have them predict *tomorrow's* schedule.

# Social Studies Time

large group · 20 minutes

**Health Skills** Remind children that washing their hands after they sneeze or use the bathroom is an important routine that they should follow every day.

## Oral Language and Academic Vocabulary

✔ **Can children discuss current and past routines using complex sentences?**

✔ **Can children use regular and irregular plurals, past tense, and possessive pronouns?**

**Daily Schedule** Ask children to name the day of the week. Tell them you will discuss what routines they normally have on this day.

● Display a calendar and help children locate today's date. Ask, **What day do we start school in a week? What day do we finish school for the week? How many days away is Friday?** *¿Qué día de la semana comenzamos la escuela? ¿Qué día de la semana terminamos la escuela? ¿Cuántos días hay entre hoy y el viernes?*

● Discuss any routines of the day that children might recognize, such as regular play times, snack foods, or class visitors, on this day. Say, for example **Yesterday was Tuesday. On Tuesdays we always have music and play outside.** *Ayer fue martes. El día siguiente al martes tenemos música y jugamos al aire libre.*

● Create a daily schedule using picture symbols with children. Include pictures to represent math and reading activities. Throughout the day, have them refer to the picture symbols to tell what the class has done so far and what they will do next. Continue the daily schedule for the rest of the week or longer.

## Understand and Participate

✔ **Can children recognize time and their common daily routines?**

**Daily Comparisons** Display the schedule showing the routines for the day. Ask children what they have done today that they normally do every day.

● Use the calendar to ask questions about time intervals. Ask: **What was today's read aloud story? What was yesterday's read aloud? Is it the same or different? What is normal for us to do after we read together?** *¿Cuál fue la lectura en voz alta de hoy? ¿Cuál fue la lectura en voz alta de ayer? ¿Es la misma o es diferente? ¿Qué hacemos normalmente después de leer juntos?*

● Continue to discuss usual routines, each day reviewing what has been the same and different from *today* and *yesterday*.

**TIP** This is a good time to have children compare and contrast regular daily events. Ask questions that include the words *same* and *different*.

**ELL** Help children make possessive pronoun statements using the words *today* and *yesterday*. **Today you are wearing your blue shirt. Yesterday I wore my green shirt. Today is her birthday. Yesterday it was his turn to help.**

# Center Time

▶ **Center Rotation** Center Time includes teacher-guided activities and independent activities. Refer to the **Learning Centers** on pages 62–63 for activities in additional centers.

 small group · 30 minutes

## Writer's Center

| | Center Tip |
|---|---|
| ☑ **Track children's ability to speak in complete sentences.** | **If...**children have trouble coming up with a sentence, **then...**prompt them with the sentence stem **In summer I like to** _____. *En el verano, me gusta* _____. |

**Materials** paper, crayons

**Fun Activity** Display pictures of summer in the center. Explain to children that the pictures show summer. Help them generalize that summer weather is warm and sunny.

- Tell children to think of a fun activity that they like to do in the summer and draw a picture of it.

- Direct children to show only one activity and to include many details in their pictures.

- Once children have completed their pictures, have them dictate a detailed sentence that tells about the activity.

## Purposeful Play

☑ **Look for children working in pairs or small groups, playing with common plans and goals.**

Children choose an open center for free playtime. Encourage cooperation skills by suggesting they play or pretend to play an activity someone drew in the Writer's Center.

## Let's Say Good-Bye

 large group · 15 minutes

 **Read Aloud** Revisit "April Clouds"/"Nubes de abril" from the *Teacher's Treasure Book,* page 134, for your afternoon Read Aloud. Ask children to tell about clouds they saw today or recently.

 **Home Connection** Refer to the Home Connection activities listed in the Materials and Resources chart on page 59. Remind children to tell their families what they learned about their daily routines. Sing the "Good-bye Song" as children prepare to leave.

---

### ☑ Learning Goals

**Social and Emotional Development**
- Child initiates play scenarios with peers that share a common plan and goal.

**Language and Communication**
- Child speaks in complete sentences of four or more words including a subject, verb, and object.
- Child uses complex sentences that include many details, tell about one topic, and communicate meaning clearly.

**Emergent Literacy: Writing**
- Child writes own name or a reasonable approximation of it.

### Writing

Recap the day. Ask children to volunteer what they learned about weather today and what weather they like best. Record their responses on chart paper or an interactive whiteboard. Have children write their names beside their contributions.

**Focus Question**

## What weather can I observe each day?

## ¿Qué tiempo puedo observar todos los días?

### Learning Goals

**Language and Communication**
• Child experiments with and produces a growing number of sounds in English words. (ELL)

• Child exhibits an understanding of instructional terms used in the classroom.

**Science**
• Child observes, identifies, compares, and discusses objects in the sky (such as clouds, sun, moon, stars).

• Child describes the effects of natural forces (such as wind, gravity).

### Vocabulary

| | | | |
|---|---|---|---|
| cause | causa | cloudy | nublado |
| sunny | soleado | weather | tiempo |
| windy | ventoso | | |

### Differentiated Instruction

 **Extra Support**

**Phonological Awareness**

**If...**children have difficulty identifying the beginning sound, **then...**say three words and have them identify the word that begins with a different sound. Say, for example, *Bat, cat, bike. What word starts with a different sound?* Bat, cat, bike. ¿Cuál de las tres palabras comienza con un sonido distinto?

⭐ **Enrichment**

**Phonological Awareness**

Challenge children to take the place of the puppet and lead a group in isolating either the beginning or ending sound of a given word.

# Let's Start the Day

▶ **Opening Routines and Transition Tips**

For **Opening Routines** and **Transition Tips** turn to pages 178–181 and visit **DLMExpressOnline.com** for more ideas.

📖 Read **"Whether the Weather"/"Si hace un tiempo..."** from the *Teacher's Treasure Book*, page 98, for your morning Read Aloud.

## Language Time

  large group · 15 minutes

### Oral Language and Vocabulary

✓ **Can children identify cause and effect?**

**Weather Changes** Before the lesson, make stick puppets of a sun and a cloud. Review with children what sunny, cloudy, and windy weather are like. Distribute the stick puppets to two children.

● Have the child with the sun puppet stand in front of the room. Discuss with children what a warm, sunny day feels like.

● Then have the child holding the cloud move in and block the sun. Discuss with children what it feels like when a sunny day becomes cloudy. Ask: **What caused the day to get colder? What caused the day to get darker?** ¿Cuál fue la causa de que refrescara? ¿Cuál fue la causa de que se pusiera oscuro?

● Next, have two children stand beside the cloud and blow like the wind. Have the cloud slowly move to the side of the room. Discuss with children what caused the cloud to go away. Discuss what it feels like on a windy day.

**ELL** Make sure each child takes a turn being the sun, the cloud, and the wind. Before the role playing, have each child state **I am the sun** (or cloud, or wind) to reinforce the nouns.

### Phonological Awareness

✓ **Can children segment words into phonemes?**

**Segmenting Phonemes** Divide children into two groups. Assign one group to be the beginning of the word and the other group to be the end. Act as the Dog Puppets to lead each group.

● Say a whole word: **land.** Have one puppet lead the beginning group like a cheerleader, repeating the beginning sound /l/.

● Then have the second puppet lead the ending group, repeating the ending sound *-and*. Have the puppets repeat several times like a chant, each a little faster: */l/...-and; /l/ -and; l-and; land!*

● Play again using the words *stone, rich, man,* and *nice.*

# Center Time

**Center Rotation** Center Time includes teacher-guided activities and independent activities. Refer to the **Learning Centers** on pages 62–63 for activities in additional centers.

small group · 60–90 minutes

## Library and Listening Center

| | Center Tip |
|---|---|

✓ **Help children set a purpose for looking at books.**

**Materials** variety of picture books about each season; sticky notes

**Season Hunt** Have children browse through picture books to find examples of one season they enjoy.

- Before children begin looking at books, have them pick just one season to search for.

- Then have pairs of children browse through the books to find two pictures they like that show that season. Instruct them to flag those pages.

- Have pairs share their pictures with another pair of children and identify the season. Encourage them to take turns saying what they like about the season and listening to the turns of others.

**Center Tip**

**If...**children have difficulty picking a season, **then...**assign them the current season and remind them of the current weather and signs of the season they can see outside the window.

## Creativity Center

**Center Tip**

**If...**children have difficulty drawing a weather symbol, **then...**draw a light-colored pattern for them to trace.

✓ **Observe how well children can talk about different kinds of weather.**

**Materials** lunch-size paper bags, glue, construction paper, scissors, crayons

**Weather Puppets** Explain to children that they are going to make a puppet for one kind of weather and then put on a puppet show about the weather.

- Model making a puppet by drawing a half-page sized weather symbol on construction paper (a lightning bolt, raindrop, sun, cloud, or snowflake). Children may wish to color or decorate the symbol. Show them how to cut it out and glue it to the bottom of the bag.

- After a group of children have made their puppets, let them make up shows where the puppets talk about the kind of weather they cause.

### Learning Goals

**Social and Emotional Development**
- Child maintains concentration/attention skills until a task is complete.

**Emergent Literacy: Reading**
- Child independently engages in pre-reading behaviors and activities (such as, pretending to read, turning one page at a time).

**Science**
- Child describes the effects of natural forces (such as wind, gravity).

**Fine Arts**
- Child uses and experiments with a variety of art materials and tools in various art activities.
- Child expresses emotions or ideas through art.
- Child expresses ideas, emotions, and moods through individual and collaborative dramatic play.

### Differentiated Instruction

 **Extra Support**

**Library and Listening Center**
**If...**children have difficulty completing the task, **then...**remind children of what they are looking for and steer them to the appropriate books.

 **Enrichment**

**Library and Listening Center**
Group children who have chosen the same season and have them compose a detailed description of the season using their pictures.

 **Special Needs**

**Vision Loss**
Provide tactile objects as weather symbols that children can glue on to their bag puppets, such as tinsel for rain or fluffy cotton for clouds.

**Focus Question**

## What weather can I observe each day?
## ¿Qué tiempo puedo observar todos los días?

### ✔ Learning Goals

**Social and Emotional Development**
• Child understands and respects the different ideas, feelings, perspectives, and behaviors of others.

**Language and Communication**
• Child demonstrates an understanding of oral language by responding appropriately.

**Emergent Literacy: Reading**
• Child names most upper- and lowercase letters of the alphabet.
• Child identifies the letter that stands for a given sound.

### Vocabulary

| | | | |
|---|---|---|---|
| carved | esculpir | lightning | relámpago |
| mountain | montaña | spirit | espíritu |
| stonecutter | picapedrero | thunder | trueno |

### Differentiated Instruction

 **Extra Support**

**Learn About Letters and Sounds**
**If...**children have difficulty identifying the letter from the clues, **then...**have them trace each letter with a finger and repeat the clue about the physical shape of the letter.

 **Enrichment**

**Read Aloud**
Let children use the flannel board pieces to retell the story.

## Literacy Time

### 📖 Read Aloud

✔ **Can children express opinions and respect the opinions of others?**

**Build Background** Tell children that you will be reading a make-believe story about a man who wanted to be something he was not. Remind children that sometimes things happen in stories that cannot really happen in life, and those are make-believe stories.

● Ask: *Do you think a man can become the sun? A cloud? The wind?* *¿Creen que un hombre puede convertirse en el Sol? ¿Y en una nube? ¿Y en el viento?*

**Listen for Enjoyment** Read aloud the flannel board story "The Stonecutter" from the *Teacher's Treasure Book*, page 329. Tell children to listen carefully to what happens every time the man changes into something new.

**Respond to the Story** Encourage children to take turns giving their opinions. Remind them that not everyone will have the same favorite part. Ask: *What was your favorite part? Show me by placing the picture on the flannel board. Why do you like this part?* *¿Cuál fue su parte favorita? Señalen una ilustración de la cartelera. ¿Por qué les gustó esa parte?*

 **TIP** To aid in understanding vocabulary and to make the story more engaging, use motions and sound effects for the stonecutter's transformations.

 **ELL** Focus on words that name what the stonecutter wishes for. Point to each flannel pattern and say the word. Provide details and ask questions. For example: *The sun gives us light. What does the sun give us?*

*Teacher's Treasure Book, page 329*

### Learn About Letters and Sounds

✔ **Can children identify the /kw/ and /w/ sounds spelled *Qq* and *Ww*?**

**Learn About the Letters *Qq* and *Ww*** Give each child an Alphabet/Letter Tile for *Qq* and *Ww*. Review the name of each letter and its sound.

● Give children clues about a letter. When children know what letter it is, have them hold the tile over their head. Say: *I am made of all straight lines. My upper- and lowercase letters look alike. I make the /w/ sound like* wig. *Tengo sólo líneas rectas. Mi mayúscula y mi minúscula son parecidas. Tengo el sonido /w/, como en la palabra* wig.

● Say: *My uppercase letter looks like the letter* O *with a tail. I make the /kw/ sound like* queen. *Mi mayúscula parece una letra* O *con una pequeña cola. Tengo el sonido /kw/, como en la palabra* queen.

● Say: *My lowercase letter is a round circle with a curled tail. You can hear my sound in* quilt *and* quart. *Mi minúscula es redonda, con una cola rizada. Puedes oírme en las palabras* quilt *y* quart.

# Math Time

**Building Blocks**

**Online Math Activity**
Children can complete Piece Puzzler 2 and Shape Parts 1 during computer time or Center Time.

### Observe and Investigate

 **Can children describe and identify the properties of a triangle?**

**Shape Parts (Triangle)** Using Pattern Blocks, show children a triangle, and ask how they know it is a triangle.

- Emphasize the parts of a shape using your fingers to trace its outline; count the shape's sides and its corners. Allow children to trace a triangle as you do it again.

- While children are completing the online math activities Piece Puzzler 2 and Shape Parts 1, ask them to name the various parts of the computer for you (keyboard, mouse, screen) and tell you how they use the parts. Encourage children to see that they can learn more about shapes by using the technology. Explain that if they want to know more about shapes, like triangles, they can go online with an adult.

# ⚇ Social and Emotional Development

### Making Good Choices

**Do children show an understanding of classroom responsibilities?**

**Classroom Helpers** Set out a popular game messily as if it were played and not put away. Act out a lighthearted but realistic scenario with the Dog Puppets. Have the puppets act as if they just finished the game. One puppet begins to move on to another activity without cleaning up. The other puppet does not know whether to go play or stay and clean up.

- Ask: *What should the first puppet do? Why? What should the second do? ¿Qué deben hacer los títeres en primer lugar? ¿Por qué? ¿Qué deben hacer en segundo lugar?*

- Ask children why they should keep their classroom clean and organized. Encourage them to discuss how the puppets can work together to get the chore done quickly.

- End by having the children help the puppets clean up the game.

Allow children to act out the same problem-solving scenario. Prompt them to use phrases, such as: *Will you help me? Let's clean up!*

## Learning Goals

**Social and Emotional Development**
• Child participates in a variety of individual, small- and large-group activities.

**Mathematics**
• Child recognizes, names, describes, matches, compares, sorts common two-dimensional shapes (such as circle, square, rectangle, triangle, rhombus).

**Technology Applications**
• Child names and uses various computer parts (such as mouse, keyboard, CD-ROM, microphone, touch screen).

• Child knows some ways that technology affects people's lives.

### Vocabulary

| | | | |
|---|---|---|---|
| corners | vértices | parts | partes |
| shape | figura | sides | lados |
| triangle | triángulo | | |

## Differentiated Instruction

 **Extra Support**
**Observe and Investigate**
**If...**children struggle with identifying the properties of a triangle, **then...**display a triangle and have children use beverage stirrers to make a triangle, then count the stirrers as the sides. Discuss shape properties as they are made.

**Enrichment**
**Observe and Investigate**
Challenge children to repeat the activity for a square and a rectangle, emphasizing the differences between the two.

 **Accommodations for 3's**
**Observe and Investigate**
**If...**children struggle with the properties of a triangle, **then...**have three children lie on the floor in the shape of a triangle. Count the number of sides. Give everyone a chance to be in the triangle and to count the number of sides.

## Learning Goals

**Language and Communication**
• Child names and describes actual or pictured people, places, things, actions, attributes, and events.
• Child uses newly learned vocabulary daily in multiple contexts.
• Child uses complex sentences that include many details, tell about one topic, and communicate meaning clearly.
• Child tries to use newly learned vocabulary and grammar. (ELL)

**Mathematics**
• Child recognizes, names, describes, matches, compares, sorts common two-dimensional shapes (such as circle, square, rectangle, triangle, rhombus).

**Science**
• Child uses senses to observe, classify, investigate, and collect data.

### Vocabulary

| | | | |
|---|---|---|---|
| cone | cono | cube | cubo |
| curved | curvado | cylinder | cilindro |
| sides | lados | sphere | esfera |
| straight | recto | | |

## Differentiated Instruction

### ✋ Extra Support

**Math Time**
**If...**children have difficulty describing the solid, **then...**ask leading questions such as, *Is it round? Is it flat? What does it remind you of?* *¿Es redondo? ¿Es plano? ¿A qué se parece?*

### ⭐ Enrichment

**Math Time**
Challenge children by placing common objects in the feely box and having children describe them using the names of the solids. For example, an orange might be described as a sphere.

# Math Time

**large group** · 20 minutes

**Language and Communication Skills** Read a book about solids, such as *Cubes, Cones, Cylinders, and Spheres* by Tana Hoban. As you show each picture, have children identify the shapes. Correct their pronunciation of math words as needed.

☑ **Can children use a wide variety of words to describe a solid shape?**

**Identify Solid Shapes** Display cube, cylinder, sphere, and cone blocks. Review the names of each solid. Discuss with children the properties of each solid.

● Ask: *Does this shape have straight sides? Does it have curved sides? Does it have both straight and curved sides?* *¿Esta figura tiene lados rectos? ¿Tiene lados curvados? ¿Tiene lados rectos y curvados?*

● Have children look for examples of similar solid shapes around the room. For example, boxes, balls, and paper towels might be easily identified as cubes, spheres, and cylinders.

☑ **Can children describe and name a common solid shape?**

**Feely Box** Secretly hide a solid shape in the feely box.

● Have one child feel the solid and describe it well enough *without using its name* for other children to name it.

● Ask children how they knew it was that solid. Repeat with each solid: cube, cylinder, sphere, cone.

● As a variation, display *Math and Science Flip Chart* page 56, and allow children to point to whichever shape they think the child giving the description can feel in the feely box.

💡 **TIP** Tell children to use some of the same words they used when working with shapes.

**ELL** Focus on the phrase *the same as*. When children describe a solid, encourage them to say **This shape is the same as** and name a familiar object. For additional suggestions on how to meet the needs of children at various levels of English proficiency, see pages 184–187.

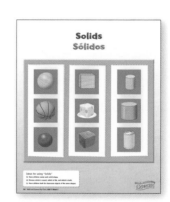

*Math and Science Flip Chart, page 56*

# Center Time

**Center Rotation** Center Time includes teacher-guided activities and independent activities. Refer to the **Learning Centers** on pages 62–63 for activities in additional centers.

 small group · 30 minutes

## Construction Center

 Track children's abilities to make something creative from three-dimensional objects.

**Materials** poster board, glue, crayons, paint; small objects for art such as beads, shells, cotton balls

**3-D Object Mural** Show children a circle and a sphere. Help children understand that a sphere is three-dimensional (they can get their fingers around it), but a circle is flat. Repeat with cylinder/rectangle, cube/square, and cone/triangle.

- Hang poster board low enough for children to reach. Instruct them to use the objects, crayons, and paint to make a 3-D picture on the poster board. Have them name the shape of objects they include.

- Encourage children to work together to make a class mural.

- When the mural is complete, hang it low enough for children to view and feel.

### Center Tip

**If…**children have trouble understanding 3-D, **then…**have them close their eyes. Give them one of the art objects, and ask if they can tell what it is by feeling it. Explain that they probably could not easily tell what the object was if it was just flat.

## Purposeful Play

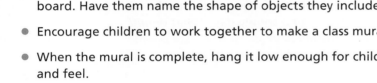

Observe children taking care of classroom materials as they play together.

Children choose an open center for free playtime. Encourage cooperation skills by suggesting they work together to create a play using their weather puppets or a conversation between two people about what to wear in a certain kind of weather.

## Let's Say Good-Bye

 large group · 15 minutes

 **Read Aloud** Revisit "Whether the Weather"/"Si hace un tiempo…" for your afternoon Read Aloud. Tell children to listen for rhyming words in the poem.

 **Home Connection** Refer to the Home Connection activities listed in the Materials and Resources chart on page 59. Remind children to tell their families the story of the stonecutter. Sing the "Good-bye Song" as children prepare to leave.

### Learning Goals

**Social and Emotional Development**
- Child uses classroom materials carefully.

**Language and Communication**
- Child uses oral language for a variety of purposes.

**Emergent Literacy: Writing**
- Child uses scribbles, shapes, pictures, symbols, and letters to represent language.

**Mathematics**
- Child recognizes, names, describes, matches, compares, sorts common two-dimensional shapes (such as circle, square, rectangle, triangle, rhombus).

**Science**
- Child uses senses to observe, classify, investigate, and collect data.

### Writing

Recap the day. Have children draw a picture of an event from "The Stonecutter." If needed, review the events in the story. Ask children to label the pictures. Prompt them to write the letters they know. Invite children to share their work with the class.

**Focus Question**
## What weather can I observe each day?
## ¿Qué tiempo puedo observar todos los días?

**Social and Emotional Development**
• Child participates in a variety of individual, small- and large-group activities.

**Emergent Literacy: Reading**
• Child removes one word from a compound word.
• Child blends syllables to form a word.
• Child deletes syllables from a word.

**Social Studies**
• Child understands basic human needs for food, clothing, shelter.

## Vocabulary

| | | | |
|---|---|---|---|
| falling | caída | hail | granizo |
| hailstones | piedras | rainbow | arco iris |
| raindrops | gotitas | rooftops | tejados |
| shelter | refugio | | |

## Differentiated Instruction

 **Extra Support**
*Phonological Awareness*
**If...**children have difficulty making chant motions, **then...**prompt them to make a motion for one repeating word such as wiggling fingers for the word *rain*.

 **Enrichment**
*Phonological Awareness*
After children have segmented a word, have them take the word ending (-*ain*) and add new beginning sounds to make real and nonsense rhyming words.

# Let's Start the Day

 **Opening Routines and Transition Tips**
For **Opening Routines** and **Transition Tips** turn to pages 178–181 and visit DLMExpressOnline.com for more ideas.

📖 Read **"Weather"/"El tiempo"** from the *Teacher's Treasure Book*, page 234, for your morning Read Aloud.

## Language Time

 large group  15 minutes

👧👦👧 **Social and Emotional Development** Encourage different children to act as the chant leader and make up motions for the class to follow as they all chant together.

### Oral Language and Vocabulary

✓ **Can children relate a chant to different kinds of weather?**

✓ **Can children understand why all people need shelter?**

**Relate to Weather** Talk with children about today's weather.

*Rhymes and Chants Flip Chart, page 30/page 62*

● Display *Rhymes and Chants Flip Chart* page 30. Chant the poem "Raindrops" with children. Ask: **Would you chant this on a rainy day or a snowy day? What would you change to chant this on a snowy day? A stormy day?** *¿Recitarías este poema un día lluvioso o un día de nieve? ¿Que deberías cambiar para recitarlo un día de nieve? ¿Y durante una tormenta?*

● Chant again with children, substituting the words *snowflakes* and *snow*, or *hailstones* and *hail*. Remind children that snow and hail are types of weather for which people need shelter. Ask: **Why do all people need shelter?** *¿Por qué necesitamos un refugio?*

ELL Read through "Raindrops" slowly. Ask children to identify any words or phrases they do not understand by raising a hand when they hear it. Use motions and picture cards to aid children in understanding unfamiliar words.

### Phonological Awareness

✓ **Can children segment compound word parts into phonemes?**

**Segmenting Phonemes** Chant "Raindrops" once more with children. Remind them that they can break a word into its beginning and ending sounds, and sometimes they can break a big word into two smaller words.

● Point to *raindrops* in the first line. Say: **Raindrops. How do we break this word? Rain, drops. Rain. /R/...** *Raindrops. ¿Cómo podemos dividir esta palabra? Rain, drops. Rain. /R/...*

● Have children complete the word as -*ain*. Repeat for *drop* (/d/ -*rop*) and *bow* (/b/ /o/). Finally, blend the sounds back together to say **Raindrops, rainbow!**

# Center Time

▶ **Center Rotation** Center Time includes teacher-guided activities and independent activities. Refer to the **Learning Centers** on pages 62–63 for activities in additional centers.

  small group 60–90 minutes

## ABC Center

**Center Tip**

 Track children's use of words beginning with the /kw/ sound.

**Materials** dress-up clothes for kings and queens; elastic headbands, construction paper, scissors, crayons; objects related to *Qq* words such as quilts, quarters, and toy ducks

**Kings and Queens** Model how to make a special crown for a Queen or a Queen's King. Write an uppercase *Q* on construction paper and decorate it using multiple colors. Cut it out. Then place a headband around your head like a crown. Tuck the *Q* into the front of the headband to make the crown.

- Review the difference between the /kw/ sound of *queen* and the /k/ sound of *king*. Let boys make a *QK* crown to wear as Queen's King.

- As children play, have them name things in the center that begin with the /kw/ sound like the word *queen*.

- Encourage children to play being silly things using *Qq* words, such as the Queen of Quilts or the Queen's King of Quarters.

**Center Tip**
**If...**you are not able to obtain many *Qq* word objects for the center, **then...**post pictures of things related to *Qq* words.

## Creativity Center

 Observe that child's artwork is somehow related to music.

**Materials** recordings of music about various types of weather such as rain or snow; drawing paper, crayons

**Art Inspired by Music** Direct children to sit quietly and listen to a song one time through. Then have them replay the song and think of what pictures form in their minds.

- Have children make pictures about the song. They can make scenes or just beautiful designs.

- Assemble the pictures into a book and put it in the Library and Listening Center with a recording of the song for children to listen to and look at independently.

**Center Tip**
**If...**children are distracted or intimidated by the idea of drawing from music with lyrics, **then...**let them draw to soothing instrumental music.

---

## Learning Goals

**Emergent Literacy: Reading**
- Child names most upper- and lowercase letters of the alphabet.

**Emergent Literacy: Writing**
- Child writes some letters or reasonable approximations of letters upon request.

**Fine Arts**
- Child uses and experiments with a variety of art materials and tools in various art activities.
- Child expresses thoughts, feelings, and energy through music and creative movement.

**Physical Development**
- Child develops small-muscle strength and control.

---

## Differentiated Instruction

✋ **Extra Support**
**ABC Center**
**If...**children are not familiar with the concept of a queen, **then...**read fairy tales and other stories that include queens. Discuss how queens dress and behave in the stories.

★ **Enrichment**
**Creativity Center**
Give children felt-tip markers and large paper and have them freely move their markers over the paper in time to the music. Then have them color in the design. Talk about what feelings they had as they listened to the music.

**Accommodations for 3's**
**Creativity Center**
Play children's music with clear, repetitive lyrics about snow or winter activities so children are steered into what kind of scene to draw.

**Focus Question**

## What weather can I observe each day?
## ¿Qué tiempo puedo observar todos los días?

## Literacy Time

 **Read Aloud**

✓ **Can children respond appropriately and give opinions about a story?**

**Build Background** Tell children that you will reread *Who Likes Rain?*

● Ask: **What do you remember about the weather in this story?** *¿Qué recuerdan del tiempo en este cuento?*

**Listen for Understanding** Display the Big Book *Who Likes Rain?* and read the title.

● Reread the story. Ask: **Which part of the story looks like the most fun?** *¿Qué parte del cuento les parece más divertida?* Remind children that not everyone likes the same things and that it is OK to like different things.

**Respond and Connect** Have children connect what they observed about weather this week with pictures in the selection. Page through the selection and ask: **Do any of these pictures look like anything you have seen this week? Have you ever seen wet, windy weather like this? What animals like rain in this story? Which season do you think this book is about? Why?** *¿Alguna de las ilustraciones se parece a algo que hayan visto esta semana? ¿Han visto alguna vez un tiempo húmedo y ventoso como éste? ¿A qué animales del cuento les gusta la lluvia? ¿De qué estación crees que habla este cuento? ¿Por qué?*

**TIP** As you read, leave off the last word in a stanza for children to complete with the rhyming word.

*Who Likes Rain?*
*¿A quién le gusta la lluvia?*

## Learn About Letters and Sounds

✓ **Can children identify letters** *Qq* **and** *Ww* **and their sounds?**

**Review Letters** *Qq* **and** *Ww* Display the *ABC Picture Card Ww.* Have children trace the letter in the air.

● Say: **Worm, /w/, /w/, /w/ worm! Worm begins with W!** *¡Worm empieza con W!* Have children echo the chant, tracing another *W* in the air. Repeat the chant using *wall, wig, web,* and *wind.*

● Display the *ABC Picture Card Qq.* Have children trace a *Q* and a *q* in the air.

● Say: **Queen, /kw/, /kw/, /kw/ queen. Queen begins with Q!** *¡Queen empieza con Q!* Have children echo the chant, tracing *Q* and *q* in the air. Repeat the chant using *quack, quick, quilt,* and *quit.*

**ELL** Provide pictures of *wall, wig, web,* duck *quacking,* and *quilt* to provide context for words in the letter chant.

*ABC Picture Cards*
*Tarjetas abecé de imágenes*

**Emergent Literacy: Reading**
● Child names most upper- and lowercase letters of the alphabet.
● Child identifies the letter that stands for a given sound.
● Child asks and answers questions about books read aloud (such as "Who?" "What?" "Where?").

**Science**
● Child observes, understands, and discusses the relationship of plants and animals to their environments.
● Child describes the effects of natural forces (such as wind, gravity).

**Vocabulary**

| | | | |
|---|---|---|---|
| autumn | otoño | season | estación |
| spring | primavera | summer | verano |
| winter | invierno | | |

## Differentiated Instruction

 **Extra Support**
**Learn About Letters and Sounds**
**If...**children have difficulty differentiating between *Qq* and *Ww,* **then...**provide multi-sensory experiences with the letters, such as writing them in sand or shaving cream.

**Enrichment**
**Learn About Letters and Sounds**
Display Alphabet/Letter Tiles of all the letters learned this year. Challenge children to name as many as they can and pull out *Qq* and *Ww.*

 **Special Needs**
**Speech/Language Delays**
**If...**children have difficulty pronouncing letters, **then...**do not overtly correct them, but simply repeat the letter names frequently, such as by saying **Yes, that is Q.** *Sí, es la Q.*

**Online Math Activity**

Children can complete Piece Puzzler 2 and Shape Parts 1 during computer time or Center Time.

# Math Time

## Observe and Investigate

✓ **Can children find and identify a shape based on its description?**

**I Spy (Properties)** Describe a shape's attributes, and ask children to name which shape you mean.

- Use Pattern Blocks or classroom objects. Guidelines for description: circles—all perfectly round; triangles—three sides; squares—four equal sides, four right angles; rhombuses—four equal sides but different angles; and parallelograms—four sides of different lengths but opposite sides are equal, no right angles.

# ⅄⅄⅄ Social and Emotional Development

## Making Good Choices

✓ **Do children assume responsibilities in the classroom?**

**Classroom Helpers** Play the song "Everybody Needs Help Sometimes"/"Todos necesitan ayuda alguna vez" from the Making Good Choices Audio CD. Allow children to sing along if they know the words. Then display *Making Good Choices Flip Chart* page 30, "How Can I Help?"

- Point to the flip chart illustration. Ask: **What did we learn about being helpful in our classroom?** *¿Qué aprendimos acerca de ayudar en el salón de clases?*

- Discuss with children what jobs should go on (or be added to) a Job Chart in your classroom. Have children work with a partner to suggest other things they can do to be helpful in the classroom.

- Have pairs act out their suggestions for the group.

**ELL** Have pairs of children role play a conversation. Pair native speakers with English language learners. Encourage English language learners to act out their words as they say them, and prompt native speakers to use simple words and grammar. One child asks, "How can I help?" The other child answers, "You can ____" and fills in a classroom chore from the group discussion. Have children switch roles and repeat.

*Making Good Choices Flip Chart, page 30*

**Social and Emotional Development**
- Child participates in a variety of individual, small- and large-group activities.

**Language and Communication**
- Child uses nonverbal cues to communicate with others who do not speak his or her home language. (ELL)

- Child uses individual words and short phrases to communicate. (ELL)

**Mathematics**
- Child recognizes, names, describes, matches, compares, sorts common two-dimensional shapes (such as circle, square, rectangle, triangle, rhombus).

### Vocabulary

| | |
|---|---|
| circle | círculo |
| parallelogram | paralelogramo |
| rhombus | rombo |
| square | cuadrado |
| triangle | triángulo |

**Differentiated Instruction**

✋ **Extra Support**

Observe and Investigate
**If...**children need more practice identifying shapes, **then...**play the I Spy game during transitions and other down times.

⭐ **Enrichment**

Observe and Investigate
Challenge children to play the I Spy game using solid shapes.

**Focus Question**
**What weather can I observe each day?**
**¿Qué tiempo puedo observar todos los días?**

 **Learning Goals**

**Social and Emotional Development**
• Child is aware of self in terms of abilities, characteristics and preferences, and respects personal boundaries.

• Child recognizes and manages feelings and impulses; increasingly maintains self-control in difficult situations (can increase or decrease intensity of emotions with guidance).

**Fine Arts**
• Child expresses thoughts, feelings, and energy through music and creative movement.

**Physical Development**
• Child coordinates body movements in a variety of locomotive activities (such as walking, jumping, running, hopping, skipping, climbing).

## Vocabulary

| | | | |
|---|---|---|---|
| lightning | relámpago | music | música |
| rain | lluvia | storm | tormenta |
| thunder | trueno | wind | viento |

**Differentiated Instruction**

 **Extra Support**
**Explore and Express**
**If...**children have difficulty moving in response to the music, **then...**prompt them by saying *Shake like thunder, sway like wind, skip like rain! ¡Tiembla como el trueno, menea como el viento, brinca como la lluvia!*

**Enrichment**
**Explore and Express**
After listening, have children tell what the music reminded them of. Encourage children to share their stormy weather experiences.

 **Special Needs**
**Hearing Impairment**
Allow children to sit with their hands on the speakers so that they can feel the vibrations the music makes.

# Music and Movement Time

 large group / 20 minutes

**Social and Emotional Development** Before the music activity, assure children that it will be very interesting, but at the beginning they will need to follow their listening rules and sit with arms folded and heads down.

## Oral Language and Academic Vocabulary

✓ **Can children identify the features of a storm?**

**Stormy Weather** Display pictures of stormy weather. Include wind, rain, and lightning.

● Ask: *Have you ever seen a storm? How is it different from rainy weather? How is it the same? ¿Has visto una tormenta? ¿En qué se diferencia del tiempo lluvioso? ¿En qué se parece?* Lead children to understand that a storm has hard rain, wind, lightning, and thunder.

● Let children share how a storm makes them feel. They may need to talk about their fears.

● Lead children in making the sounds of a storm by tapping their fingers on the desk harder and faster for raindrops, making wind noises, and clapping their hands for thunder. Encourage children to think of the activity as fun and not scary.

## Explore and Express

✓ **Can children imagine and identify parts of a storm?**

**The Storm** Explain that like the way children made the sounds of a storm with their hands, musicians can use instruments to make the sounds of a storm.

● Instruct children to lay their heads down and use their ears to listen and imagine a storm. Play a few minutes of a recording of Tchaikovsky's "The Storm" Overture Op. 76.

● Have children raise their hands when they hear sounds like thunder and again when they hear sounds like wind.

● Play the same segment of the recording a second time. Have children stand up and move their bodies in time to show thunder, wind, and rain.

**TIP** This is a popular recording that has been done by many orchestras. It is available on many CDs or the Internet.

**ELL** Rain and thunder sound effects are readily available on the Internet. Play each and prompt children to say the sentences *I hear rain. I hear thunder.*

# Center Time

▶ **Center Rotation** Center Time includes teacher-guided activities and independent activities. Refer to the **Learning Centers** on pages 62–63 for activities in additional centers.

small group 30 minutes

## Pretend and Learn Center

☑ **Observe that children cooperate, share in role-playing scenarios, and follow a sequence of events.**

☑ **Observe children using regular and irregular plurals, past tense, and subject-verb agreement.**

**Materials** flannel board patterns and cut outs for "The Stonecutter"

**The Stonecutter** Review "The Stonecutter" from the *Teacher's Treasure Book,* page 329, rereading it if time allows.

● Invite children to assume roles and act out the story together.

● As needed, prompt children to help them remember the sequence of events and the mood of the story.

### Center Tip

**If...**children are unsure what to do when portraying the mountain or a type of weather, **then...** review the object or weather and help children come up with appropriate movements and descriptions.

### ✓ Learning Goals

**Social and Emotional Development**
• Child initiates play scenarios with peers that share a common plan and goal.

**Language and Communication**
• Child understands and uses regular and irregular plural nouns, regular past tense verbs, personal and possessive pronouns, and subject-verb agreement.

**Emergent Literacy: Writing**
• Child writes own name or a reasonable approximation of it.

**Fine Arts**
• Child expresses ideas, emotions, and moods through individual and collaborative dramatic play.

**Physical Development**
• Child develops small-muscle strength and control.

## Purposeful Play

☑ **Observe children initiating play with others.**

Children choose an open center for free playtime. Encourage cooperation skills by suggesting they pretend they are playing outdoors in different types of weather.

## Let's Say Good-Bye

large group 15 minutes

### Writing

Recap the day and week. Say: *Tell me one thing you learned about weather this week. Digan una cosa que hayan aprendido esta semana acerca del tiempo.* Record children's answers on chart paper or an interactive whiteboard. Share the pen with children as you write. Have children write their names (all or part of them) beside their entries.

**Read Aloud** Revisit "Weather"/"El tiempo" from the *Teacher's Treasure Book,* page 234, for your afternoon Read Aloud. Remind children to listen for familiar weather words.

**Home Connection** Refer to the Home Connection activities listed in the Materials and Resources chart on page 59. Remind children to tell their families what they learned this week about weather and the four seasons. Sing the "Good-bye Song" as children prepare to leave.

# Week 3

## Focus Question

# What can I learn about day and night?

# ¿Qué puedo aprender sobre el día y la noche?

This week children will compare day and night. They will learn about and describe changes in the sky over time, write a class book about day and night activities, and create day and night sky mobiles. Children will also observe and make shadows, and discuss what they do during the day and night using ordinal terms such as *first, second,* and *third.*

| Social and Emotional Development | Day 1 | 2 | 3 | 4 | 5 |
|---|---|---|---|---|---|
| Child demonstrates appropriate conflict-resolution strategies, requesting help when needed. | ✓ | ✓ | ✓ | ✓ | ✓ |

| Language and Communication | Day 1 | 2 | 3 | 4 | 5 |
|---|---|---|---|---|---|
| Child demonstrates an understanding of oral language by responding appropriately. | | | | ✓ | ✓ |
| Child demonstrates some understanding of English spoken by teachers and peers. (ELL) | | | | ✓ | |
| Child uses oral language for a variety of purposes. | | | ✓ | | ✓ |
| Child communicates relevant information for the situation (for example, introduces herself; requests assistance). | | | | | ✓ |
| Child matches language to social setting. | ✓ | | | | |
| Child experiments with and produces a growing number of sounds in English words. (ELL) | ✓ | | | ✓ | |
| Child names and describes actual or pictured people, places, things, actions, attributes, and events. | ✓ | ✓ | ✓ | | ✓ |
| Child exhibits an understanding of instructional terms used in the classroom. | | ✓ | | ✓ | |
| Child uses newly learned vocabulary daily in multiple contexts. | ✓ | ✓ | ✓ | ✓ | ✓ |
| Child uses words to identify and understand categories. | ✓ | | ✓ | ✓ | |
| Child understands and uses regular and irregular plural nouns, regular past tense verbs, personal and possessive pronouns, and subject-verb agreement. | ✓ | ✓ | | | |
| Child understands and uses sentences of increasing length and complexity. | | | | | ✓ |
| Child uses nonverbal cues to communicate with others who do not speak his or her home language. (ELL) | | | | | ✓ |
| Child uses individual words and short phrases to communicate. (ELL) | | | | | ✓ |

| Emergent Literacy: Reading | 1 | 2 | 3 | 4 | 5 |
|---|---|---|---|---|---|
| Child enjoys and chooses reading-related activities. | | | | | ✓ |
| Child explores books and other texts to answer questions. | | ✓ | ✓ | | |
| Child combines two words to form a compound word. | ✓ | | | | ✓ |
| Child removes one word from a compound word. | ✓ | | | | ✓ |
| Child blends two phonemes to form a word. | | | | ✓ | |
| Child names most upper- and lowercase letters of the alphabet. | ✓ | ✓ | ✓ | ✓ | ✓ |
| Child identifies the letter that stands for a given sound. | ✓ | ✓ | ✓ | ✓ | ✓ |
| Child asks and answers questions about books read aloud (such as "Who?" "What?" "Where?"). | ✓ | ✓ | | | ✓ |

| Emergent Literacy: Writing | 1 | 2 | 3 | 4 | 5 |
|---|---|---|---|---|---|
| Child uses scribbles, shapes, pictures, symbols, and letters to represent language. | | | | ✓ | ✓ |

| Mathematics | Day 1 | 2 | 3 | 4 | 5 |
|---|---|---|---|---|---|
| Child divides sets from 2 to 10 objects into equal sets, using informal techniques. | | | | | ✓ |
| Child recognizes, names, describes, matches, compares, sorts common two-dimensional shapes (such as circle, square, rectangle, triangle, rhombus). | | ✓ | | | |
| Child creates two-dimensional shapes; recreates two-dimensional shapes from memory. | ✓ | ✓ | ✓ | ✓ | ✓ |
| Child understands and uses words that describe position/location in space (such as *under, over, beside, between, on, in, near, far away*). | ✓ | ✓ | | | |
| Child manipulates (flips, rotates) and combines shapes. | | | | ✓ | ✓ |
| Child measures the length and height of people or objects using standard or non-standard tools. | ✓ | | | | |
| Child measures passage of time using standard or non-standard tools. | | | ✓ | | |

| Science | 1 | 2 | 3 | 4 | 5 |
|---|---|---|---|---|---|
| Child investigates and describes energy sources (light, heat, electricity). | ✓ | ✓ | ✓ | | |
| Child observes, identifies, compares, and discusses objects in the sky (such as clouds, sun, moon, stars). | ✓ | ✓ | ✓ | | ✓ |
| Child describes the effects of natural forces (such as wind, gravity). | ✓ | ✓ | ✓ | | ✓ |
| Child follows basic health and safety rules. | ✓ | | | | ✓ |

| Social Studies | 1 | 2 | 3 | 4 | 5 |
|---|---|---|---|---|---|
| Child identifies common events and routines. | | | ✓ | | |
| Child participates in voting for group decision-making. | | ✓ | | | |

| Fine Arts | 1 | 2 | 3 | 4 | 5 |
|---|---|---|---|---|---|
| Child shares opinions about artwork and artistic experiences. | | ✓ | | | ✓ |
| Child participates in a variety of music activities (such as listening, singing, finger plays, musical games, performances). | ✓ | ✓ | ✓ | | |
| Child expresses ideas, emotions, and moods through individual and collaborative dramatic play. | | | | ✓ | ✓ |

| Physical Development | 1 | 2 | 3 | 4 | 5 |
|---|---|---|---|---|---|
| Child develops small-muscle strength and control. | ✓ | ✓ | ✓ | ✓ | |
| Child completes tasks that require eye-hand coordination and control. | | | | | ✓ |

| Technology Applications | 1 | 2 | 3 | 4 | 5 |
|---|---|---|---|---|---|
| Child opens and correctly uses age-appropriate software programs. | ✓ | ✓ | | | |
| Child uses voice/sound players and recorders, and touch screens correctly. | ✓ | | ✓ | ✓ | |
| Child uses computer software or technology to express original ideas. | | ✓ | | | |

# Materials and Resources

| DAY 1 | DAY 2 | DAY 3 | DAY 4 | DAY 5 |
|-------|-------|-------|-------|-------|

## Program Materials

| DAY 1 | DAY 2 | DAY 3 | DAY 4 | DAY 5 |
|-------|-------|-------|-------|-------|
| • Alphabet Wall Card *Ww*<br>• Building Blocks Math Activities<br>• Home Connections Resource Guide<br>• Making Good Choices Flip Chart<br>• Math and Science Flip Chart<br>• *Matthew and the Color of the Sky* Big Book<br>• Oral Language Development Cards 66 and 67<br>• Photo Library CD-ROM<br>• Rhymes and Chants Flip Chart<br>• Teacher's Treasure Book | • Alphabet/Letter Tiles *Ww* and *Zz*<br>• ABC Picture Card *Ww*<br>• Building Blocks Math Activities<br>• Concept Big Book 4: *The Earth and Sky*<br>• Dog Puppets<br>• Making Good Choices Flip Chart<br>• Math and Science Flip Chart<br>• *Matthew and the Color of the Sky* Big Book<br>• Pattern Blocks<br>• Shape Sets<br>• Teacher's Treasure Book | • Alphabet/Letter Tiles<br>• Building Blocks Math Activities<br>• Concept Big Book 4: *The Earth and Sky*<br>• Dog Puppets<br>• Farm Animal Counters<br>• Making Good Choices Flip Chart<br>• Oral Language Development Card 68<br>• Photo Library CD-ROM<br>• Rhymes and Chants Flip Chart<br>• Shape Sets<br>• Teacher's Treasure Book | • ABC Big Book<br>• Alphabet/Letter Tiles<br>• Alphabet Wall Card *Zz*<br>• Building Blocks Math Activities<br>• Dog Puppets<br>• Flannel Board Patterns for "The Stolen Soup Smell"<br>• Home Connections Resource Guide<br>• Math and Science Flip Chart<br>• Pattern Blocks<br>• Sequence Cards: "The Little Red Hen" and "Making Bee Bim Bop"<br>• Teacher's Treasure Book | • Alphabet/Letter Tiles<br>• ABC Picture Cards *Ww* and *Zz*<br>• Building Blocks Math Activities<br>• Making Good Choices Flip Chart<br>• *Matthew and the Color of the Sky* Big Book<br>• Pattern Blocks<br>• Pattern Block Puzzles (Teacher's Treasure Book, pp. 512–517)<br>• Photo Library CD-ROM<br>• Rhymes and Chants Flip Chart<br>• Teacher's Treasure Book |

## Other Materials

| DAY 1 | DAY 2 | DAY 3 | DAY 4 | DAY 5 |
|-------|-------|-------|-------|-------|
| • adjustable desk lamp<br>• beverage stirrers cut into pieces (see p. 105)<br>• black paper and drawing paper<br>• craft supplies (see p. 103)<br>• crayons<br>• glue<br>• index cards<br>• pictures of daytime and nighttime objects (see p. 103)<br>• paper dolls<br>• rectangular container of soil<br>• sticks or branches | • box or bag for Feely Box<br>• camera<br>• cardstock (various colors)<br>• crayons and markers<br>• dark cloth<br>• dashed outlines of *Ww* and *Zz*<br>• dot stickers<br>• hole-punch<br>• index cards<br>• masking tape<br>• plastic hangers or paper towel rolls<br>• pretzel sticks<br>• white pipe cleaners, yarn<br>• yellow circles (large) | • beverage stirrers or straws cut into pieces (see p. 117)<br>• butcher paper<br>• crayons<br>• dark cloth<br>• drawing paper with writing lines<br>• glue<br>• lamp (adjustable)<br>• masking tape<br>• three-column chart labeled *Morning, Afternoon, Night* (see p. 118)<br>• labeled time-related picture cards (see p. 118)<br>• stickers<br>• voice/sound recorder | • beverage stirrers or straws cut into pieces (see p. 124)<br>• cardstock<br>• craft sticks<br>• crayons<br>• dark cloth<br>• dot stickers<br>• fiction and nonfiction books about day and night<br>• masking tape and clear tape<br>• tablecloth<br>• toy cars<br>• white block letter *Zz* cut-outs<br>• zebra picture card | • black wash (diluted black paint)<br>• blue wash (diluted blue paint)<br>• colored butcher paper and colored construction paper (see p. 130)<br>• crayons<br>• resealable plastic bags<br>• sentence-strip puzzle pieces (see p. 127)<br>• graham crackers<br>• tempera paint and paintbrushes<br>• yard sticks<br>• yarn |

## Home Connection

| DAY 1 | DAY 2 | DAY 3 | DAY 4 | DAY 5 |
|-------|-------|-------|-------|-------|
| Remind children to talk with families about day and night. Send home the Weekly Family Letter, Home Connections Resource Guide, pp. 65–66. | Remind children to tell families about the shapes that they described in Math Time. Encourage them to play "I Spy" at home with their families. | Remind children to tell families about the morning, afternoon, and nighttime activities they discussed in Social Studies Time. | Send home Take-Home Storybook 20, Home Connections Resource Guide, pp. 157–160. Remind children to read the storybook with their families. | Remind children to tell families what they learned this week about day and night and the play they put on together. |

## Assessment

As you observe children throughout the week, you may fill out an Anecdotal Observational Record Form to document an individual's progress toward a goal or signs indicating the need for developmental or medical evaluation. You may also choose to select work for each child's portfolio. The Anecdotal Observational Record Form and Weekly Assessment rubrics are available in the assessment section of DLMExpressOnline.com.

## More Literature Suggestions

- **Night in the Country** by Cynthia Rylant and Mary Szilagyi
- **Night Becomes Day** by Richard McGuire
- **Black? White! Day? Night! A Book of Opposites** by Laura Vaccaro Seeger
- **What Makes Day and Night?** by Franklyn M. Branley

- **A Cloak for the Dreamer** by Aileen Friedman
- **Buenas noches, Luna** por Margaret Wise Brown
- **Las sombras** por Deanna Calvert
- **Un monstruo debajo de la cama** por Angelika Glitz y Joana Claverol
- **Perro y Gato** por Ricardo Alcantara
- **Pequeño vaquero** por Sue Heap

# Daily Planner

| | | DAY 1 | DAY 2 |
|---|---|---|---|
| **Let's Start the Day**<br>**Language Time** | large group | **Opening Routines** p. 102<br>**Morning Read Aloud** p. 102<br>**Oral Language and Vocabulary** p. 102 Spring Showers<br>**Phonological Awareness** p. 102 Segmenting Phonemes | **Opening Routines** p. 108<br>**Morning Read Aloud** p. 108<br>**Oral Language and Vocabulary** p. 108 Day and Night<br>**Phonological Awareness** p. 108 Segmenting Phonemes |
| **Center Time** | small group | **Focus On:**<br>**Library and Listening Center** p. 103<br>**Creativity Center** p. 103 | **Focus On:**<br>**ABC Center** p. 109<br>**Pretend and Learn Center** p. 109 |
| **Circle Time**<br>**Literacy Time** | large group | **Read Aloud**<br>*Matthew and the Color of the Sky/*<br>*Matías y el color del cielo* p. 104<br><br>**Learn About Letters and Sounds:**<br>*Ww* p. 104 | **Read Aloud**<br>*Matthew and the Color of the Sky/*<br>*Matías y el color del cielo* p. 110<br><br>**Learn About Letters and Sounds:**<br>*Ww* and *Zz* p. 110 |
| **Math Time** | large group | **Building Shapes** p. 105 | **Feely Box (Describe)** p. 111 |
| **Social and Emotional Development** | large group | **Solving a Problem** p. 105 | **Solving a Problem** p. 111 |
| **Content Connection** | large group | **Science:**<br>**Oral Language and Academic Vocabulary** p. 106<br>Comparing Day and Night<br>**Observe and Investigate** p. 106 Looking Outside | **Math:**<br>**Snapshots (Shapes)** p. 112 Naming Simple and Complex Shapes<br>**Pattern Block Pictures** p. 112 Creating Pictures and Designs |
| **Center Time** | small group | **Focus On:**<br>**Math and Science Center** p. 107<br>**Purposeful Play** p. 107 | **Focus On:**<br>**Construction Center** p. 113<br>**Purposeful Play** p. 113 |
| **Let's Say Good-Bye** | large group | **Read Aloud** p. 107<br>**Writing** p. 107<br>**Home Connection** p. 107 | **Read Aloud** p. 113<br>**Writing** p. 113<br>**Home Connection** p. 113 |

**Focus Question**

## What can I learn about day and night?
## ¿Qué puedo aprender sobre el día y la noche?

# DAY 3

**Opening Routines** p. 114
**Morning Read Aloud** p. 114
**Oral Language and Vocabulary**
p. 114 Shadow Talk
**Phonological Awareness**
p. 114 Segmenting Phonemes

**Focus On:**
**Writer's Center** p. 115
**Pretend and Learn Center** p. 115

**Read Aloud**
*Concept Big Book 4:*
*The Earth and Sky/*
*La Tierra y el cielo* p. 116
**Learn About Letters and Sounds:**
*Ww* and *Zz* p. 116

**Snapshots (Shape Parts)** p. 117

**Solving a Problem** p. 117

**Social Studies:**
**Oral Language and Academic Vocabulary**
p. 118 Time of Day
**Understand and Participate**
p. 118 Time Sequence Charts

**Focus On:**
**Math and Science Center** p. 119
**Purposeful Play** p. 119

**Read Aloud** p. 119
**Writing** p. 119
**Home Connection** p. 119

# DAY 4

**Opening Routines** p. 120
**Morning Read Aloud** p. 120
**Oral Language and Vocabulary**
p. 120 Real or Make-Believe?
**Phonological Awareness**
p. 120 Review Blending Phonemes

**Focus On:**
**Library and Listening Center** p. 121
**ABC Center** p. 121

**Read Aloud** p. 122
"The Stolen Soup Smell"/
"El robo del olor de la sopa"
**Learn About Letters and**
**Sounds:** *Ww* and *Zz* p. 122

**Slide, Turn, Flip** p. 123

**Solving a Problem** p. 123

**Math:**
**Snapshots (Shape Parts)**
p. 124 Making Simple and Complex Shapes

**Focus On:**
**Construction Center** p. 125
**Purposeful Play** p. 125

**Read Aloud** p. 125
**Writing** p. 125
**Home Connection** p. 125

# DAY 5

**Opening Routines** p. 126
**Morning Read Aloud** p. 126
**Oral Language and Vocabulary**
p. 126 Day and Night
**Phonological Awareness**
p. 126 Segmenting Phonemes

**Focus On:**
**ABC Center** p. 127
**Writer's Center** p. 127

**Read Aloud**
*Matthew and the*
*Color of the Sky/Matías*
*y el color del cielo* p. 128
**Learn About Letters**
**and Sounds:** *Ww* and *Zz*
p. 128

**Pattern Block Puzzles** p. 129

**Solving a Problem** p. 129

**Dramatic Play:**
**Oral Language and Academic Vocabulary**
p. 130 Recalling Story Details
**Explore and Express**
p. 130 Dramatizing the *Big Book* Story

**Focus On:**
**Creativity Center** p. 131
**Purposeful Play** p. 131

**Read Aloud** p. 131
**Writing** p. 131
**Home Connection** p. 131

# Week 3

**Day and Night**

# Learning Centers

## Math and Science Center

### Tree Shadow
Children make a model of a tree and use the model to create shadows. They examine and record light effects. See p. 107.

### Shadow Shapes
Child pairs make shadows using shapes and trace them. Children discuss how shadow sizes change. See p. 119.

### Shadow Puppets
Children use their hands or stick puppets by a sunny window to cast shadows, and then explain how the shadows are formed.

### Comparing Shadows
Child pairs stand in a place where they cast shadows. They compare the lengths of their shadows and their actual heights.

## ABC Center

### Walk the *W*
Children form the letter *Ww* using pipe cleaners. They then walk along a *W* shape on the floor while acting out *W* words. See p. 109.

### Zigzag *Z*
Children decorate a letter *Zz* cutout, identify words beginning with the /z/ sound, and move a toy car along a *Z* shape on the floor. See p. 121.

### Letter Trade
Children rearrange Alphabet/Letter Tiles to spell words starting with *Ww* and *Zz*. See p. 127.

### Super *Z* Sound Effects
Children act like superheroes and use words that begin with *Zz*, such as *zap, zing, zip,* and *zoom* to accompany their actions.

### Sticky Letters
Children use pasta to form and glue upper- and lowercase *Zz* and *Ww* to a sheet of paper.

## Creativity Center

### Shoe Shadow
Children create shadows. Then they trace their shoes on white and black paper and depict the tracings as shoes and shoe shadows. See p. 103.

### Paint Colors of the Sky
Children draw night or day sky objects in crayon and paint over them using light or dark paint. See p. 131.

### Shadow Portraits
Child pairs draw silhouettes of each other by tracing their shadows cast on butcher paper with sidewalk chalk.

### Sky Object Masks
Children use paper plates to create masks of the sun and moon.

## Library and Listening Center

**Sorting Day and Night**
Children sort picture cards showing day and night activities, and then make additional cards. See p. 103.

**Real and Make-Believe in Books**
Children find pictures of day and night in books and identify whether the scenes are real or make-believe. See p. 121.

**Daytime Setting**
Children look through books and put sticky notes on pages showing daytime.

**Starry Night Pictures**
Children draw night sky objects on black paper while listening to songs about the night sky. They poke small holes in the paper and hang the paper in the window to see the "starry" light effects.

## Construction Center

**Day and Night Mobiles**
Child pairs assemble mobiles of day and night sky objects. See p. 113.

**Puppet Theater**
Children build a theater and make stick puppets to retell "The Stolen Soup Smell" in sequential order. See p. 125.

**Building Flying Objects**
Children use blocks to build airplanes, rockets, and kites and describe when they see the objects in the sky.

## Writer's Center

**Day and Night Book**
Children copy sentences about day and night and illustrate them. Pages are collected in a class book. See p. 115.

**Compound Word Puzzles**
Children combine word cards to make compound words such as *daytime* and *nighttime*. See p. 127.

**Day and Night Poem**
Children identify rhyming words for *day* or *night* and dictate a two line rhyming poem. They illustrate the poem.

## Pretend and Learn Center

**Sun Talk**
Children make a sun and discuss its effects during role play. See p. 109.

**The Shy Sun**
Children discuss how the sun would behave if it were shy. They suggest ways to help the sun recover from shyness. See p. 115.

**Astronaut Talk**
Children pretend to be astronauts flying through space. They discuss what they see in the sky.

# DAY 1

## Focus Question
**What can I learn about day and night?**
**¿Qué puedo aprender sobre el día y la noche?**

### Learning Goals

**Language and Communication**
• Child understands and uses regular and irregular plural nouns, regular past tense verbs, personal and possessive pronouns, and subject-verb agreement.

**Emergent Literacy: Reading**
• Child combines two words to form a compound word.
• Child removes one word from a compound word.

**Fine Arts**
• Child participates in a variety of music activities (such as listening, singing, finger plays, musical games, performances).

### Vocabulary

| | | | |
|---|---|---|---|
| puddle | charco | raincoat | impermeable |
| raindrops | gotas | spring | primavera |
| umbrella | paraguas | | |

### Differentiated Instruction

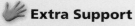 **Extra Support**
**Phonological Awareness**
**If...**children have difficulty separating words, **then...**have them clap or tap as they say each sound, or use two-phoneme words.

 **Enrichment**
**Phonological Awareness**
Challenge children to segment four-phoneme words such as *hand* and *what*.

 **Special Needs**
**Hearing Impairment**
**If...**children have difficulty hearing the song, **then...**sign or create simple gestures for verses that they can do with you as the group sings.

# Let's Start the Day

 **Opening Routines and Transition Tips**
For **Opening Routines** and **Transition Tips** turn to pages 178–181 and visit **DLMExpressOnline.com** for more ideas.

Read **"The Princess and the Pea"/**"La princesa y la arveja" from the *Teacher's Treasure Book*, page 225, for your morning Read Aloud.

## Language Time

 large group  15 minutes

**Social and Emotional Development** Ask children to show and tell you what they should do when they want to ask questions.

### Oral Language and Vocabulary

✓ **Can children use descriptive words and plurals to tell about rainy days?**

**Spring Showers** Talk about what happens on rainy days. Discuss how rainy days can sometimes be dark like nighttime. Share that on a rainy day, like at night, the sun is not visible. Ask: *Why do we need a raincoat and umbrella when it rains? How is a rainy day like nighttime? How do rainy days make you feel? Do you like the sound of rain at night? ¿Por qué necesitamos un impermeable y un paraguas cuando llueve? ¿En qué se parecen un día lluvioso y la noche? ¿Cómo te sientes en los días lluviosos? ¿Te gusta el sonido de la lluvia por la noche?*

● Display *Oral Language Development Card 66*. Point out the raindrops and name the different parts of the child's attire. Ask: *What words do we put together to make the word raincoat? What word can we take away from raindrops to make the word rain? ¿Qué palabras unimos para formar la palabra raincoat? ¿Qué palabra tenemos que quitar de raindrops para formar rain?*

● Follow the suggestions on the back of the card.

### Phonological Awareness

✓ **Can children separate the individual phonemes of a word?**

**Segmenting Phonemes** Display *Rhymes and Chants Flip Chart* page 31. Sing "Making Shadows" until children are comfortable joining in. Then tell children to listen carefully as you stretch out a word. Say: *Make. /m/ /a/, may, /k/, make.* Have children repeat after you. Then ask: *How many sounds are in the word? ¿Cuántos sonidos hay en la palabra?* (3) Repeat with *can* and *put*.

**ELL** Use familiar body words such as *teeth, feet,* and *nose* to review segmenting words. Point to your feet and say: *Feet, /f/ /e/, fee, /t/, feet.* Have children repeat after you.

*Oral Language Development Card 66*

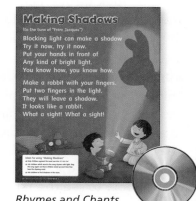
*Rhymes and Chants Flip Chart, page 31/ page 63*

# Center Time

▶ **Center Rotation** Center Time includes teacher-guided activities and independent activities. Refer to the **Learning Centers** on pages 100–101 for activities in additional centers.

 small group 60–90 minutes

## Library and Listening Center

 **Observe children cooperating and solving problems together.**

**Materials** picture cards of daytime and nighttime objects (such as: sun, moon, star, rainbow, ball, bed, flashlight); index cards, crayons

**Sorting Day and Night** Make an index card that says *daytime* and a card that says *nighttime*. Explain to children that people see and do different things during the day and night.

● Read the cards and segment the words *day* and *night* with children.

● Distribute the picture cards for partners to sort below the category names *daytime* and *nighttime*. Ask: **Which pictures show daytime things? Which pictures show nighttime things?** *¿Qué ilustraciones muestran algo que vemos de día? ¿Cuáles muestran algo que vemos de noche?*

● Have children use index cards to make their own pictures for daytime and nighttime.

### Center Tip

**If...**children have difficulty deciding how to sort the picture cards, **then...** suggest that they think of when they see or use that object most often.

## Creativity Center

 **Listen for words children use to describe a shadow.**

**Materials** lamp or light source, paper dolls or shapes, wall for projecting shadows, black paper, white paper, scissors, crayons

**Shoe Shadow** Remind children that shadows are formed when objects block light. Ask: **What causes light outside? Inside?** *¿Qué nos da luz cuando estamos afuera? ¿Y adentro?* Encourage children to turn the light on and off to explore the source of light and electricity.

● Tell children to hold up a paper doll or shape in front of the light. Ask: **How does the shadow look different from the paper? What happens when you move the paper?** *¿En qué se diferencia la sombra del objeto real? ¿Qué sucede cuando mueven el papel?*

● Have children trace their shoes on white paper, then color and cut them out. Have them make shoe "shadows" out of black paper.

### Center Tip

**If...**children have difficulty tracing the shoe, **then...**have them take off their shoes to trace, or have partners help each other.

### ✓ Learning Goals

**Social and Emotional Development**
• Child demonstrates appropriate conflict-resolution strategies, requesting help when needed.

**Language and Communication**
• Child uses words to identify and understand categories.

**Science**
• Child investigates and describes energy sources (light, heat, electricity).

**Fine Arts**
• Child expresses emotions or ideas through art.

### Differentiated Instruction

**✋ Extra Support**

**Library and Listening Center**
**If...**children have difficulty sorting the picture cards, **then...**show them only two cards at a time, one for day and the other for night. Ask: **Which object do you use more during the day? Which one do you use more at night?** *¿Qué objeto usan más durante el día? ¿Cuál usan más durante la noche?*

**⭐ Enrichment**

**Library and Listening Center**
Have children write the object's name below the picture they draw for their day and night cards.

**♥ Special Needs**

**Delayed Motor Development**
**If...**children have difficulty cutting paper or controlling their arms, **then...**give them precut paper shoes to color for the shoe and the shadow. Tape the precut shoes to the table top so they do not have to hold them as they color.

**Focus Question**

## What can I learn about day and night?
## ¿Qué puedo aprender sobre el día y la noche?

 **Learning Goals**

**Emergent Literacy: Reading**
• Child identifies the letter that stands for a given sound.
• Child asks and answers questions about books read aloud (such as "Who?" "What?" "Where?").

**Science**
• Child describes the effects of natural forces (such as wind, gravity).

**Technology Applications**
• Child uses voice/sound players and recorders, and touch screens correctly.

### Vocabulary

| changing | cambiante | color | color |
|----------|-----------|-------|-------|
| different | diferente | rain | lluvia |
| real | real | make-believe | fantasía |

 **Differentiated Instruction**

### ✋ Extra Support
**Learn About Letters and Sounds**
**If...**children have difficulty identifying the letter *Ww*, **then...**give them a large *W* cutout to feel and describe with their eyes closed. Have them show you the orientation of the letter. After they open their eyes, say: *I see something in the room that begins with the /w/ sound. What do I see?* (wall, window) *Veo algo en el salón de clases que tiene el sonido /w/. ¿Qué veo?*

### ⭐ Enrichment
**Learn About Letters and Sounds**
Challenge children to look through stories to find words that have letter *Ww* in the beginning, middle, or end of the word. Have them copy the words with Alphabet/Letter Tiles.

### Accommodations for 3's
**Learn About Letters and Sounds**
**If...**children have trouble remembering what words start with the /w/ sound, **then...**have them repeat and act out *W* words: *walk, waddle, wiggle, wag, wash, warm, wind, wave.*

## Literacy Time
 **Read Aloud**

✅ Can children describe what happens during changes in the sky?

**Build Background** Tell children that you will be reading a book about the sky changing colors. Ask if any children have seen the sky change. Ask: *What colors have you seen in the sky in the day? In the night? ¿Qué colores has visto en el cielo de día? ¿Y de noche?*

**Listen for Enjoyment** Display the Big Book *Matthew and the Color of the Sky*, and read aloud the title.

● Browse through the pictures before you read the story. Point to the sky and the animals. Ask: *What color is the sky in this picture? What are the animals doing? How are these animals different from real animals? ¿De qué color es el cielo en esta ilustración? ¿Qué están haciendo los animales? ¿En qué se diferencian estos animales de los reales?*

● Help children distinguish between real and make-believe in the story as you read it aloud. Ask: *What do you see in this picture that happens in real life? What doesn't? ¿Qué cosa de esta ilustración sucede en la vida real? ¿Qué cosa no?*

**Respond to the Story** Have children tell what is happening in each picture. Refer to details in the story. Ask: *Why is Matthew upset? What does the sky look like early in the day? What happens to the sky at night? How does it change? ¿Por qué está enojado Matías? ¿Cómo es el cielo por la mañana? ¿Cómo es el cielo de noche?*

## Learn About Letters and Sounds

✅ Can children identify the /w/ sound and the letter *Ww* in words?

**Letter Hunt for *Ww*** Use *Alphabet Wall Card* to review the sound and shape of *Ww*. Remind children that *Ww* makes the /w/ sound. Have them trace the letter with their fingers. Have them say after you: *W is for /w/.../w/ /w/ /w/.*

● Display the following sentence, and read it aloud: *What will you wear to warm up?* Say: *Find a word that begins with W. Busquen una palabra que empiece con W.* Invite volunteers to underline or trace the *Ww* in each word on chart paper or an interactive whiteboard (touch screen board).

**ELL** Play "Follow the Leader." Say: *Repeat after me. Say and do what I say and do.* Say and model for children: *Walk this way...walk, walk, walk...waddle, waddle, waddle...wiggle, wiggle, wiggle...wave, wave, wave.*

 large group | 15 minutes

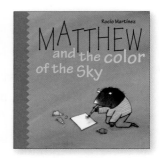

*Matthew and the Color of the Sky*
*Matías y el color del cielo*

*Alphabet Wall Cards*
*Tarjetas abecé de pared*

# Math Time

## Observe and Investigate

✓ **Can children create shapes?**

**Building Shapes** Cut flat beverage stirrers into 2", 4", and 6" pieces to give to children. Have children make a triangle that you show them from the Shape Set. Make sure they accurately form the sides and corners.

● Have them make other triangles. Ask: *How are your triangles alike? How are they different? How many sides and corners does every triangle have? ¿En qué se parecen los triángulos? ¿En qué se diferencian? ¿Cuántos lados y vértices tiene cada triángulo?*

● Repeat for squares and rectangles. Have children compare the shapes. Ask: *How many sides and corners does every square have? How many sides and corners does every rectangle have? How are rectangles and squares alike? ¿Cuántos lados y vértices tiene cada cuadrado? ¿Cuántos lados y vértices tiene cada rectángulo? ¿En qué se parecen los rectángulos y los cuadrados?*

### Building Blocks

**Online Math Activity**

Introduce Shapes Part 2, in which children build shapes from parts. Some shapes are rotated and less familiar. Each child should complete the activity this week.

# ☰☰☰ Social and Emotional Development

## Making Good Choices

✓ **Do children use different problem-solving strategies to resolve conflicts?**

**Solving a Problem** Discuss how children have solved problems. Display *Making Good Choices Flip Chart* page 31. Point to the two children holding the ball.

● Ask: *What is happening in this picture? What do you think is the problem? How might they solve it? ¿Qué está pasando en este dibujo? ¿Qué problema creen que tienen los niños? ¿Cómo lo resolverán?*

● If necessary, explain that both children in the picture want the ball. Ask children how they might solve the problem. Discuss what it means to share a toy or other material item with someone. Ask: *Why is it good to share things with each other? ¿Por qué es bueno compartir cosas con otros?*

🔲 Review the meaning of *toy box, watching, pulling,* and *playground.* Point to each example in the picture as you say the word, and have children repeat after you. Write the word on a sticky note and put it on the example. Track the print as you read the word. Have children repeat after you.

*Making Good Choices Flip Chart, page 31*

## ✓ Learning Goals

**Social and Emotional Development**
● Child demonstrates appropriate conflict-resolution strategies, requesting help when needed.

**Mathematics**
● Child creates two-dimensional shapes; recreates two-dimensional shapes from memory.

**Physical Development**
● Child develops small-muscle strength and control.

### Vocabulary

| | | | |
|---|---|---|---|
| corner | vértice | problem | problema |
| rectangle | rectángulo | side | lado |
| solve | resolver | square | cuadrado |
| triangle | triángulo | | |

## Differentiated Instruction

✋ **Extra Support**

**Observe and Investigate**

**If...**children have difficulty forming the sides and corners accurately, **then...**display examples of shapes for reference, or have them use balls of modeling clay to join the corners together.

⭐ **Enrichment**

**Observe and Investigate**

Challenge children to make a shape using all of their pieces or a specific number. For example, say: *Make a shape that has five sides that are all the same length. Hagan una figura que tenga cinco lados del mismo largo.*

### Accommodations for 3's

**Observe and Investigate**

**If...**children struggle building different shapes, **then...**have them focus only on making different triangles (all sides the same length, two sides the same length, all sides different lengths).

## Learning Goals

**Language and Communication**
- Child matches language to social setting.
- Child experiments with and produces a growing number of sounds in English words. (ELL)
- Child names and describes actual or pictured people, places, things, actions, attributes, and events.

**Science**
- Child investigates and describes energy sources (light, heat, electricity).
- Child observes, identifies, compares, and discusses objects in the sky (such as clouds, sun, moon, stars).
- Child describes the effects of natural forces (such as wind, gravity).
- Child follows basic health and safety rules.

### Vocabulary

| clouds | nubes | light | luz |
|--------|-------|-------|-----|
| moon | luna | night | noche |
| shine | brillar | sky | cielo |

## Differentiated Instruction

### Extra Support

**Oral Language and Academic Vocabulary**
**If...**children have difficulty comparing day and night, **then...**point to objects in the day scene of the flip chart, and have children look for them on the night side (and vice versa).

### Enrichment

**Oral Language and Academic Vocabulary**
Challenge children to make their own day and night posters. They might draw themselves doing something they do during the day and something they do at night.

# Science Time

large group  20 minutes

**Personal Safety Skills** Tell children not to look directly at the sun, but only to glance around it. Allow children to wear sunglasses if they have them.

## Oral Language and Academic Vocabulary

✓ **Can children use words to describe and compare day and night?**

**Comparing Day and Night** Point to both pictures of *Math and Science Flip Chart* page 57. Say: *This is the same place. It is the same on Earth both day and night.* *Éste es el mismo lugar. Es el mismo lugar de la Tierra, ya sea de de día o de noche.*

- Have children compare the different characteristics of the day and night scenes. Ask: *What do you see in the sky during the day? What do you see at night? Where is light coming from in each picture?* *¿Qué ven en el cielo durante el día? ¿Y durante la noche? ¿De dónde viene la luz en cada ilustración?*

- Display *Oral Language Development Card 67*. Ask: *Which picture on the chart is similar to this one? Why?* *¿Qué ilustración del rotafolio se parece a ésta? ¿Por qué?* Point to the moon on the card. Explain that the moon appears to change shape during the month, and sometimes cannot be seen. Then follow the suggestions on the back of the card.

## Observe and Investigate

✓ **Can children investigate sources of energy such as heat and light?**

✓ **Can children identify, observe, and discuss objects in the sky?**

**Looking Outside** Take children outside to observe the sky and the earth. Tell children to look at the sky, but not straight at the sun. Then have them look around the ground. Ask: *How many different things do you see? ¿Cuántas cosas diferentes ven?*

- After a few minutes, have partners discuss what they observed. Monitor children matching their language to this social aspect of the activity. Then talk about it. Ask: *What did you discuss? Did your partner see anything you didn't? ¿Sobre qué hablaron? ¿Vio su compañero algo que ustedes no vieron?* Explain that often by working together we can notice more than we can notice alone.

- If there are shadows that day, ask children what shadows they can see. Ask if they can find the objects blocking the light to create the shadows.

- Prompt children to consider changes that will happen to the sky at night. Ask: *How will the sky change tonight? Will the sun give heat and light? ¿Cómo cambiará el cielo esta noche? ¿El sol dará luz y calor?*

**ELL** Pair English language learners with native speakers for the partner discussion. Encourage them to use the same intonation as their native speaking partner by prompting them to mimic the partner's voice. Ask: *How does it sound?*

*Math and Science Flip Chart, page 57*

*Oral Language Development Card 67*

# Center Time

▶ **Center Rotation** Center Time includes teacher-guided activities and independent activities. Refer to the **Learning Centers** on pages 100–101 for activities in additional centers.

small group   30 minutes

## Math and Science Center

**Center Tip**

✓ **Observe children investigating and describing light and shadows.**

**Materials** container of soil, short sticks or branches, desk lamp with adjustable neck, drawing paper, crayons

**Tree Shadow** Tell children they will make a model of a tree and explore its shadow. Help children stand a stick "tree" securely in soil.

- Have children turn on the lamp and put it in front of their tree. Ask: **Was the shadow there before we turned on the light? What has to happen to make a shadow?** *¿Había una sombra antes de que encendiéramos la luz?¿Qué hizo aparecer una sombra?*

- Have children adjust and move the lamp to different positions. Ask: **What happens to the shadow when you move the light? How does the size and position change? What is longer, the shadow or tree?** *¿Qué sucedió con la sombra cuando movieron la luz? ¿Cómo cambió el tamaño y la posición de la sombra? ¿Qué es más grande: la sombra o el árbol?*

- Have children draw their tree, including the lamp and shadow. Have them describe their drawings and how a shadow is made.

**If...**children cannot decide where to move the lamp, **then...**prompt them with positional words and phrases, such as *higher, lower, to the right, to the left.*

## Purposeful Play

✓ **Observe children appropriately handling classroom materials.**

Children choose an open center for free playtime. Encourage cooperation and problem-solving skills by suggesting they work together to explore shadows in the room and what causes them.

## Let's Say Good-Bye

large group   15 minutes

 **Read Aloud** Revisit "The Princess and the Pea"/*"La princesa y la arveja"* for your afternoon Read Aloud. Tell children to listen for the /w/ sound.

 **Home Connection** Refer to the Home Connection activities listed in the chart on page 97. Remind children to tell their families what they learned about shadows. Sing the "Good-bye Song" as children prepare to leave.

---

### ✓ Learning Goals

**Language and Communication**
- Child names and describes actual or pictured people, places, things, actions, attributes, and events.

**Mathematics**
- Child understands and uses words that describe position/location in space (such as *under, over, beside, between, on, in, near, far away*).
- Child measures the length and height of people or objects using standard or non-standard tools.

**Science**
- Child investigates and describes energy sources (light, heat, electricity).
- Child describes the effects of natural forces (such as wind, gravity).

### Writing

Recap the day. Ask children: **What did you learn about day and night? What happens when the sky changes? Did you see the sky change today?** *¿Qué aprendieron sobre el día y la noche? ¿Qué sucede cuando el cielo cambia? ¿Vieron cómo cambió hoy el cielo?* Have children name objects seen in the sky and on the ground during the day and night, and what they observed specifically today. Record their answers. Read them back as you track the print, and emphasize the correspondence between speech and print.

# DAY 2

**Focus Question**

**What can I learn about day and night?**

**¿Qué puedo aprender sobre el día y la noche?**

 **Learning Goals**

**Social and Emotional Development**
• Child demonstrates appropriate conflict-resolution strategies, requesting help when needed.

**Language and Communication**
• Child uses oral language for a variety of purposes.

• Child understands and uses regular and irregular plural nouns, regular past tense verbs, personal and possessive pronouns, and subject-verb agreement.

**Science**
• Child investigates and describes energy sources (light, heat, electricity).

• Child describes the effects of natural forces (such as wind, gravity).

## Vocabulary

| | | | |
|---|---|---|---|
| bright | brillante | earth | Tierra |
| energy | energía | light | luz |
| moon | Luna | night | noche |

## Differentiated Instruction

 **Extra Support**
**Oral Language and Vocabulary**
**If...**children have difficulty understanding the meaning of descriptive words, **then...**illustrate and role play the meanings of the words.

 **Enrichment**
**Oral Language and Vocabulary**
Expand children's vocabularies during the discussion by having them take turns saying something they know about light and where it comes from during the day and night.

# Let's Start the Day

 **Opening Routines and Transition Tips**

For **Opening Routines** and **Transition Tips** turn to pages 178–181 and visit **DLMExpressOnline.com** for more ideas.

Read **"Counting My Blessings"/**"Mis tesoros" from the *Teacher's Treasure Book*, page 95, for your morning Read Aloud.

## Language Time

large group  15 minutes

**Social and Emotional Development** Ask children what they know about taking turns and how to talk nicely to one another if they disagree.

### Oral Language and Vocabulary

Can children use language associated with day and night?

Can children describe sources of light, heat, and electricity?

**Day and Night** Review the pictures from *The Earth and Sky,* pages 5–13. Reread the labels on images. Reread the text on pages 8–9 and 12–13.

● Ask: *What do you see here that happens only in the day? What do you see that happens only at night? Where does light come from at different times? ¿Qué ven aquí que sólo ocurre de día? ¿Qué ven que sólo ocurre de noche? ¿De dónde viene la luz en los diferentes momentos?*

● Encourage children to share their experiences with daytime and nighttime light and energy sources. Ask: *What gave light outside yesterday? What made it warm? What gave light to your house last night? ¿Qué nos dio luz ayer, cuando estuvimos al aire libre? ¿Qué nos dio calor? ¿Qué les dio luz anoche en sus casas?*

### Phonological Awareness

Can children separate the individual phonemes of a word?

**Segmenting Phonemes** Display the Dog Puppets. Tell children to listen carefully as each dog slowly says a word. Tell children to use their fingers to show the number of sounds they hear in the word. Confirm the answer. For example, the Dog Puppet says: *Me, /m/ /e/. There are two sounds in the word me, /m/ /e/. Me. Hay dos sonidos en la palabra me: /m/ /e/.* Repeat with other two-phoneme words. As children advance with the activity, make mistakes with the puppet that the children can correct. For example, *Me. There are two sounds in me: /t/ /e/. Is that me? Me. Hay dos sonidos en la palabra me: /t/ /e/. Eso forma me?*

**ELL** Point to an object shown in *Concept Big Book 4: The Earth and Sky.* Say the name as you point to the object. Then say each sound of the word. For example: *sun, /s/ /u/ /n/.* Have children repeat after you.

# Center Time

▶ **Center Rotation** Center Time includes teacher-guided activities and independent activities. Refer to the **Learning Centers** on pages 100–101 for activities in additional centers.

small goup | 60–90 minutes

## ABC Center

✓ **Track children's ability to recognize and show letters in the correct orientation.**

**Materials** *ABC Picture Card Ww*, index cards, white pipe cleaners, wide masking tape

**Walk the *W*** Review with children the shape and letter sound for *Ww*. Have children use the letter card to trace the shape with their fingers.

● Have children use a white pipe cleaner to form a *W*. Point out that *white* begins with the /w/ sound and *Ww*.

● Write and display the words *walk, wiggle,* and *wave* on index cards. Point out that they begin with *Ww*. Read aloud each word.

● Use wide tape to make a large *W* on the floor. Have children walk on the *W* from left to right. Then have them wiggle and wave along the way.

### Center Tip

**If...**children have difficulty forming *W* from a single pipe cleaner, **then...**let them use four pipe cleaners laid flat on the table.

## Pretend and Learn Center

✓ **Look for examples of children asking and answering questions thoughtfully about changes in the sky.**

**Materials** large yellow circles, scissors, crayons

**Sun Talk** Tell children to pretend to be the sun. Prompt them to look out the window to see if they can find the sun right now. Then ask children what they think the sun would say if it could talk.

● Give each child a yellow circle. Model how to cut zigzag around the circle to make rays. Help children cut peep holes in their suns.

● Have children take turns pretending to be the sun talking about daytime. Have them hold up their sun masks as they share their thoughts about how "they" change during the day.

● Encourage classmates to ask questions to the "sun," such as: *Where do we see you? When do we see you? What do you give Earth?* *¿Dónde te vemos? ¿Cuándo te vemos? ¿Qué le das a la Tierra?*

### Center Tip

**If...**children have difficulty cutting a zigzag around the circle, **then...**draw zigzag lines for them to cut around the circle, or place your hand near theirs as you cut together.

## ✓ Learning Goals

**Language and Communication**
● Child uses newly learned vocabulary daily in multiple contexts.

**Emergent Literacy: Reading**
● Child names most upper- and lowercase letters of the alphabet.

● Child identifies the letter that stands for a given sound.

**Science**
● Child observes, identifies, compares, and discusses objects in the sky (such as clouds, sun, moon, stars).

● Child describes the effects of natural forces (such as wind, gravity).

## Differentiated Instruction

### ✋ Extra Support

**ABC Center**

**If...**children have difficulty remembering the sound of *Ww*, **then...**suggest that they think of the word *wow* for /w/.

### ⭐ Enrichment

**ABC Center**

Challenge children to name words that begin with *Ww*. Have them give clues for others to guess the word. For example: *My word tells what you get when you stand in the rain.* (wet) *Mi palabra dice cómo quedas cuando te paras bajo la lluvia.*

### ♥ Special Needs

**Vision Loss**

**If...**children have difficulty seeing the orientation of *Ww* or any letter, **then...**provide large, tactile letters at the center so children can physically feel the orientation of the letters.

## Focus Question

**What can I learn about day and night?**

**¿Qué puedo aprender sobre el día y la noche?**

## Literacy Time

 **Read Aloud**

✓ **Can children distinguish between real and make-believe?**

**Build Background** Tell children that you will be reading about the sky changing colors. Remind them that sometimes stories are make-believe even though they include real parts. Ask: **When does the real sky change colors?** *¿Cuándo cambia de color el cielo real?*

**Listen for Understanding** Read *Matthew and the Color of the Sky*. Point out that the sky in the story changes color just like the real sky. Have children compare the different color changes.

● Compare pages 5, 7, 17 and 18. Ask: **How is the sky different in these pictures? What happens to the sky when it changes from day to night?** *¿Cuál es la diferencia entre el cielo en estas dos ilustraciones? ¿Qué pasa en el cielo cuando el día se convierte en noche?*

**Respond to the Story** Have children explain the problem that Matthew is trying to solve. Encourage children to ask you to reread or explain the meaning of text on the pages. Have them name the animals in the story. Ask: **Whose skin is the color of the sky at sunrise? Whose hair is the color of a cloudy sky?** *¿Qué animal es del color del cielo al amanecer? ¿Qué animal es del color del cielo nublado?*

● Help children distinguish between real and make-believe. Ask: **How do we know this story is make-believe? What parts are not real?** *¿Cómo sabemos que este cuento es de fantasía? ¿Qué partes no son reales?*

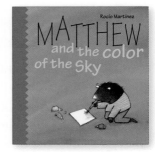

*Matthew and the Color of the Sky*
*Matías y el color del cielo*

## Learn About Letters and Sounds

✓ **Can children distinguish between letters *Ww* and *Zz*?**

**Compare *Ww* and *Zz*** Display upper- and lowercase Alphabet/Letter Tiles for *Ww* and *Zz* for children to compare. Review the letter sounds with children.

● Have children put matching pairs together, showing the correct orientation.

● Give children dashed outlines of *W* and *Z* to trace. Have them put a green dot where each letter starts and a red dot where each letter ends. Then have them use their finger to trace each letter from beginning to end. Point out the different shapes and direction of the letters.

● Have children use pretzel sticks to make upper- and lowercase *Ww* and *Zz*. Children can break or bite the pretzels to make shorter lines for each letter.

**ELL** Have children feel a sponge cutout of *W*. Dip the sponge in water as you say: */w/*, **water.** Have children repeat. Give children the sponge as you say: */w/*, **wet.** Have children repeat while they squeeze out the water.

---

## Learning Goals

**Emergent Literacy: Reading**

● Child explores books and other texts to answer questions.

● Child names most upper- and lowercase letters of the alphabet.

● Child identifies the letter that stands for a given sound.

● Child asks and answers questions about books read aloud (such as "Who?" "What?" "Where?").

**Science**

● Child describes the effects of natural forces (such as wind, gravity).

### Vocabulary

| | | | |
|---|---|---|---|
| cloudy | nublado | color | color |
| hair | pelo | make-believe | fantasía |
| skin | piel | sunrise | amanece |
| upset | enfurruñado | | |

## Differentiated Instruction

 **Extra Support**

**Learn About Letters and Sounds**

**If...**children have difficulty writing or distinguishing between *Ww* and *Zz*, **then...** hold the child's writing hand to write the letters together. Point out that *Ww* is drawn up and down, and *Zz* is drawn side to side.

**Enrichment**

**Learn About Letters and Sounds**

Challenge children to make large block letters of *W* and *Z* that show words or pictures inside them of things or actions that begin with that letter.

large group · 15 minutes

# Math Time

## Observe and Investigate

 **Can children identify and describe common shapes?**

**Feely Box (Describe)** Explain to children that they are going to describe a secret shape for classmates to name.

- Secretly hide a Shape Set shape in the feely box. Use a simple shape, such as a square. Have one child feel the shape and describe it *without saying its name*. Invite classmates to guess the shape. Ask: **What is the shape's name?** *¿Cuál es el nombre de esta figura?*

- Repeat with different shapes, including the trapezoid, hexagon, and rhombus. Prompt children to compare the shapes from the box.

- As you introduce Piece Puzzler 3, ask children to show you how to open the program.

### Building Blocks

**Online Math Activity**

Introduce Piece Puzzler 3: Make Pictures, in which children drag and sometimes flip shapes into place. Each child should complete the activity this week.

large group · 15 minutes

# ✗✗✗ Social and Emotional Development

## Making Good Choices

 **Do children use different strategies to solve problems?**

**Solving a Problem** Revisit *Making Good Choices Flip Chart* page 31.

- Display a Dog Puppet. Say: **Who can tell the puppet what these two children are doing? Tell a way for the children to solve their problem.** *¿Quién puede decirle al títere qué están haciendo estos dos niños? Digan una forma en que los niños pueden resolver su problema.*

- Provide each child a turn to tell the puppet about the two children both wanting the ball and how they can solve their problem. Encourage children to provide answers that haven't been given yet by other children.

- Have the puppet coordinate a vote for what children think is a good solution to the problem in the picture.

**ELL** Let children use drawing software to create and express their ideas about what the children in the flip chart picture should do. Model how to draw in the software and let them use it freely to express their ideas. Then discuss their pictures with them using sentence frames: **I see _____. Do you mean the boy and girl should _____?** As children respond, type their responses and add them to the pictures. Read and print out their creations for them to keep.

*Making Good Choices Flip Chart, page 31*

### Learning Goals

**Social and Emotional Development**
- Child demonstrates appropriate conflict-resolution strategies, requesting help when needed.

**Mathematics**
- Child recognizes, names, describes, matches, compares, sorts common two-dimensional shapes (such as circle, square, rectangle, triangle, rhombus).

**Social Studies**
- Child participates in voting for group decision-making.

**Technology Applications**
- Child uses computer software or technology to express original ideas.

### Vocabulary

| | | | |
|---|---|---|---|
| circle | círculo | hexagon | hexágono |
| rhombus | rombo | shape | figura |
| square | cuadrado | trapezoid | trapecio |

### Differentiated Instruction

✋ **Extra Support**
*Observe and Investigate*
**If...**children struggle identifying or describing shapes during the activity, **then...**have them trace each shape on paper, counting as they make crayon strokes along each side.

⭐ **Enrichment**
*Observe and Investigate*
Have children use templates to draw shapes. Have them turn the shapes into "feely shapes," such as a *soft square*, a *rough rectangle*, and a *smooth circle* by gluing material textures to the shape.

**Accommodations for 3's**
*Observe and Investigate*
**If...**children struggle describing shapes during the activity, **then...**prompt them by asking questions, such as: **Is it flat or round? Does it have three sides?** *¿Es redondo? ¿Tiene 3 lados?*

✓ **Learning Goals**

**Social and Emotional Development**
• Child demonstrates appropriate conflict-resolution strategies, requesting help when needed.

**Language and Communication**
• Child exhibits an understanding of instructional terms used in the classroom.

**Mathematics**
• Child recognizes, names, describes, matches, compares, sorts common two-dimensional shapes (such as circle, square, rectangle, triangle, rhombus).

### Vocabulary

| build | construir | compare | comparar |
|-------|-----------|---------|----------|
| pattern | patrón | picture | imagen |
| position | posición | same | igual |
| shape | figura | | |

## Differentiated Instruction

### 👋 Extra Support

**Math Time**

**If...**children have difficulty creating their own picture with pattern blocks, **then...**build one as a model for them to replicate.

### ⭐ Enrichment

**Math Time**

Challenge children to teach classmates how to make complicated patterns and pictures by displaying their design for a classmate to replicate. Encourage partners to help each other.

---

large group — 20 minutes

# Math Time

**Language and Communication Skills** Check children's understanding of math terms. Pause to correct any misunderstandings before moving on.

✓ **Can children create and name simple and complex shapes?**

**Snapshots (Shapes)** Give children colored Pattern Blocks. Secretly make a simple house with a square and triangle. Cover the house with a dark cloth.

- Tell children to look carefully and take a snapshot in their minds as you show your Pattern Block picture. Reveal your house for two seconds, and then cover it again. Challenge children to build what they saw.

- After a short while, reveal your house for two more seconds so children can check and change their picture if needed. Ask: **Does your picture use the same shapes as my picture? Are the shapes in the same position?** *¿Contienen sus imágenes las mismas figuras que contiene la mía? ¿Están las figuras en la misma posición?*

- Reveal your picture for the last time, leaving the cloth off. Have children compare their picture to yours. Ask: **How did you decide which shapes to use to make your picture the same as mine?** *¿Cómo decidieron qué figuras usar para que sus imágenes fueran iguales que las mías?*

- Repeat with other pictures, as complex as children's ability allows.

✓ **Can children use shapes to create pictures and designs?**

**Pattern Block Pictures** Have children create pictures and designs using paper Pattern Blocks copied onto different colored cardstock. Suggest they make pictures of objects seen in the sky and on the earth.

- Display *Math and Science Flip Chart* page 58. Discuss the two pictures and the locations and attributes of the shapes used to make them. Ask: **Which picture shows something you see in the sky? What is it next to? What are over the squares?** *¿Qué imagen muestra algo que pueden ver en el cielo? ¿Qué está cerca de esta imagen? ¿Qué hay sobre los cuadrados?*

- Distribute the design materials and observe children as they create pictures. Ask: **What object are you making? What shapes are you using? Which shapes are above?** *¿Qué objeto están haciendo? ¿Qué figuras están usando? ¿Qué figuras están arriba?*

💡 **TIP** Tell children to keep their finished design until you have time to take a photograph of it.

**ELL** Hold up each shape and name it. Give the shapes to children to hold and repeat the names after you. Build up to simple actions, narrating as you go. For example: **Hexagon. I flip the hexagon.**

*Math and Science Flip Chart, page 58*

# Center Time

▶ **Center Rotation** Center Time includes teacher-guided activities and independent activities. Refer to the **Learning Centers** on pages 100–101 for activities in additional centers.

  small group

## Construction Center

| **Center Tip** |
|---|

 **Observe and assist children as they assemble their mobiles.**

**Materials** cardstock, crayons, markers, scissors, hole-punch, yarn, plastic hangers or paper-towel rolls

**Day and Night Mobiles** Tell children that they are going to work with a partner to make mobiles of the day and night skies. Have each pair make one mobile for day and one for night.

- Have pairs draw and cut out pictures for each sky. Prompt them to include anything they can see in the sky (rainbows, sun, airplanes).

- Help children punch a hole in the top of each piece and use different lengths of yarn to attach the pieces to a hanger or tube frame.

- Hang the mobiles. Encourage children to ask about others' mobiles.

**Center Tip**

**If…**children have difficulty arranging and assembling the parts of their mobile, **then…**have them tape the yarn to the back of the paper instead of looping it through a hole.

## Purposeful Play

 **Observe children sharing classroom resources and working cooperatively.**

Children choose an open center for free playtime. Encourage children to use drawing or painting software to create ideas for a new story about Matthew and the other storybook characters.

## Let's Say Good-Bye

 large group 15 minutes

 **Read Aloud** Revisit "Counting My Blessings"/"Mis tesoros" from the *Teacher's Treasure Book,* page 95, for your afternoon Read Aloud. Remind children to listen for objects in the sky.

 **Home Connection** Refer to the Home Connection activities listed in the Materials and Resources chart on page 97. Remind children to tell their families about the shapes they described in Math Time. Sing the "Good-bye Song" as children prepare to leave.

### ✓ Learning Goals

**Social and Emotional Development**
• Child demonstrates appropriate conflict-resolution strategies, requesting help when needed.

**Language and Communication**
• Child names and describes actual or pictured people, places, things, actions, attributes, and events.

**Science**
• Child describes the effects of natural forces (such as wind, gravity).

**Fine Arts**
• Child shares opinions about artwork and artistic experiences.

**Physical Development**
• Child develops small-muscle strength and control.

**Technology Applications**
• Child uses computer software or technology to express original ideas.

### Writing

Recap the day. Have children name objects seen in the sky during the day and night. Ask: *Why does the sky change colors from day to night? ¿Por qué cambia de color el cielo entre el día y la noche?* Have children draw and label a picture of the sky.

**Focus Question**

**What can I learn about day and night?**

**¿Qué puedo aprender sobre el día y la noche?**

 **Learning Goals**

**Social and Emotional Development**
• Child demonstrates appropriate conflict-resolution strategies, requesting help when needed.

**Language and Communication**
• Child names and describes actual or pictured people, places, things, actions, attributes, and events.

**Fine Arts**
• Child participates in a variety of music activities (such as listening, singing, finger plays, musical games, performances).

### Vocabulary

| | | | |
|---|---|---|---|
| behind | atrás | dark | oscuro |
| shadow | sombra | sidewalk | acera |
| sunlight | luz del sol | | |

 **Differentiated Instruction**

 **Extra Support**

**Phonological Awareness**
**If...**children have difficulty separating the sounds of a word, **then...**have them pull apart two connected cubes as they say each sound of a two-phoneme word, such as /m/ /e/, /b/ /e/, /i/ /t/.

**Enrichment**

**Phonological Awareness**
Challenge children to segment the sounds of their own names.

**Special Needs**

**Cognitive Challenges**
**If...**children have difficulty separating the sounds of a word, **then...**have them separate two-phoneme nonsense words that start with the same consonant, such as ba, bey, bi, bo, bu.

# Let's Start the Day

 **Opening Routines and Transition Tips**
For **Opening Routines** and **Transition Tips** turn to pages 178–181 and visit DLMExpressOnline.com for more ideas.

 Read **"The Wind and the Sun"/**"El viento y el sol" from the Teacher's Treasure Book, page 185, for your morning Read Aloud.

## Language Time

large group — 15 minutes

**ÅÅÅ Social and Emotional Development** Ask children to tell you what the rules are about speaking politely, taking turns, and listening carefully so that they can solve problems together.

### Oral Language and Vocabulary

✓ **Can children use new and descriptive words to tell about shadows?**

**Shadow Talk** Invite children to share what they know about shadows. Ask: **Do you see shadows outside during the day or during the night? How can you make a shadow appear? Can you see a shadow in the dark?** ¿Ven las sombras durante el día o durante la noche? ¿Cómo pueden hacer que aparezca una sombra? ¿Se puede ver una sombra en la oscuridad?

● Display Oral Language Development Card 68. Ask children to describe what they see in the picture. Follow the suggestions on the back of the card.

*Oral Language Development Card 68*

### Phonological Awareness

✓ **Can children separate the individual phonemes of a word?**

**Segmenting Phonemes** Revisit Rhymes and Chants Flip Chart page 31, and sing "Making Shadows" with children. Then give children Farm Animal Counters. Tell them that you will say words from the song that they should break into sounds. They should move their animals once for each sound. Model by saying **Try** and moving an animal three times while saying /t/ /r/ /i/. Supply the words for the rest of the line "Try it now, try it now" as children segment the words and move their counters.

 Have children hop or jump for each sound of a word they repeat after you. Use simple words such as go, do, see, we, day.

*Rhymes and Chants Flip Chart, page 31/ page 63*

go
do
see
we
day

# Center Time

▶ **Center Rotation** Center Time includes teacher-guided activities and independent activities. Refer to the **Learning Centers** on pages 100–101 for activities in additional centers.

small group  60–90 minutes

## Writer's Center | Center Tip

✓ **Track children's ability to identify the separate sounds in a word.**

**Materials** drawing paper with writing lines, crayons, voice recorders

**Day and Night Book** Tell children they are going to help make and record a class book about daytime and nighttime activities.

- Display these sentences to read with children: *Good day, Sun! Good night, Moon!* Help children record themselves segmenting the words. Review the use of the voice recorder if necessary.

- Have children copy the first sentence at the top of their papers. Have them copy the second sentence on the back.

- Have children draw and label daytime activities on the front of their papers. Have them draw and label nighttime activities on the back. Bind the pages together to make a class book.

**Center Tip**

**If...**children have difficulty labeling their pictures, **then...**have them dictate descriptive words and sentences for you to write for them.

## Pretend and Learn Center | Center Tip

✓ **Track children's ability to identify and describe points of view.**

**The Shy Sun** Have children pretend that the sun has feelings, and that the sun is shy. Remind them that this is a make-believe game; the real sun does not have feelings.

- Review the word *shy*. Say the word for children to repeat. Discuss its meaning. Ask: **What might a shy sun do?** *¿Qué haría un sol tímido?* (hide; be afraid to shine) (esconderse; tener miedo de brillar) **What might happen to daytime if the sun is shy?** *¿Qué le pasaría al día si el sol fuera tímido?*

- Have children take turns playing the shy sun. Tell them to think of ways to help the sun feel better. Ask: **What happens when the sun hides or goes away? What can someone say or do to help the sun feel better?** *¿Cómo lo podrán resolver? ¿Qué podrá hacer o decir alguien para ayudar al sol sentirse mejor?*

- Have children act out their stories and solutions.

**Center Tip**

**If...**children have difficulty getting started with their play, **then...** encourage them to think of the story "The Sun and the Moon" and what happened when the sun went away.

## ✓ Learning Goals

**Language and Communication**
- Child names and describes actual or pictured people, places, things, actions, attributes, and events.

**Emergent Literacy: Writing**
- Child uses scribbles, shapes, pictures, symbols, and letters to represent language.

**Science**
- Child describes the effects of natural forces (such as wind, gravity).

**Fine Arts**
- Child expresses ideas, emotions, and moods through individual and collaborative dramatic play.

**Technology Applications**
- Child uses voice/sound players and recorders, and touch screens correctly.

## Differentiated Instruction

 **Extra Support**

**Pretend and Learn Center**
**If...**children have difficulty deciding what to draw for their story, **then...**help them plan their story. Fold a sheet of paper into fourths to organize what happens *first, next, then, last.* Provide story prompts such ask: **Where is the sun? What is her problem? Who helps her? How does the problem get solved?** *¿Dónde está el sol? ¿Cuál es su problema? ¿Quién lo ayuda? ¿Cómo se resuelve el problema?*

**Enrichment**

**Pretend and Learn Center**
Challenge children to write captions to go with their pictures, or have them make another picture book about the sun.

## Accommodations for 3's

**Writer's Center**
**If...**children have difficulty copying letters in the two sentences, **then...**give them a photocopy of the sentences with the letters written in dotted lines for them to trace. Have them glue those sentences to the front and back of their papers.

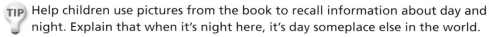

## ✔ Learning Goals

**Language and Communication**
• Child demonstrates an understanding of oral language by responding appropriately.

**Emergent Literacy: Reading**
• Child explores books and other texts to answer questions.
• Child names most upper- and lowercase letters of the alphabet.
• Child identifies the letter that stands for a given sound.

**Science**
• Child observes, identifies, compares, and discusses objects in the sky (such as clouds, sun, moon, stars).
• Child describes the effects of natural forces (such as wind, gravity).

### Vocabulary

| | | | |
|---|---|---|---|
| bright | brillante | earth | Tierra |
| moon | luna | night | noche |
| shining | radiante | sky | cielo |
| warm | cálido | | |

## Differentiated Instruction

 **Extra Support**

**Learn About Letters and Sounds**
**If...**children have difficulty saying or distinguishing between /w/ and /z/, **then...**model how you keep your teeth close to say the /z/ sound, and how you purse your lips to say the /w/ sound. You might also record children saying each sound and have them listen to themselves to help self-correct.

 **Enrichment**

**Learn About Letters and Sounds**
Challenge children to share additional questions for the guessing game. For an extra challenge, include another consonant in the game.

## Literacy Time

 large group — 15 minutes

### 📖 Read Aloud

✅ **Can children recall important story details about the earth and sky?**

**Build Background** Tell children you will be rereading a story about the earth and sky. They should listen carefully for information about day and night. Ask: **What do you already know about day and night?** *¿Qué saben sobre día y noche?*

**Listen for Understanding** Read aloud *Concept Big Book 4: The Earth and Sky*, pointing out details in the pictures as you read. Discuss the information on pages 13–14. Encourage children to ask you to reread or explain the meaning of certain text.

● Ask: **How does each new day begin? What happens when the sun isn't shining here?** *¿Cómo empieza cada día? ¿Qué pasa cuando el sol no brilla aquí?*

**Respond to the Book** Have children compare the book's facts about the sun and the moon with their own experiences of day and night. Ask: **Which object in the sky is both bright and warm? Which object in the sky is only bright?** *¿Qué objeto del cielo es brillante y cálido? ¿Qué objeto es sólo brillante?*

**TIP** Help children use pictures from the book to recall information about day and night. Explain that when it's night here, it's day someplace else in the world.

*The Earth and Sky*
*La Tierra y el cielo*

### Learn About Letters and Sounds

✅ **Can children distinguish between the /w/ and /z/ sounds of Ww and Zz?**

**Which Is It: Ww or Zz?** Review the sounds made by *Ww* and *Zz*, emphasizing that upper and lower case versions of each letter make the same sound. Give children Alphabet/Letter Tiles for *Ww* and *Zz* to play "Guess the Letter."

● Tell children to hold up the correct letter tile to answer questions that you ask them about *Ww* and *Zz*.

● Ask, for example: **Which letter makes the /w/ sound? Which letter makes the /z/ sound? Which letter comes first in the ABC song? Which letter opens upward? Which letter zigzags from side to side?** *¿Qué letra tiene el sonido /w/? ¿Qué letra tiene el sonido /z/? ¿Qué letra está primero en el alfabeto? ¿Qué letra está abierta arriba? ¿Qué letra zizaguea?*

**ELL** Prepare word cards for *we, wag, win, zig, zag, zoo*. Show each card one at a time, and read it for children to repeat. Help children use letter tiles *Ww* and *Zz* to find those letters in the words. Have children place the letter tile below the written letter. When they find a match, have them trace the letter and make the letter sound.

# Math Time

**Online Math Activity**

Children can complete Shape Parts 2 and Piece Puzzler 3 during computer time or Center Time.

## Observe and Investigate

 **Can children make shapes correctly?**

**Snapshots (Shape Parts)** This is a variation of the activity on Day 2. Cut straws into 2", 4", and 6" pieces to distribute to children. Use some pieces to make a shape secretly, such as a rectangle. Cover the shape with a dark cloth.

● Tell children to look carefully and take a snapshot in their minds as you show your hidden shape. Reveal the shape for two seconds, and then cover it again. Have children use their straws to build the shape they saw. Monitor their demonstrated small-muscle control as they grasp the straws.

● After a few minutes, reveal your shape for two more seconds so children can check and change their shape if needed. Ask: **Does your shape have the same number of sides and corners as mine? Is it the same size?** *¿Tienen sus formas el mismo número de lados y vértices que la mía? ¿Tienen el mismo tamaño?*

● Then reveal your shape for the last time, leaving the cloth off. Have children compare it to theirs. Ask: **What did you see that helped you decide what to do?** *¿Qué vieron que los ayudó a decidir qué hacer?*

**ELL** Review the meaning of *compare* with children. Focus on the aspect of looking at different objects closely in order to compare them.

# ✸✸✸ Social and Emotional Development

## Making Good Choices

 **Do children use different strategies to solve a problem?**

**Solving a Problem** Display *Making Good Choices Flip Chart* page 31. Ask: **What is one way the boy and girl can solve their problem? What is another way? What would you try first?** *¿De qué manera pueden el niño y la niña resolver su problema? ¿De qué otra manera pueden lograrlo? ¿Qué intentarían primero ustedes?*

● With the puppet, role play other problems to solve at school. For example, explain that someone cut in line ahead of the puppet. Have volunteers model what to say and do to help the puppet with the problem.

● After the role play, ask: **How did you help the puppet? When should the puppet ask for help?** *¿Cómo ayudaron al títere? ¿Cuándo debe el títere pedirle ayuda a la maestra?*

*Making Good Choices Flip Chart, page 31*

## Learning Goals

**Social and Emotional Development**
• Child demonstrates appropriate conflict-resolution strategies, requesting help when needed.

**Mathematics**
• Child creates two-dimensional shapes; recreates two-dimensional shapes from memory.

**Physical Development**
• Child develops small-muscle strength and control.

## Vocabulary

| | | | |
|---|---|---|---|
| corners | vértices | shape | figura |
| sides | lados | size | tamaño |
| snapshot | fotos | | |

## Differentiated Instruction

 **Extra Support**

*Observe and Investigate*

**If...**children have difficulty duplicating your shape, **then...**leave the cloth off for longer periods of time, and prompt them to look at specific attributes, such as: **Count the number of sides and corners you see in my shape.** *Cuenten el número de lados y vértices que ven en mi figura.*

**Enrichment**

*Observe and Investigate*

Have partners do the activity on their own, each taking turns hiding and revealing their shape for the other person to duplicate. Challenge them to use more complex shapes than rectangles.

## Accommodations for 3's

*Observe and Investigate*

**If...**children struggle to recall the hidden shape accurately, **then...**leave the shape uncovered for a longer time, use fewer straws, or have them work with a partner.

## Learning Goals

**Social and Emotional Development**
• Child demonstrates appropriate conflict-resolution strategies, requesting help when needed.

**Language and Communication**
• Child uses words to identify and understand categories.

**Mathematics**
• Child measures passage of time using standard or non-standard tools.

**Science**
• Child describes the effects of natural forces (such as wind, gravity).

**Social Studies**
• Child identifies common events and routines.

### Vocabulary

| | | | |
|---|---|---|---|
| after | después | afternoon | tarde |
| beginning | principio | morning | mañana |
| night | noche | noon | mediodía |

## Differentiated Instruction

### Extra Support

**Oral Language and Academic Vocabulary**
**If...**children have difficulty distinguishing between the labels *morning, afternoon*, and *night,* **then...**point out that *afternoon* is the label in the middle, and that time comes between morning and night.

### Enrichment

**Understand and Participate**
Have children label their pictures for the sequence chart. Help them write the words. You might also challenge children to make a sequence chart for the categories *yesterday, today, tomorrow.*

# Social Studies Time

large group  20 minutes

## Oral Language and Academic Vocabulary

✓ **Can children explain the difference between *morning, afternoon, and night*?**

**Time of Day** Explain to children that we use charts and calendars to help us plan ahead or remember what we have already done.

● Display a three-column chart, with the first column showing a sunrise and the title *Morning*, the second showing a full sun and the title *Afternoon*, and the third showing a moon and the title *Night*.

● Explain to children that *morning* is the beginning of the day; *afternoon* is after lunch, while the sun is still out; and *night* is when the sun goes down and the moon comes out.

● Ask: **What do you do in the morning? What do you do after lunch at school? What do you do just before you go to bed?** *¿Qué hacen por la mañana? ¿Qué hacen en la escuela después del almuerzo? ¿Qué hacen antes de dormir?*

## Understand and Participate

✓ **Can children organize their activities by time (morning, afternoon, night)?**

**Time Sequence Charts** Create and display cards labeled with pictures for *dinner* (dinner food), *bedtime* (bed), *shower,* (shower), *breakfast* (bowl of cereal), *recess* (playground), and *math time* (colored shapes). Read each word or phrase aloud, and have children repeat after you.

● Have children help sort the activities into the three categories. For example, read the word *dinner,* show the picture, and ask: **Do we eat dinner in the morning, afternoon, or at night?** *¿Cenamos a la mañana, a la tarde o a la noche?*

● Give children a three-column chart and sticker labels to make their own time sequence chart. Have them draw pictures showing what they do in the morning, afternoon, and night.

**ELL** Display fewer labeled picture cards for the activities being sorted. Read aloud the label as you point to the picture. Work with children to put the cards in the correct time-of-day categories.

# Center Time

▶ **Center Rotation** Center Time includes teacher-guided activities and independent activities. Refer to the **Learning Centers** on pages 100–101 for activities in additional centers.

 small group 30 minutes

## Math and Science Center

☑ **Monitor children as they explore and trace shadow shapes.**

**Materials** Shape Sets, butcher paper, white tape, lamp, crayons, glue

**Shadow Shapes** Cover a wall with butcher paper. Use tape to mark the floor at two distances from the wall. Shine a lamp from behind the farther distance to project shadows. Children will work with a partner to make and compare shadow shapes.

● One child holds a shape in the light while standing on the line close to the wall. The partner traces the shadow projected on the paper. Then the first child steps to the second line and holds the shape directly in front of the first drawing, so the new shadow covers the old. The partner then traces the new shadow.

● Have children write their names by their shapes as partners switch roles. Ask: *How are the shapes the same? How are they different? ¿En qué se parecen las figuras? ¿En qué se diferencian?*

### Center Tip

**If...**children have difficulty drawing around the shadow shape, **then...**suggest they draw dots in the corners of the shadow and then later connect the dots to show the shape.

## Purposeful Play

☑ **Observe children as they work in pairs or small groups.**

Children choose an open center for free playtime. Encourage teamwork by suggesting that they work together to create a shadow puppet show.

## Let's Say Good-Bye

 large group 15 minutes

 **Read Aloud** Revisit "The Wind and the Sun"/"El viento y el sol" for your afternoon Read Aloud. Ask children to listen and tell you if the story happens in the day or at night.

 **Home Connection** Refer to the Home Connection activities listed on page 97. Remind children to talk to families about morning, afternoon, and night. Sing the "Good-bye Song" as children prepare to leave.

### ☑ Learning Goals

**Language and Communication**
• Child uses newly learned vocabulary daily in multiple contexts.
• Child uses words to identify and understand categories.

**Mathematics**
• Child creates two-dimensional shapes; recreates two-dimensional shapes from memory.
• Child measures passage of time using standard or non-standard tools.

**Science**
• Child investigates and describes energy sources (light, heat, electricity).

**Social Studies**
• Child identifies common events and routines.

###  Writing

Recap the day. Have children tell the difference between *morning, afternoon,* and *night,* and tell where the sun is during those times of the day. Ask: *What usually happens at school in the morning? What usually happens at school in the afternoon? ¿Qué suele pasar en la escuela por la mañana? ¿Qué suele pasar en la escuela por la tarde?* Record their answers on chart paper. Have children help write letters and words.

# DAY 4

# Let's Start the Day

**Focus Question**

**What can I learn about day and night?**

**¿Qué puedo aprender sobre el día y la noche?**

---

## ▶ Opening Routines and Transition Tips

For **Opening Routines** and **Transition Tips** turn to pages 178–181 and visit **DLMExpressOnline.com** for more ideas.

 Read **"Sing Me a Rainbow"/**"Cántame un arco iris" from the *Teacher's Treasure Book,* page 165, for your morning Read Aloud.

## Language Time

 large group · 15 minutes

 **Social and Emotional Development** Encourage children to work through problems with peers on their own. Ask children what it means to be good team members who are helpful to each other.

### Oral Language and Vocabulary

 **Can children distinguish real from make-believe?**

**Real or Make-Believe?** Remind children that some stories are make-believe. A make-believe story tells about things that do not happen in real life. Tell children to listen to you tell them about some animals. If they think what you tell them can really happen, they should show you a thumbs-up.

- Say: ***The bird sings a song. The bird eats a worm. The worm eats a bird. The dog takes the bone. The dog takes the smell.*** *El pájaro canta una canción. El pájaro se come un gusano. El gusano se come un pájaro. El perro huele un hueso. El perro toma el olor. El perro toma el hueso.*

- Show children the *Sequence Card* sets "The Little Red Hen" and "Making Bee Bim Bop." Ask: ***Which of these shows something that can happen in real life?*** *¿Qué tarjetas muestran algo que podría suceder en la vida real?*

- Have children take turns telling sentences about things that can or cannot happen. Have the rest of the children respond by saying *real* or *make-believe.*

### Phonological Awareness

 **Can children blend two phonemes with pictorial support?**

**Review Blending Phonemes** Use the Dog Puppets to play "Which is Mine?" Display three objects or photo cards that have a two-phoneme name, such as *key, bee, toe.* Provide clues to help children identify which object belongs to each dog. For example, one puppet says: ***The first sound is /b/. Which one is mine?*** *El primer sonido es /b/. ¿Qué es?* (Child blends "bee.") Then the other puppet says: ***The last sound is /e/. Which one is mine?*** *El último sonido es /e/. ¿Qué es?* (Child blends "key.")

**ELL** Display a picture card of a two-phoneme word, such as *bee.* As you say each phoneme, put a Vehicle Counter below the picture, in a row from left to right. Then give a child the Vehicle Counters to repeat the process.

---

# Center Time

▶ **Center Rotation** Center Time includes teacher-guided activities and independent activities. Refer to the **Learning Centers** on pages 100–101 for activities in additional centers.

 small group | 60–90 minutes

## Library and Listening Center

### Center Tip

**If...**children think only photographs show real things, **then...**have them draw something they know is real and something they know is make-believe. Explain that drawings can show real things just like photos can.

✓ Track children's ability to distinguish real from make-believe.

**Materials** fiction and nonfiction books about day and night

**Real and Make-Believe in Books** Have children browse through fiction and nonfiction books about day and night to distinguish real pictured items from pictures of make-believe things.

- Explain to children that some books show and tell things that do not happen in real life. Say: *Look carefully at the pictures. Which pictures show something that you see in real life? Which pictures do not? Miren atentamente las fotos. ¿Qué fotos muestran algo que ven en la vida real? ¿Cuáles no?*

- Encourage children to use the terms *real* and *make-believe* in their responses.

## ABC Center

### Center Tip

**If...**children have difficulty remembering the sound of *Zz*, **then...**have them think of the ending sound of a buzzing bee...*buzzzz.*

✓ Track children's ability to recognize and show letters in the correct orientation.

**Materials** Alphabet/Letter Tile *Zz*, zebra picture card, white *Zz* block-letter cutouts, black crayons, wide masking tape, toy cars

**Zigzag Zz** Review with children the shape and letter sound for *Zz*. Have children use the card to trace the zigzag shape with a finger.

- Display the picture card. Point out that *zebra* begins with *Zz*, /z/. Give children a *Zz* cutout to color black and white like a zebra.

- Display the words *zigzag, zip, zoom.* Point out that all the words begin with *Zz*. Read aloud each word, and have children repeat after you.

- Have children use masking tape to make a large *Z* on the floor. Have them move a toy car along the *Z* path from top to bottom. Tell them to zip and zoom down the zigzag.

---

 **Learning Goals**

**Language and Communication**
- Child uses newly learned vocabulary daily in multiple contexts.

**Emergent Literacy: Reading**
- Child names most upper- and lowercase letters of the alphabet.
- Child identifies the letter that stands for a given sound.
- Child produces the most common sound for a given letter.

---

### Differentiated Instruction

 **Extra Support**

**ABC Center**

**If...**children have difficulty forming the letter *Zz* on the floor, **then...**give them three yardsticks to use as guide lines (top, middle, bottom). Check that they align the yardsticks correctly for the *Zz*.

⭐ **Enrichment**

**Library and Listening Center**

Challenge children to use self-stick notes to label the pictures with *R* or *M* for *Real* and *Make-Believe*. Have them compare pictures of the sun and sky shown in nonfiction books and tell how they are alike and different.

**Accommodations for 3's**

**ABC Center**

**If...**children have difficulty with the orientation of letter *Zz*, **then...**draw the letter to make it look like a zebra's head (top snout, middle neck, bottom connected to the body) and display it in the center.

**Focus Question**
## What can I learn about day and night?
## ¿Qué puedo aprender sobre el día y la noche?

 **Learning Goals**

**Social and Emotional Development**
• Child demonstrates appropriate conflict-resolution strategies, requesting help when needed.

**Language and Communication**
• Child demonstrates an understanding of oral language by responding appropriately.

**Emergent Literacy: Reading**
• Child names most upper- and lowercase letters of the alphabet.
• Child identifies the letter that stands for a given sound.

**Technology Applications**
• Child uses voice/sound players and recorders, and touch screens correctly.

### Vocabulary

| hungry | hambriento | hurt | lastimar |
|--------|------------|------|----------|
| shadow | sombra | smell | oler |
| soup | sopa | steal | robar |
| stick | palo | | |

**Differentiated Instruction**

 **Extra Support**
**Learn About Letters and Sounds**
**If...**children have difficulty finding *Ww* or *Zz* in the written words, **then...**give them a Letter Tile to compare with the written letters.

 **Enrichment**
**Learn About Letters and Sounds**
Challenge children to draw and label pictures to go with the sentences about Wally and Zeta.

## Literacy Time

📖 **Read Aloud**

✔ **Can children answer questions about information read aloud?**

**Build Background** Tell children that you will be reading a story about a hungry woman and her shadow.

● Ask: ***Does it hurt a shadow when you step on it? Why or why not?*** *¿Lastima la sombra cuando la pisan? ¿Por qué o por qué no?*

**Listen for Enjoyment** Read "The Stolen Soup Smell" from the *Teacher's Treasure Book,* page 331. Use the flannel board patterns.

● Tell children to listen carefully to what happens to the shadow. Ask: ***Why is the rich woman upset? What does she do to the shadow? Why?*** *¿Por qué se molesta la mujer rica? ¿Qué le hace a la sombra? ¿Por qué?*

**Respond to the Story** Have children explain why the rich woman was upset and how the wise man helped solve the problem. Ask: ***Why was it silly for the woman to hit the shadow with a stick? What did the rich woman learn?*** *¿Por qué fue ridículo que la mujer le pegara a la sombra con un palo? ¿Qué aprendió la mujer?*

**TIP** Use voice inflection to emphasize the different moods of the characters—the timid hungry woman, the angry selfish woman, and the calm wise man.

## Learn About Letters and Sounds

✔ **Can children distinguish letters *Ww* and *Zz* from other written letters?**

**Animals for *Ww* and *Zz*** Display *ABC Big Book* page 49, showing a worm for *Ww;* and *Alphabet Wall Card Zz,* showing a zebra. Review the /w/ and /z/ sounds.

● Display the following sentences on chart paper or an interactive whiteboard:

> *Wally Worm is on the wall. Wally likes to wiggle and wave.*
>
> *Zeta Zebra is in the zoo. Zeta likes to zip, zigzag, and zoom!*

● Read aloud the first two sentences. Say: ***Let's draw a line under each word that has a W.*** *Dibujemos una línea debajo de cada palabra que tenga una W.* Model with the first word, *Wally.* Invite children to find and underline the words using the pen or touch screen.

● Read each underlined word aloud to children. Have children take turns coming up to trace a *Ww* with their fingers. Use the next pair of sentences to repeat the process for *Zz.*

**ELL** If children have difficulty knowing where words start and stop on the chart paper or board, allow them to come up to trace a *W* or *Z* with their finger after you model the action.

*Teacher's Treasure Book, page 331*

*ABC Big Book, page 49*
*Superlibro abecé*

 large group · 15 minutes

# Math Time

**Online Math Activity**

Children can complete Shape Parts 2 and Piece Puzzler 3 during computer time or Center Time.

## Observe and Investigate

 **Can children slide, turn, and flip shapes to make them fit?**

**Slide, Turn, Flip** Photocopy pairs of congruent Pattern Blocks in either the same or different orientations. Give children only one of the Pattern Blocks to go with each photocopied set.

- Tell children to fit their block exactly on top of the first picture shape. Then say: *Without lifting your block, how can you move your block to fit exactly on top of the second shape?* *Sin levantar sus bloques, ¿cómo pueden moverlos para que encajen justo encima de la segunda figura?* Model how to slide and/or turn the block to fit exactly on top of the second picture.

- Then have children exchange their shape for a congruent one with a dot sticker on it. Model how to flip the block before turning and sliding it into place to match the second picture.

- Have children repeat several times using different sets of photocopied shapes. Ask: *What three ways can you move your block to match the second shape exactly?* (slide, turn, flip) *Does the shape change?* *¿De qué tres formas pueden mover sus bloques para que encajen justo con el segundo dibujo?* (deslizar, girar, voltear) *¿Cambia la figura?*

# ⁂ Social and Emotional Development

## Making Good Choices

 **Do children use different strategies to solve problems?**

**Solving a Problem** Display the Dog Puppets and a set of Pattern Blocks. Tell children that the puppets are disagreeing about who gets to use the blocks. Ask what children know about solving disagreements.

- Ask children why sharing might be a good way to solve this problem. Ask what could happen if the puppets decided to take turns.

- Finally, call on volunteers to model how the puppets could resolve their problem fairly as the group discussed.

 Use voice inflections to help convey meaning. During the discussion, restate native-speaking children's complex sentences simply for the benefit of English language learners, such as: *We do not shout. We are fair.*

---

✓ **Learning Goals**

**Social and Emotional Development**
- Child demonstrates appropriate conflict-resolution strategies, requesting help when needed.

**Mathematics**
- Child manipulates (flips, rotates) and combines shapes.

**Vocabulary**

| | | | |
|---|---|---|---|
| exactly | justo | flip | voltear |
| move | mover | shape | figura |
| slide | deslizar | turn | girar |

## Differentiated Instruction

✋ **Extra Support**

*Observe and Investigate*

**If**...children have difficulty seeing how to move their block to match the second picture, **then...** put a dot stick on the two photocopied shapes as well as the pattern block. Ask: *How do you move your block so that the dots are in the same place?* *¿Cómo mueven sus bloques para que los puntos estén en el mismo lugar?*

⭐ **Enrichment**

*Observe and Investigate*

Give children a series of four photocopied pictures of the same shape. Challenge them to figure out whether to slide, turn, and/or flip their blocks to get from one shape to the next. Or show them a pattern of turns and flips to duplicate.

♥ **Special Needs**

*Cognitive Challenges*

**If**...children have difficulty seeing how to move their block onto the photocopied shape, **then...** show them a row of four identical shapes in different orientations, and have them stack a duplicate set of blocks on top of it. Show children how to turn or flip their shape to fit exactly on top.

Focus Question
**What can I learn about day and night?**
*¿Qué puedo aprender sobre el día y la noche?*

## Learning Goals

**Language and Communication**
• Child follows two- and three-step oral directions.
• Child demonstrates some understanding of English spoken by teachers and peers. (ELL)

**Mathematics**
• Child creates two-dimensional shapes; recreates two-dimensional shapes from memory.

**Physical Development**
• Child develops small-muscle strength and control.

### Vocabulary

| corner | vértice | length | largo |
|---|---|---|---|
| position | posición | same | mismo |
| shape | figura | side | lado |
| size | tamaño | | |

## Differentiated Instruction

 **Extra Support**
**Math Time**
**If...**children have difficulty positioning the straws to form shapes, **then...**have children place their straw pieces along the sides of paper shapes to create their design.

 **Enrichment**
**Math Time**
Challenge children to make each other's picture by following oral directions. Have partners sit back to back, one child giving the directions for the other child to follow. If needed, model how to give step-by-step directions to build shapes.

 **Special Needs**
**Vision Loss**
Allow children to take a snapshot with their hands by feeling the straw shapes gently.

# Math Time

large group    20 minutes

**Language and Communication Skills** After you model building shapes from straw pieces, provide 2-step directions for children to follow. For example: ***Find three straw pieces that are the same size. Now put them together to make a triangle.*** *Encuentren tres popotes que tengan el mismo tamaño. Ahora, júntenlos para formar un triángulo* Then ask children to help create steps with you that they can follow, by asking: ***What can we do next?*** *¿Qué haremos ahora?*

✓ **Can children make simple and complex shapes correctly?**

**Snapshots (Shape Parts)** This lesson is a variation of the activity on Day 3. Cut straws into 2", 4", and 6" pieces to distribute to children. Use some pieces secretly to make a two-part shape, such as a triangle on top of a square to show a house. Cover the shape with a dark cloth.

● Tell children to look carefully and take a snapshot in their minds as you show them your hidden shape briefly. Reveal the shape for two seconds, and then cover it again. Have children use their straws to build the same two-part shape. Monitor their demonstrated small-muscle control as they grasp the straws.

● After a few minutes, reveal your shape for two more seconds so children can check and change their shape if needed. Ask: ***Does your shape have the same parts as mine? Is it the same size? Are the parts in the same positions?*** *¿Sus figuras tienen las mismas partes que la mía? ¿Son del mismo tamaño? ¿Están las partes en las mismas posiciones?*

● Then reveal your shape for the last time, leaving the cloth off. Have children compare it to theirs. Ask: ***How did you decide which straws you needed to make the shape? How many sides and corners do you see?*** *¿Cómo decidieron qué popotes usar para hacer la figura? ¿Cuántos costados y vértices ven?*

● Repeat with more complex shapes as children's ability allows.

**TIP** Refer to *Math and Science Flip Chart* page 58, "Pattern Block Pictures." Show children that their straw pieces can be used as the sides of the shapes, forming an outline.

**ELL** Focus on the words *side, length,* and *corner.* Give children a paper shape and straw pieces that match the lengths of the sides. Have children glue the straw pieces along each side to form the shape. Help children decide which straw to use for each side. Say: ***This straw is the same length as this side.*** Monitor the understanding children show of your language as you review the words and concepts.

**Pattern Block Pictures**
*Imágenes de bloques con patrones*

*Math and Science Flip Chart, page 58*

# Center Time

>  **Center Rotation** Center Time includes teacher-guided activities and independent activities. Refer to the **Learning Centers** on pages 100–101 for activities in additional centers.

  small group 30 minutes

## Construction Center

✓ **Observe as children build a puppet theater to retell the folktale.**

**Materials** flannel board patterns (*Teacher's Treasure Book* page 436), cardstock, crayons, scissors, craft sticks, tape, tablecloth

**Puppet Theater** Have children make stick puppets to retell "The Stolen Soup Smell." Have them put the tablecloth on the table and sit behind it as their curtain.

- Have children work in small groups. Give them story patterns to color, cut out, and tape onto craft sticks to make stick puppets.

- Have children practice using their puppets. Help them decide their story sequence. Ask: *What happens first in the story? Next? Last?* *¿Qué sucede primero en el cuento? ¿Qué sucede después? ¿Y por último?*

- Invite children to present their puppet show.

### Center Tip

**If...**children have difficulty cutting out the story patterns, **then...**give them pre-cut figures to color and tape onto the sticks.

### Learning Goals

**Social and Emotional Development**
- Child demonstrates appropriate conflict-resolution strategies, requesting help when needed.

**Language and Communication**
- Child uses newly learned vocabulary daily in multiple contexts.
- Child uses words to identify and understand categories.

**Fine Arts**
- Child expresses ideas, emotions, and moods through individual and collaborative dramatic play.

### Writing

Recap the day. Have children tell what is true and not true about shadows. Ask: *What did you hear about shadows in the folktale?* *¿Qué aprendieron sobre las sombras en el cuento?* Record their answers in a Real/Make-Believe chart. Read them back as you track the print, and emphasize the correspondence between speech and print.

## Purposeful Play

✓ **Observe children appropriately handling classroom materials and supplies.**

Children choose an open center for free playtime. Encourage cooperation skills by suggesting that they dramatize their own make-believe story using dress-up clothes.

## Let's Say Good-Bye

 large group 15 minutes

 **Read Aloud** Revisit "Sing Me a Rainbow"/"Cántame un arco iris" from the *Teacher's Treasure Book,* page 165, for your afternoon Read Aloud. Remind children to listen for words about things in the sky.

 **Home Connection** Refer to the Home Connections activities listed in the Materials and Resources chart on page 97. Remind children to tell families about what good choices they learned for solving problems. Sing the "Good-bye Song" as children prepare to leave.

# DAY 5

**Focus Question**

**What can I learn about day and night?**

*¿Qué puedo aprender sobre el día y la noche?*

## ✓ Learning Goals

**Social and Emotional Development**
• Child demonstrates appropriate conflict-resolution strategies, requesting help when needed.

**Language and Communication**
• Child communicates relevant information for the situation (for example, introduces herself; requests assistance).

• Child names and describes actual or pictured people, places, things, actions, attributes, and events.

### Vocabulary

| | | | |
|---|---|---|---|
| dark | oscuro | light | claro |
| night | noche | sky | cielo |
| shadow | sombra | | |

## Differentiated Instruction

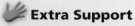

**Extra Support**

**Oral Language and Vocabulary**
**If...**children have difficulty describing day, **then...**have them look out the window.

⭐ **Enrichment**

**Oral Language and Vocabulary**
Challenge children to make shadow puppets using a desk lamp projected on the wall. Have them explain how shadows are made.

💜 **Special Needs**

**Speech/Language Delays**
If children cannot pronounce words correctly: say the word correctly, allow the child to practice it after you, and give the child additional time during the day to practice the word with you. Praise every time a child comes closer to the correct pronunciation of a word.

# Let's Start the Day

▶ **Opening Routines and Transition Tips**
For **Opening Routines** and **Transition Tips** turn to pages 178–181 and visit DLMExpressOnline.com for more ideas.

 Read **"The Sun and the Moon"**/*"El Sol y la Luna"* from the *Teacher's Treasure Book*, page 241, for your morning Read Aloud.

## Language Time

large group    15 minutes

👪 **Social and Emotional Development** Ask children what they know to do when they have a disagreement or a problem. Have them tell you what ideas they might use for solving problems, including when they should get an adult's help.

### Oral Language and Vocabulary

✓ **Can children provide appropriate information about day and night?**

**Day and Night** Talk about what children have learned this week about day and night. Ask: **What happens to the sky when day turns into night? Why is it dark at night?** *¿Qué le pasa al cielo cuando el día se convierte en noche? ¿Por qué está oscuro durante la noche?*

● Display *Rhymes and Chants Flip Chart* page 31. Sing "Making Shadows" again with children. Point to the children in the picture. Ask: **How are these children making shadows in their room? How can they make the shadow move?** *¿Cómo hacen estos niños sombras en su habitación? ¿Cómo hacen que la sombra se mueva?*

● Then ask: **What causes shadows?** *¿Por qué aparecen las sombras?*

### Phonological Awareness

✓ **Can children separate the individual phonemes of a word?**

**Segmenting Phonemes** As you revisit *Rhymes and Chants Flip Chart* page 31, stop at the word *now* at the end of the second sentence. Have children repeat each sound of the word: **now, /n/ -ow.** Ask: **Which word rhymes with** now? *¿Qué palabra rima con now?* Have children say the answer and segment the sounds: **how, /h/ -ow.**

**ELL** Create and display picture cards for *pie, key, bee.* Have children repeat after you as you say the sounds of each word: **pie, /p/ /i/; key, /k/ /e/.** Ask: **Which one do you like to eat?** Have children say the answer, segment the sounds, and mime eating. Repeat for *key* **(Which do you use to lock a door?)** and *bee* **(Which goes bzzz?)**.

*Rhymes and Chants Flip Chart, page 31/page 63*

# Center Time

▶ **Center Rotation** Center Time includes teacher-guided activities and independent activities. Refer to the **Learning Centers** on pages 100–101 for activities in additional centers.

 small group 60–90 minutes

## ABC Center

**Center Tip**

✓ **Track children's abilities to distinguish between Ww and Zz and to identify the traded letter.**

**Materials** Alphabet/Letter Tiles *a, b, e, g, i, n, p, t, w, z*

**Letter Trade** Review with children the shape and sound of letters *Ww* and *Zz*. Tell them they will be putting together letters to form new words that begin with *Ww* or *Zz*.

- Display this word train: *web–wet–wit–wig–win*. Say the first word, sounding out the phonemes for children to repeat. Ask: **What three letters are in the first word?** *¿Cuáles son las tres letras de la primera palabra?* (*w, e, b*)

- Then ask: **Which one letter do I trade to make the next word?** (trade *b* to *t* to make *wet*) *¿Qué letra debo cambiar para formar la siguiente palabra? (cambiar b por t para formar wet)*

- Do the next pair of words, *wet–wit*. Have children finish the rest of the train on their own. Repeat the process for *zip–zig–zag–zap*.

**Center Tip**

If...children have difficulty identifying which letter to trade, **then...**show children only two words at a time, and underline the letter to trade.

## Writer's Center

✓ **Track children's ability to write compound words correctly.**

**Materials** sentence-strip puzzle pieces, resealable bags, paper

**Compound Word Puzzles** Explain to children that some words are formed by putting two smaller words together, just like puzzle pieces.

- In advance, make two each of two-part puzzle pieces, with *day, night,* being identical front-end pieces, and *time, light,* being identical back-end pieces. Store each set in a resealable bag.

- Distribute the puzzle pieces. Show children how to put together *day* and *time* to form *daytime*. Say and write: **day + time = daytime.**

- Repeat for *nighttime*. Have children complete the other word puzzles and copy them on paper.

**Center Tip**

If...children have difficulty copying the compound words, **then...**have them glue the puzzle pieces onto paper and trace the words.

---

## Differentiated Instruction

 **Extra Support**
**Writer's Center**
**If...**children have difficulty recognizing compound words, **then...**have them use different colors to box each word within a word.

 **Enrichment**
**Writer's Center**
Challenge children to write additional compound words. Have them use index cards to make their own, or have them use self-stick notes.

**Accommodations for 3's**
**Writer's Center**
**If...**children have difficulty writing, **then...**have them do only the first set of compound words. Have them tape the matching pairs together on the back, and use a crayon to trace over the compound word on the front.

**Focus Question**

## What can I learn about day and night?
## ¿Qué puedo aprender sobre el día y la noche?

# Circle Time

## Literacy Time

large group · 15 minutes

### 📖 Read Aloud

 **Can children distinguish between real and make-believe?**

**Build Background** Tell children you will be rereading *Matthew and the Color of the Sky*. Ask them what about the story is real and what is make-believe.

- Ask: ***What happens to the color of the sky throughout the day?*** *¿Qué le pasa al color del cielo a medida que avanza el día?*

**Listen for Understanding** Reread the story to children. Stop after each spread and have children summarize what is happening. Refer to details in the text.

- Ask: ***What is Matthew trying to do? Why is it difficult? What causes the color of the sky to change? How does Matthew remember the different colors of the sky?*** *¿Qué está tratando de hacer Matías? ¿Qué hace que el color del cielo cambie? ¿Cómo recuerda Matías los diferentes colores del cielo?*

**Respond and Connect** Have children connect their new learning to their daily lives. Instruct them to look out the window at the sky. Ask: ***What color is the sky right now? What color will the sky be when you go to bed tonight?*** *¿De qué color es el cielo en este momento? ¿De qué color será el cielo cuando se vayan a dormir esta noche?*

**TIP** Help children relate information from the story to their lives. Point out that the story is make-believe but still includes true information about the sky changing colors due to weather, position of the sun, and time.

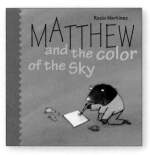

*Matthew and the Color of the Sky*
*Matías y el color del cielo*

### Learn About Letters and Sounds

 **Can children distinguish between *Ww* and *Zz*?**

**Wiggle and Buzz with *Ww* and *Zz*** Tell children that bees wiggle and buzz when they communicate. Say that *wiggle* starts with the /w/ sound, made by *Ww*. The word *buzz* ends with the /z/ sound, made by *Zz*. Say: ***Let's /w/, /w/, wiggle and buzz, /z/, /z/, to tell about W and Z!***

- Display 8 to 12 short words beginning with *Ww* or *Zz*. As you point to each word, tell children to wiggle or buzz to indicate whether the word begins with *Ww* or *Zz*. Confirm the correct answer by saying the word. After you finish the list, go back to each word that begins with *Ww* or *Zz*, and have children read the word with you.

- Repeat the process, this time with words ending with *Zz*.

**ELL** Prepare picture cards for *web, wall, worm, wagon, shadow, zebra, zipper, zoo*. Prepare corresponding word cards that have a line instead of the *Ww* or *Zz*. Show and read the cards one at a time. Help children decide which tile completes each word.

*ABC Picture Cards*
*Tarjetas abecé de imágenes*

## Online Math Activity

Children can complete Shape Parts 2 and Piece Puzzler 3 during computer time or Center Time.

How Do I Solve a Problem? ¿Cómo resuelvo este problema?

*Making Good Choices Flip Chart, page 31*

# Math Time

## Observe and Investigate

✓ **Can children identify common shapes?**

**Pattern Block Puzzles** Provide sets of Pattern Blocks and copies of Pattern Block Puzzles (*Teacher's Treasure Book,* pages 512–517).

● Demonstrate how to fit Pattern Blocks onto a Pattern Block Puzzle. Point to one of the puzzle shapes and ask: *How do I know which Pattern Block to choose for this shape?* *¿Cómo puedo saber qué bloque usar para formar esta figura?* Model how to count the sides and corners to find the congruent shape. Then ask: *How do I move this block to fit inside that shape? Do I turn it, flip it, or slide it?* *¿Cómo muevo este bloque para que encaje dentro de la figura? ¿Lo debo girar, voltear o deslizar?*

● Have children choose a puzzle to complete. As you observe them fitting the shapes into the puzzle, ask: *Are you sliding, turning, or flipping that shape to fit it into the puzzle?* *¿Estás deslizando, girando o volteando esta pieza para encajarla en el rompecabezas?*

**ELL** Use hand motions to help convey the meaning of directional words *slide, flip, turn.* Say *slide* as you slide your hand across the desk. Say *flip* as you flip your hand over. Say *turn* as you use your hand to show a turning motion.

# ✖✖✖ Social and Emotional Development

## Making Good Choices

✓ **Do children use different strategies to solve problems?**

**Solving a Problem** Display *Making Good Choices Flip Chart* page 31. Ask: *What did we learn about how to solve problems?* *¿Qué aprendimos acerca de cómo resolver problemas?*

● Show a stack of graham crackers equal to half the number of children in the group. Ask: *How do we share this fairly?* *¿Cómo podemos dividir esto de manera justa?*

● Ask a volunteer to count the crackers and the children. Then assign pairs to discuss what the problem is and how to solve it. Call on pairs to propose solutions. After every proposed solution ask: *Would that be fair? Why?* *¿Esto sería justo? ¿Por qué?*

● End by breaking the crackers in half to give to the children equally.

✓ **Learning Goals**

**Social and Emotional Development**
• Child demonstrates appropriate conflict-resolution strategies, requesting help when needed.

**Mathematics**
• Child divides sets from 2 to 10 objects into equal sets, using informal techniques.

• Child creates two-dimensional shapes; recreates two-dimensional shapes from memory.

• Child manipulates (flips, rotates) and combines shapes.

## Vocabulary

| fit | encajar | flip | voltear |
|---|---|---|---|
| inside | adentro | move | mover |
| shape | figura | slide | deslizar |
| turn | girar | | |

**Differentiated Instruction**

### ✋ Extra Support
**Observe and Investigate**
**If...**children have difficulty choosing which Pattern Blocks to use for the puzzle, **then...**give them the exact set of shapes to use. Tell them to do the biggest shapes first. Model how to flip, turn, or slide the shape into the correct spot.

### ⭐ Enrichment
**Observe and Investigate**
Challenge children to make their own unique puzzle by tracing Pattern Blocks onto paper. Have partners trade puzzles and complete them.

### Accommodations for 3's
**Observe and Investigate**
**If...**children have difficulty completing the Pattern Block puzzles, **then...**have them put together Pattern Blocks to make their own pictures. Observe them as they put their pictures together, and point out when they turn, slide, or flip a shape into position.

Focus Question
## What can I learn about day and night?
## ¿Qué puedo aprender sobre el día y la noche?

## Learning Goals

**Social and Emotional Development**
• Child demonstrates appropriate conflict-resolution strategies, requesting help when needed.

**Language and Communication**
• Child uses oral language for a variety of purposes.
• Child understands and uses sentences of increasing length and complexity.

**Emergent Literacy: Reading**
• Child enjoys and chooses reading-related activities.
• Child asks and answers questions about books read aloud (such as "Who?" "What?" "Where?").

**Science**
• Child describes the effects of natural forces (such as wind, gravity).
• Child follows basic health and safety rules.

**Fine Arts**
• Child expresses ideas, emotions, and moods through individual and collaborative dramatic play.

### Vocabulary

| change | cambiar | color | color |
|---|---|---|---|
| daytime | día | different | diferente |
| morning | mañana | nighttime | noche |

## Differentiated Instruction

### Extra Support
**Explore and Express**
**If...**children have difficulty remembering details about the story, **then...**display the *Big Book* for children to refer to for the play.

### Enrichment
**Explore and Express**
Have children add details to the different daytime and nighttime skies for the play, such as the sun, rain clouds, rainbow, moon, stars.

# Dramatic Play Time

large group    20 minutes

**Personal Safety Skills** Model how to use play props safely, such as not running with yardsticks. Remind children to be careful and respectful of the others around them.

## Oral Language and Academic Vocabulary

☑ **Can children describe the characters and the scenery of a story?**

**Recalling Story Details** Have children recall details about this week's *Big Book*. Have them focus on the changing colors of the sky and the related colors of the animals. Prompt them to speak in complete, complex sentences.

● Ask: *Why is Matthew upset? How does Penny help him remember the different colors of the sky? How does the sky change from day to night? ¿Por qué está triste Matías? ¿Cómo lo ayuda Penélope a recordar los diferentes colores del cielo? ¿Cómo cambia el cielo del día a la noche?*

● Have children name the color to complete each of these complex sentences:

Juan's skin and the sky at sunrise are both _____ (pink).
The baby birds' feathers and the midday sky are both _____ (blue).
Tina's hair and the rainy sky are both _____ (gray and white).
Matthew's hair and the night sky are both _____ (black).

## Explore and Express

☑ **Can children dramatize the story of *Matthew and the Color of the Sky*?**

**Dramatizing the *Big Book* Story** Tell children that they will put on a play for *Matthew and the Color of the Sky*.

● Tie yarn through two holes punched at the top of colored paper to make yarn necklaces matching the colors of the characters. Have children work together to draw a picture of each character onto the correct colored sheet.

● For each sky background, make a color flag by taping a yardstick to the ends of a long strip of colored paper. Have two children hold the flag during that part of the play. You might also have children add details to each of the skies.

● Have children form groups and practice acting out the story while you guide and monitor their progress. Have groups take turns using the props to act out their play. Remind the audience to be good listeners.

**TIP** Have children take turns playing different roles. Monitor the use and storage of the props.

**ELL** Point to the colors used in props, and ask children to name them. Let them use their home languages. Repeat the colors in English. Hand them crayons in the shades as you say: *This is (color). This is a (color) crayon.*

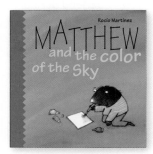

*Matthew and the Color of the Sky*
*Matías y el color del cielo*

# Center Time

**Center Rotation** Center Time includes teacher-guided activities and independent activities. Refer to the **Learning Centers** on pages 100–101 for activities in additional centers.

small group | 30 minutes

## Learning Goals

**Social and Emotional Development**
• Child demonstrates appropriate conflict-resolution strategies, requesting help when needed.

**Language and Communication**
• Child uses newly learned vocabulary daily in multiple contexts.

• Child uses nonverbal cues to communicate with others who do not speak his or her home language. (ELL)

• Child uses individual words and short phrases to communicate. (ELL)

**Science**
• Child describes the effects of natural forces (such as wind, gravity).

**Fine Arts**
• Child expresses emotions or ideas through art.

• Child shares opinions about artwork and artistic experiences.

## Creativity Center

### Center Tip

✓ **Monitor children as they paint pictures of the earth and sky.**

**Materials** tempera paint, white paper, paint brushes, containers of water, jars of diluted black paint (black wash), jars of diluted blue paint (blue wash), white and yellow crayons

**Paint Colors of the Sky** Tell children they are going to paint the colors of the sky, just like Matthew from the *Big Book*.

• Let children paint any color of the sky. Show them how to draw details with crayon (such as white clouds or stars) and paint over the details with diluted paint so the crayon still appears.

• Invite children to share their work and ask questions of each other.

**If...**children need help using the supplies or thinking of ideas to paint for their pictures, **then...** assign peer helpers to offer assistance. You might also limit the number of supplies a child can have so children must trade for new colors.

## Purposeful Play

✓ **Track English learners' use of nonverbal means or simple phrases to communicate.**

Children choose an open center for free playtime. Encourage cooperation skills by suggesting they paint other pictures of the earth and sky together.

## Writing

Recap the day and week. Say: *Tell me one thing you learned about day and night this week. How are shadows made? How does day change into night?* *Mencionen una cosa que hayan aprendido esta semana acerca del día y la noche.* Record children's answers on chart paper. Share the pen with children as you write. Invite volunteers to write the next letter or word in the sentence. Have each child write or scribble his or her name beside the entry.

## Let's Say Good-Bye

large group | 15 minutes

 **Read Aloud** Revisit "The Sun and the Moon"/"El Sol y la Luna" for your afternoon Read Aloud. Remind children to listen for real and make-believe parts of the story.

 **Home Connection** Refer to the Home Connection activities listed in the Materials and Resources chart on page 97. Remind children to tell their families what they learned this week about day and night, and about the play they put on. Sing the "Good-bye Song" as children prepare to leave.

## Focus Question

# Why is caring for the earth and sky important?

# ¿Por qué es importante cuidar la Tierra y el cielo?

This week children will learn about reducing, reusing, and recycling to preserve natural resources. They will read about how recycling helps keep the earth and sky clean, learn what they can do to conserve natural resources at school and home, build a class recycling center, and create a skit about ways to care for Earth.

# ✓ Learning Goals

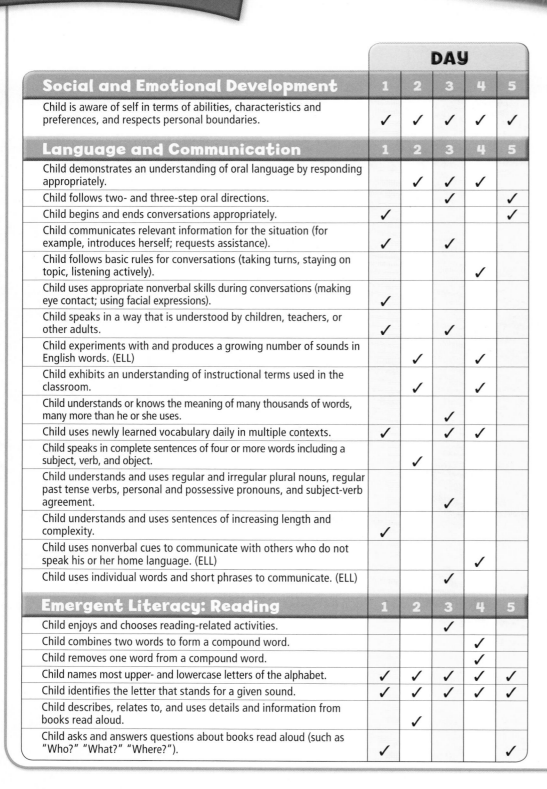

| Social and Emotional Development | 1 | 2 | 3 | 4 | 5 |
|---|---|---|---|---|---|
| Child is aware of self in terms of abilities, characteristics and preferences, and respects personal boundaries. | ✓ | ✓ | ✓ | ✓ | ✓ |

| Language and Communication | 1 | 2 | 3 | 4 | 5 |
|---|---|---|---|---|---|
| Child demonstrates an understanding of oral language by responding appropriately. |  | ✓ | ✓ | ✓ |  |
| Child follows two- and three-step oral directions. |  |  | ✓ |  | ✓ |
| Child begins and ends conversations appropriately. | ✓ |  |  |  | ✓ |
| Child communicates relevant information for the situation (for example, introduces herself; requests assistance). | ✓ |  | ✓ |  |  |
| Child follows basic rules for conversations (taking turns, staying on topic, listening actively). |  |  |  | ✓ |  |
| Child uses appropriate nonverbal skills during conversations (making eye contact; using facial expressions). | ✓ |  |  |  |  |
| Child speaks in a way that is understood by children, teachers, or other adults. | ✓ |  | ✓ |  |  |
| Child experiments with and produces a growing number of sounds in English words. (ELL) |  | ✓ |  | ✓ |  |
| Child exhibits an understanding of instructional terms used in the classroom. |  | ✓ |  | ✓ |  |
| Child understands or knows the meaning of many thousands of words, many more than he or she uses. |  |  | ✓ |  |  |
| Child uses newly learned vocabulary daily in multiple contexts. | ✓ |  | ✓ | ✓ |  |
| Child speaks in complete sentences of four or more words including a subject, verb, and object. |  | ✓ |  |  |  |
| Child understands and uses regular and irregular plural nouns, regular past tense verbs, personal and possessive pronouns, and subject-verb agreement. |  |  | ✓ |  |  |
| Child understands and uses sentences of increasing length and complexity. | ✓ |  |  |  |  |
| Child uses nonverbal cues to communicate with others who do not speak his or her home language. (ELL) |  |  |  | ✓ |  |
| Child uses individual words and short phrases to communicate. (ELL) |  |  | ✓ |  |  |

| Emergent Literacy: Reading | 1 | 2 | 3 | 4 | 5 |
|---|---|---|---|---|---|
| Child enjoys and chooses reading-related activities. |  |  | ✓ |  |  |
| Child combines two words to form a compound word. |  |  |  | ✓ |  |
| Child removes one word from a compound word. |  |  |  | ✓ |  |
| Child names most upper- and lowercase letters of the alphabet. | ✓ | ✓ | ✓ | ✓ | ✓ |
| Child identifies the letter that stands for a given sound. | ✓ | ✓ | ✓ | ✓ | ✓ |
| Child describes, relates to, and uses details and information from books read aloud. |  | ✓ |  |  |  |
| Child asks and answers questions about books read aloud (such as "Who?" "What?" "Where?"). | ✓ |  |  |  | ✓ |

| Emergent Literacy: Writing | 1 | 2 | 3 | 4 | 5 |
|---|---|---|---|---|---|
| Child uses scribbles, shapes, pictures, symbols, and letters to represent language. |  | ✓ |  |  | ✓ |
| Child experiments with and uses some writing conventions when writing or dictating. |  |  |  |  | ✓ |

| Mathematics | 1 | 2 | 3 | 4 | 5 |
|---|---|---|---|---|---|
| Child understands that objects, or parts thereof, can be counted. | ✓ |  |  |  |  |
| Child demonstrates that the numerical counting sequence is always the same. |  | ✓ |  |  |  |
| Child understands and uses ordinal numbers (such as *first, second, third*) to identify position in a series. |  | ✓ |  | ✓ | ✓ |
| Child tells how many are in a group of up to 5 objects without counting. |  |  | ✓ |  |  |
| Child uses concrete objects or makes a verbal word problem to add up to 5 objects. | ✓ |  | ✓ | ✓ | ✓ |

| Science | 1 | 2 | 3 | 4 | 5 |
|---|---|---|---|---|---|
| Child knows the importance of and demonstrates ways of caring for the environment/planet. | ✓ | ✓ | ✓ | ✓ | ✓ |

| Social Studies | 1 | 2 | 3 | 4 | 5 |
|---|---|---|---|---|---|
| Child understands basic human needs for food, clothing, shelter. |  |  | ✓ |  |  |
| Child understands basic concepts of buying, selling, and trading. |  |  | ✓ |  |  |

| Fine Arts | 1 | 2 | 3 | 4 | 5 |
|---|---|---|---|---|---|
| Child expresses emotions or ideas through art. |  |  | ✓ |  | ✓ |
| Child shares opinions about artwork and artistic experiences. |  |  | ✓ |  | ✓ |
| Child expresses thoughts, feelings, and energy through music and creative movement. |  |  |  |  | ✓ |

| Physical Development | 1 | 2 | 3 | 4 | 5 |
|---|---|---|---|---|---|
| Child engages in a sequence of movements to perform a task. |  |  |  |  | ✓ |
| Child develops small-muscle strength and control. |  | ✓ |  |  |  |

| Technology Applications | 1 | 2 | 3 | 4 | 5 |
|---|---|---|---|---|---|
| Child names and uses various computer parts (such as mouse, keyboard, CD-ROM, microphone, touch screen). |  |  |  | ✓ |  |
| Child uses voice/sound players and recorders, and touch screens correctly. | ✓ | ✓ |  |  |  |
| Child knows some ways that technology affects people's lives. | ✓ | ✓ | ✓ |  |  |

# Materials and Resources

| DAY 1 | DAY 2 | DAY 3 | DAY 4 | DAY 5 |
|---|---|---|---|---|
| **Program Materials** | | | | |
| • ABC Big Book<br>• *Ada, Once Again!* Big Book<br>• Building Blocks Math Activities<br>• Farm Animal Counters<br>• Home Connections Resource Guide<br>• Making Good Choices Flip Chart<br>• Math and Science Flip Chart<br>• Oral Language Development Card 69<br>• Photo Library CD-ROM<br>• Rhymes and Chants Flip Chart<br>• Teacher's Treasure Book | • ABC Big Book<br>• *Ada, Once Again!* Big Book<br>• Alphabet/Letter Tiles<br>• Building Blocks Math Activities<br>• Dog Puppets<br>• Magnetic Wands<br>• Making Good Choices Flip Chart<br>• copies of Pizza Game 2 for each child (Teacher's Treasure Book, p. 503)<br>• Teacher's Treasure Book | • ABC Big Book<br>• Building Blocks Math Activities<br>• Concept Big Book 4: *The Earth and Sky*<br>• Dog Puppets<br>• Making Good Choices Flip Chart<br>• Oral Language Development Card 70<br>• Rhymes and Chants Flip Chart<br>• Sequence Cards: "From Field to Table"<br>• Teacher's Treasure Book<br>• Vehicle Counters | • Alphabet/Letter Tiles<br>• Building Blocks Math Activites<br>• Dog Puppets<br>• Flannel Board Patterns for "Johnny Appleseed"<br>• Home Connections Resource Guide<br>• Math and Science Flip Chart<br>• Teacher's Treasure Book<br>• Vehicle Counters | • ABC Picture Cards<br>• *Ada, Once Again!* Big Book<br>• Building Blocks Math Activities<br>• Making Good Choices Flip Chart and Audio CD<br>• Rhymes and Chants Flip Chart<br>• Teacher's Treasure Book<br>• Vehicle Counters |
| **Other Materials** | | | | |
| • nonfiction books about recycling<br>• pebbles and rocks<br>• pictures of recyclable materials<br>• potting soil<br>• sand<br>• seashells<br>• three empty shoe boxes or plastic trays<br>• twigs<br>• voice/sound recorders | • 10 paper cups<br>• chart paper<br>• construction paper squares<br>• counters<br>• crayons<br>• glue<br>• index cards (large)<br>• marker<br>• number cubes<br>• voice/sound recorders | • blocks<br>• clean or play food containers<br>• clean socks, one per child<br>• colored dot stickers<br>• crayons and markers<br>• drawing paper<br>• fabric paint and glue<br>• fabric scraps<br>• magazines<br>• play money in various colors (see p. 156)<br>• picture books of trees<br>• scissors<br>• shop toys (cash register, grocery bags, play food, clean cartons)<br>• sticky notes | • 5 paper cups<br>• blue paper<br>• construction paper<br>• crayons<br>• fish crackers, at least ten per child<br>• illustrated children's books of folktales<br>• recordings of children's folktales<br>• red, yellow, and green paint<br>• small circle sponges | • 5 bean bags<br>• ball<br>• boxes and blocks<br>• buttons, bottle caps<br>• colored paper clips<br>• crayons and markers<br>• drawing paper<br>• fabric scraps<br>• glitter, paint, glue<br>• hula hoop<br>• index cards<br>• music for dancing and musical games<br>• newspapers<br>• recyclable materials (clean and safe) |

## Home Connection

| | | | | |
|---|---|---|---|---|
| Remind children to tell their families what they learned about recycling in Science Time. Send home the Weekly Family Letter, Home Connections Resource Guide, pp. 67–68. | Encourage children to use the ordinal words that they learned in Math Time at home with their families. | Remind children to tell their families what they bought in a play store in Social Studies Time. | Remind children to tell their families about what they did first, second, and third today. Send home Take-Home Storybook 21, Home Connections Resource Guide, pp. 161–164. | Encourage children to share with their families what games they played today during Outdoor Play, and to play them at home. |

## Assessment

As you observe children throughout the week, you may fill out an Anecdotal Observational Record Form to document an individual's progress toward a goal or signs indicating the need for developmental or medical evaluation. You may also choose to select work for each child's portfolio. The Anecdotal Observational Record Form and Weekly Assessment rubrics are available in the assessment section of DLMExpressOnline.com.

## More Literature Suggestions

• **On Earth** by G. Brian Karas
• **I Can Save the Earth!** by Alison Inches
• **10 Things I Can Do to Help My World** by Melanie Walsh
• **Mission: Addition** by Loreen Leedy

• **Un paseo por el parque** por Ricardo Alcántara
• **Cuentos ecológicos** por Saúl Schkolnik
• **El agua y tú** por Clarita Kohen
• **Grande la tierra, pequeño yo** por Thom Wiley

| | | **DAY 1** | **DAY 2** |
|---|---|---|---|
| **Let's Start the Day**<br>Language Time | *large group* | **Opening Routines** p. 140<br>**Morning Read Aloud** p. 140<br>**Oral Language and Vocabulary**<br>p. 140 Helping at the Beach<br>**Phonological Awareness**<br>p. 140 Segmenting Phonemes | **Opening Routines** p. 146<br>**Morning Read Aloud** p. 146<br>**Oral Language and Vocabulary**<br>p. 146 Question and Answer<br>About Earth<br>**Phonological Awareness**<br>p. 146 Segmenting Phonemes |
| **Center Time** | *small group* | **Focus On:**<br>**Library and Listening Center** p. 141<br>**Pretend and Learn Center** p. 141 | **Focus On:**<br>**ABC Center** p. 147<br>**Writer's Center** p. 147 |
| **Circle Time**<br>Literacy Time | *large group* | **Read Aloud**<br>*Ada, Once Again!!¡Otra vez Ada!* p. 142<br>**Learn About Letters and<br>Sounds:** Review *Ww* p. 142 | **Read Aloud**<br>*Ada, Once Again!!¡Otra vez Ada!* p. 148<br>**Learn About Letters and Sounds:**<br>Make an ABC Wall p. 148 |
| **Math Time** | *large group* | Farm Animal Shop p. 143 | Pizza Game 2 p. 149 |
| **Social and<br>Emotional<br>Development** | *large group* | Being Respectful p. 143 | Being Respectful p. 149 |
| **Content<br>Connection** | *large group* | **Science:**<br>**Oral Language and Academic Vocabulary**<br>p. 144 Talk About Recycling<br>**Observe and Investigate**<br>p. 144 School Recycling | **Math:**<br>**Lining Up—Who's First?**<br>p. 150 Learning Ordinal Terms<br>**What is First?**<br>p. 150 Using Ordinal Terms |
| **Center Time** | *small group* | **Focus On:**<br>**Math and Science Center** p. 145<br>**Purposeful Play** p. 145 | **Focus On:**<br>**Math and Science Center** p. 151<br>**Purposeful Play** p. 151 |
| **Let's Say<br>Good-Bye** | *large group* | **Read Aloud** p. 145<br>**Writing** p. 145<br>**Home Connection** p. 145 | **Read Aloud** p. 151<br>**Writing** p. 151<br>**Home Connection** p. 151 |

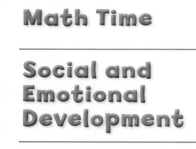

## Why is caring for the earth and sky important?
## ¿Por qué es importante cuidar la Tierra y el cielo?

# DAY 3

**Opening Routines** p. 152
**Morning Read Aloud** p. 152
**Oral Language and Vocabulary**
p. 152  Arbor Day
**Phonological Awareness**
p. 152  Segmenting Phonemes

**Focus On:**
**Pretend and Learn Center** p. 153
**Creativity Center** p. 153

**Read Aloud**
*Concept Big Book 4:*
*The Earth and Sky/*
*La Tierra y el cielo* p. 154
**Learn About Letters and Sounds:**
*Qq, Ww,* and *Zz* p. 154

**Snapshots** p. 155

**Being Respectful** p. 155

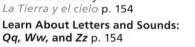

**Social Studies:**
**Oral Language and Academic Vocabulary**
p. 156  Talking About Shopping
**Understand and Participate**
p. 156  Let's Go Shopping

**Focus On:**
**Construction Center** p. 157
**Purposeful Play** p. 157

**Read Aloud** p. 157
**Writing** p. 157
**Home Connection** p. 157

# DAY 4

**Opening Routines** p. 158
**Morning Read Aloud** p. 158
**Oral Language and Vocabulary**
p. 158  Folktales
**Phonological Awareness**
p. 158  Segmenting Phonemes

**Focus On:**
**ABC Center** p. 159
**Library and Listening Center** p. 159

**Read Aloud**
"The Story of Johnny Appleseed"/
"La historia de Juan Semillita" p. 160
**Learn about Letters and Sounds:**
*Qq, Ww,* and *Zz* p. 160

**Vehicle Shop (Make It Right)** p. 161

**Being Respectful** p. 161

**Math:**
**Talk About Ordinal Numbers**
p. 162 Using Ordinal Numbers
**Gone Fishing**
p. 162 Identifying Ordinal Positions

**Focus On:**
**Creativity Center** p. 163
**Purposeful Play** p. 163

**Read Aloud** p. 163
**Writing** p. 163
**Home Connection** p. 163

# DAY 5

**Opening Routines** p. 164
**Morning Read Aloud** p. 164
**Oral Language and Vocabulary**
p. 164  Our Earth
**Phonological Awareness**
p. 164  Segmenting Phonemes

**Focus On:**
**Creativity Center** p. 165
**Writer's Center** p. 165

**Read Aloud**
*Ada, Once Again!!*
*¡Otra vez Ada!* p. 166
**Learn About Letters and**
**Sounds: Review Letters and**
**Sounds** p. 166

**Making 5** p. 167

**Being Respectful** p. 167

**Outdoor Play:**
**Oral Language and Academic Vocabulary**
p. 168  Caring for the Outdoors
**Move and Learn** p. 168  Let's Play Games

**Focus On:**
**Construction Center** p. 169
**Purposeful Play** p. 169

**Read Aloud** p. 169
**Writing** p. 169
**Home Connection** p. 169

# Week 4

**Taking Care of the World**

# Learning Centers

## Math and Science Center

### Surface Sorting
Children sort natural materials and group them by properties. See p. 145.

### Where Is It?
Children use ordinal numbers while asking about objects hidden under cups. See p. 151.

### Sort Recyclable Materials
Children look through a prepared recycling bin and sort clean, blunt items by paper, plastic, or metal properties.

### Reuse Inventory
Children tour the classroom and count the number of items that are reused.

## ABC Center

### Find the Letter
Children fish for letters *Qq*, *Ww*, and *Zz*. They identify upper- and lowercase letters and name words beginning with the letter sounds. See p. 147.

### Play Concentration
Children match letter tiles, trace the letters, and make the letter sounds. See p. 159.

### Noodle Around
Children locate letters *Qq*, *Ww*, and *Zz* in bags of alphabet noodles or magnetic letters.

### Buzzing *Zz* Bees
Children flip through storybook pages, pretending to be bees buzzing /z/ sounds. They should keep buzzing until they find a letter *Zz* in print.

## Creativity Center

### Planting a Tree Collage
Children cut out pictures of trees from magazines and assemble them on paper. See p. 153.

### Apple Stories
Children use sponge stamps to print different colored apples. They add the colored apples and write the total number. See p. 163.

### Treasure Box
Children use recycled materials to decorate boxes. See p. 165.

### Earth-Friendly Art
Children use glue, recycled materials, paint, and cardboard to create their own 3-D recycled art.

## Library and Listening Center

### Browsing Nonfiction Books

Children look at recycling books, discuss illustrations, and dictate favorite books for a Book Log. See p. 141.

### Browsing Books

Child partners browse through or listen to folktales, discuss them, and dictate their favorite titles for a Book Log. See p. 159.

### Characters with Character

Children identify storybook characters that care for the earth and tell a partner what the character did to conserve resources or clean the earth.

## Construction Center

### Build a Store

Groups of children use blocks to build stores and pretend to be store owners and customers. See p. 157.

### Build a Recycling Center

Child pairs use boxes and blocks to make a recycling center and describe and label its parts. See p. 169.

### Fantastic Machines

Children use recycled materials to form "pollution-fighting machines." They explain to a partner how the machines would be used to clean the earth, water, or air.

## Writer's Center

### Class Story

Children dictate sentences about what they have learned so far. Then they find and circle particular letters in the recorded sentences. See p. 147.

### Our World Pictures

Children draw pictures of activities that help preserve natural resources and dictate picture descriptions. See p. 165.

### Conservation Labels

Children draw pictures of things people do to care for the earth and label them *reuse* or *recycle*.

## Pretend and Learn Center

### Pantomiming

Children act out the suggestions in "Our Beautiful Earth." See p. 141.

### Making Sock Puppets

Children reuse materials by making sock puppets. They use the puppets to describe ways to care for Earth. See p. 153.

### Community Helpers

Children act like sanitation workers by pretending to sort objects into trash or recycling bins.

WE RECYCLE

**Focus Question**

## Why is caring for the earth and sky important? ¿Por qué es importante cuidar la Tierra y el cielo?

### ✓ Learning Goals

**Social and Emotional Development**
• Child is aware of self in terms of abilities, characteristics and preferences, and respects personal boundaries.

**Language and Communication**
• Child understands and uses sentences of increasing length and complexity.

### Vocabulary

| | | | |
|---|---|---|---|
| bags | bolsas | beach | playa |
| clean | limpiar | garbage | basura |
| litter | desperdicios | pick up | recoger |
| trash | basurero | | |

### Differentiated Instruction

 **Extra Support**

**Phonological Awareness**

**If...**children have difficulty segmenting one syllable words, **then...**identify the initial letter sound (onset) and say the rest of the word (rime). Have children say the whole word. Say: *Listen carefully: /b/ -us. What's the word? Escuchen atentamente: /b/ -us. ¿Qué palabra es?*

⭐ **Enrichment**

**Phonological Awareness**

Challenge children to segment the words *space* and *place* sound by sound.

 **Special Needs**

**Speech/Language Delays**

**If...**children have difficulty segmenting words, **then...**just focus on the sounds of the initial letters of words.

# Let's Start the Day

▶ **Opening Routines and Transition Tips**

For **Opening Routines** and **Transition Tips** turn to pages 178–181 and visit **DLMExpressOnline.com** for more ideas.

 Read **"My Father Picks Oranges"/**"Mi papá cosecha naranjas" from the *Teacher's Treasure Book*, page 186, for your morning Read Aloud.

## Language Time

  large group · 15 minutes

**Social and Emotional Development** Ask children as they work on an activity what their rules are for respecting each other's space.

### Oral Language and Vocabulary

✓ **Can children describe the picture using complex sentences?**

**Helping at the Beach** Ask children to share experiences they have had at the beach or with litter. Help them combine their ideas into complex sentences.

● Ask: ***Do you think it is important for a beach to be clean? Why?*** *¿Por qué es importante que la playa esté limpia?*

● Display *Oral Language Development Card 69*. Ask children to describe what is happening in the picture. Say: ***What do you see the people doing? What is on the ground?*** *¿Qué están haciendo estas personas? ¿Qué hay en el suelo?* Follow the suggestions on the back of the card.

### Phonological Awareness

✓ **Can children segment words into individual phonemes?**

**Segmenting Phonemes** Display *Rhymes and Chants Flip Chart* page 32. Recite "Our Beautiful Earth." Talk about how riding the bus is good for the sky (it cuts down on smog in the air) and how recycling helps the earth (there is less trash).

● Remind children that words are made up of sounds. For example, the word *big* is made up of the first sound /b/ and the remaining sounds /i/ and /g/. Say: ***Listen, /b/ /i/ /g/,*** **big.** *Eschuchen, /b/ /i/ /g/, big.*

● Guide children to segment the words *out* and *up* by stating the first sound, then the rest of the word.

**ELL** As you display the *Oral Language Development Card*, help children talk about the picture by providing this sentence frame: **People pick up _____ to _____ the beach.**

*Oral Language Development Card 69*

**Our Beautiful Earth**

Our beautiful Earth is a wonderful place.
It's like a big house, but built out in space!
Earth is a place we all want to keep clean,
The prettiest planet that we've ever seen!
So turn off the lights before leaving a room.
Gather the trash with a swish of a broom.
Recycle plastic. Don't toss it away!
Save plastic bags to use some other day.
Ask Mom to consider, instead of the car,
A train or a bus when you go near or far.

*Rhymes and Chants Flip Chart, page 32/ page 64*

# Center Time

▶ **Center Rotation** Center Time includes teacher-guided activities and independent activities. Refer to the **Learning Centers** on pages 138–139 for activities in additional centers.

small group  60–90 minutes

## Library and Listening Center

 **Track understanding of ways people can keep Earth beautiful.**

**Materials** nonfiction books about recycling, voice recorders

**Browsing Nonfiction Books** Show children how to operate the voice recorder. Explain that they will browse books about recycling. Explain to children that they can also help care for Earth. Ask: *Can you name one way to care for Earth? ¿Pueden nombrar una manera en que cuidamos la Tierra?* Have children record their comments about the illustrations and how they can care for Earth.

- Ask: *Which is your favorite book? Why? ¿Cuál de los libros es su favorito? ¿Por qué?* List children's responses on a Book Log for future reference.

- Allow them to listen to their peers' recordings and then discuss the ideas they heard with their classmates. Later, you can use the recordings to assess how well children's speech can be understood, and individualize future instruction as appropriate.

### Center Tip
**If...**children have difficulty recalling ways to recycle, **then...**give them a clue in the form of a question such as: *What should I do with plastic bottles when they are empty? ¿Qué debemos hacer con las botellas plásticas cuando están vacías?*

## Pretend and Learn Center

 **Track children's awareness of their bodies in space.**

**Pantomiming** Explain to children that they will act out the rhyme "Our Beautiful Earth." Refer to the *Rhymes and Chants Flip Chart*, page 32, and recite "Our Beautiful Earth" with the children.

- Invite children to pantomime each action described (turning off lights, sweeping, recycling plastic, riding a bus or train) as you recite the poem again.

- Continue by assigning groups of children to act out each action.

- Ask children to share their experiences doing things to care for the earth at home or school.

### Center Tip
**If...**children have difficulty acting out actions without bumping into other children, **then...**have children take turns.

**Focus Question**
## Why is caring for the earth and sky important?
## ¿Por qué es importante cuidar la Tierra y el cielo?

### Learning Goals

**Emergent Literacy: Reading**
- Child names most upper- and lowercase letters of the alphabet.
- Child identifies the letter that stands for a given sound.
- Child asks and answers questions about books read aloud (such as "Who?" "What?" "Where?").

**Science**
- Child knows the importance of and demonstrates ways of caring for the environment/planet.

### Vocabulary

| declares | declarar | glistens | brillante |
|----------|----------|----------|-----------|
| pity | lástima | stuck | atrapada |
| teardrop | lágrima | wavering | menearse |

### Differentiated Instruction

#### ✋ Extra Support

**Learn About Letters and Sounds**
**If...**children have difficulty writing the letter *Ww*, **then...**model how to bend pipe cleaners to form upper and lower case *Ww*. Children can also shape the pipe cleaners on traced letters.

#### ⭐ Enrichment

**Learn About Letters and Sounds**
Assign *Qq, Ww,* or *Zz* to each pair of children. Have each pair find three words that begin with their assigned letters. Have them copy the words. Encourage children to use a classroom picture dictionary.

## Literacy Time

 **Read Aloud**

✓ **Can children demonstrate the importance of caring for our planet?**

**Build Background** Tell children that you will be reading a book about an amazing plastic bag. Ask: **What do we do with plastic bags? Why?** *¿Qué hacemos con las bolsas plásticas? ¿Por qué?*

**Listen for Enjoyment** Display *Ada, Once Again!* and read the title. Conduct a picture walk. Ask: **What are the children doing in the story? Why do you think they are in the garden?** *¿Qué hacen los niños del cuento? ¿Por qué creen que están en el jardín?*

- Read the story aloud to children, encouraging them to blow like the wind to get Ada out of the tree in the appropriate scene.

**Respond to the Story** Review the pictures with children as you ask: **How do you think Ada got stuck in the tree? Have you ever seen a plastic bag in a tree? Where do you think the bag should be?** *¿Cómo creen que Ada se quedó atrapada en el árbol? ¿Han visto alguna vez una bolsa de plástico en un árbol? ¿Dónde creen que debería estar esa bolsa?*

- Point out that Ada gets recycled into something new. Explain that this helps keep Earth clean, since Ada is no longer stuck in the tree as litter.

- Ask: **Why do you think Ada is happy at the end of the story?** *¿Por qué creen que Ada está feliz al final del cuento?*

**TIP** Help children use the picture details to understand that Ada wants the children to find her.

**ELL** As you browse the *Big Book* illustrations, have children identify the things they know in English. Ask them to point to things that they do not know in English, so you can say the words aloud and have them repeat.

## Learn About Letters and Sounds

✓ **Can children identify the /w/ sound spelled *Ww*?**

**Review the Letter *Ww*** Page through the *ABC Big Book*, stopping when you get to *Ww*. Point to the "wagon" photo. Remind children that the word *wagon* begins with the /w/ sound. Have them chant with you **Willie Winkle washes with warm water.**

- Model how to write uppercase *W*. Have children trace *W* on their desks or in the air with their fingers.

- Have children make the /w/ sound each time they trace the letter.

- Repeat for the lowercase *w*. Remind children of the similarities in upper- and lowercase *Ww*.

*Ada, Once Again!*
*¡Otra vez Ada!*

*ABC Big Book, page 48*
*Superlibro abecé*

**large group** | 15 minutes

## Building Blocks

**Online Math Activity**

Introduce Dinosaur Shop 4: Make It Right, in which children hear two orders for dinosaurs, but the customer wants them in one box. The child has to click the numeral that tells how many (the sum of two numerals) will be in the single box.

**large group** | 15 minutes

*Making Good Choices Flip Chart, page 32*

# Math Time

## Observe and Investigate

✓ **Can children understand that adding one or more objects to a set will increase the number of objects in the set?**

**Farm Animal Shop** Show children a box with four of the Farm Animal Counters. Say: *I have four animals. How can I make five animals? Tengo cuatro animales. ¿Cómo puedo tener cinco animales?*

● Follow children's suggestions for making the set five, and count to check.

● Repeat several times, changing the beginning number. For example, start with five to make six; start with three to make five, and so on.

● Using horse and cow counters, ask children to count the legs and see how you can make four legs into eight, and how many parts of the animal counter can be counted.

**ELL** Have children use Two-Color Counters. They show four red counters, and then add one yellow counter. Help children see that the number can be shown in two parts.

# ⚇ Social and Emotional Development

## Making Good Choices

✓ **Are children aware of the space their bodies take up?**

✓ **Do children show respect for each other?**

**Being Respectful** Display *Making Good Choices Flip Chart* page 32. Point to the illustrations. Ask children what their rules are for being respectful of others' space. Ask them what they think it means to be respectful of other people.

● Ask: *How are the children in the picture sitting? Which children are not sitting like the other children? How should they sit? ¿Cómo están sentados los niños de la ilustración? ¿Qué niños no están sentados como el resto? ¿Cómo deberían sentarse?*

● Ask: *Which is the most respectful way to sit? Why? ¿Cuál es la manera más respetuosa de sentarse? ¿Por qué?*

● Have children pause to note how they are sitting during this exercise. Ask them how they should move over or sit straight or still, as appropriate. Then have them follow their own suggestions. Praise their efforts to respect each other.

---

### Learning Goals

**Social and Emotional Development**
● Child is aware of self in terms of abilities, characteristics and preferences, and respects personal boundaries.

**Mathematics**
● Child understands that objects, or parts thereof, can be counted.

● Child uses concrete objects or makes a verbal word problem to add up to 5 objects.

### Vocabulary

| | |
|---|---|
| altogether | en total |
| counters | fichas |
| how many more | cuántas |
| respectful | respetuoso |

---

### Differentiated Instruction

 **Extra Support**
**Observe and Investigate**
**If...**children struggle adding up to 5, **then...** have them review simple addition problems with their fingers.

 **Enrichment**
**Observe and Investigate**
Challenge children to add counters up to 10 by adding 1 or 2 more. Say: *Start with 5. How many more to make 6? Comienzo con cinco. ¿Cuántas necesito para tener seis?* Have children show how they made 6. Say: *Start with 7. How many more to make 9? Comienzo con siete. ¿Cuántas necesito para tener nueve?*

**Accommodations for 3's**
**Making Good Choices**
**If...**children struggle with the term *respectful*, **then...**define it for them as being nice to others.

## Learning Goals

**Social and Emotional Development**
• Child is aware of self in terms of abilities, characteristics and preferences, and respects personal boundaries.

**Language and Communication**
• Child begins and ends conversations appropriately.

• Child communicates relevant information for the situation (for example, introduces herself; requests assistance).

• Child uses appropriate nonverbal skills during conversations (making eye contact; using facial expressions).

**Science**
• Child knows the importance of and demonstrates ways of caring for the environment/planet.

**Technology Applications**
• Child knows some ways that technology affects people's lives.

### Vocabulary

| | | | |
|---|---|---|---|
| bottles | botellas | clean | limpiar |
| paper | papel | plastic | plástico |
| recycle | reciclar | reuse | reutilizar |

## Differentiated Instruction

 **Extra Support**

**Oral Language and Academic Vocabulary**
**If...**children have difficulty focusing on the illustration on the chart, **then...**suggest specific things for them to look for in the recycling bin.

 **Enrichment**

**Oral Language and Academic Vocabulary**
Challenge children to find a classroom item that they could reuse for a new purpose.

# Science Time

## Oral Language and Academic Vocabulary

☑ **Do children understand how and why to care for the environment?**

**Talking About Recycling** Display *Math and Science Flip Chart* page 59. Point to the children in the picture. Ask: **What do you think they are about to do?** *¿Qué creen que van a hacer los niños?*

● Point out the recycling bin and the recycling logo. Say: **When you see this label, you know the bin is for recycling. Have you seen this before?** *Cuando ven esta etiqueta, saben que ésta es una caja de reciclaje. ¿Han visto este tipo de cajas antes?*

● Ask: **What kinds of things are in the recycling bin? What do you think the children will do next? Why?** *¿Qué objetos hay en la caja de reciclaje? ¿Qué creen que van a hacer ahora los niños? ¿Por qué?*

● Explain that children can learn more about recycling by going online with an adult. Ask: **If you want more information, where can you go?** *¿Adónde pueden ir si quieren más información?*

## Observe and Investigate

☑ **Can children engage in conversations about caring for the environment?**

**School Recycling** Discuss your school's recycling plan with children.

● Take children on a trip to see how the maintenance people at your school recycle or bag the trash. Ask questions to help children learn about how things are sorted. Observe them respecting personal space on the visit.

● Visit other classes to see how older children recycle or reuse materials. Look (don't touch) to see what types of items are in the trash and recycling bins.

● Back in your class, have pairs discuss their recycling trip. Ask them to brainstorm ways they could inform others about what goes in recycling bins and trash cans. Observe them engaging appropriately in conversations.

**ELL** Use objects and pictures from the Photo Library CD-ROM to review words: *jar, can, bottle, bag, bin, paper.* Post pictures of recyclable items on or around the class recycling bin.

*Math and Science Flip Chart, page 59*

# Center Time

▶ **Center Rotation** Center Time includes teacher-guided activities and independent activities. Refer to the **Learning Centers** on pages 138–139 for activities in additional centers.

small group · 30 minutes

## Math and Science Center

| | Center Tip |
|---|---|

✓ **Observe children as they explore and compare earth materials.**

**Materials** pebbles, rocks, sand, soil, seashells, twigs; three empty shoe boxes or plastic trays; plastic tray of water

**Surface Sorting** Remind children that Earth's surface is made up of soil, rocks, sand, and water. Ask: **What do we build with rocks? What do we use water for?** *¿Qué podemos construir con rocas? ¿Para qué usamos el agua?* Point out that water is in oceans, lakes, ice and rivers. Encourage children to discuss and compare the materials' uses.

- Encourage children to sort the rocks by size, color, or smoothness.

- Add seashells and twigs, and fill two of the trays part way each with soil and sand. Watch where children put the earth materials.

**Center Tip**

**If...**children need help sorting,

**then...**choose a characteristic for them and model how to sort the types of rocks, such as by size only.

## Purposeful Play

✓ **Observe children respecting each other's personal space and engaging in conversations.**

Children choose an open center for free playtime. Encourage respecting each other by modeling appropriate standing and sitting distance, not interrupting, and asking permission before borrowing materials.

## Let's Say Good-Bye

large group · 15 minutes

 **Read Aloud** Revisit "My Father Picks Oranges"/"Mi papá cosecha naranjas" for your afternoon Read Aloud. Tell children that oranges, like many foods, need the earth and sky to be clean in order to grow.

 **Home Connection** Refer to the Home Connection activities listed in the Materials and Resources chart on page 135. Remind children to tell families what they learned about recycling in Science Time. Sing the "Good-bye Song" as children prepare to leave.

---

### ✓ Learning Goals

**Social and Emotional Development**
- Child is aware of self in terms of abilities, characteristics and preferences, and respects personal boundaries.

**Language and Communication**
- Child names and describes actual or pictured people, places, things, actions, attributes, and events.

- Child begins and ends conversations appropriately.

- Child communicates relevant information for the situation (for example, introduces herself; requests assistance).

- Child uses appropriate nonverbal skills during conversations (making eye contact; using facial expressions).

**Science**
- Child observes, identifies, explores, describes, and compares earth materials (such as rocks, soil, sand, water) and their uses.

---

### Writing

Recap the day. Have children name some of the things they can do to care for the earth. Ask: **Why is it important to care for the earth?** *¿Por qué es importante cuidar el planeta?* Record their answers. Read them back as you track the print, and emphasize the correspondence between speech and print.

# DAY 2

## Focus Question

**Why is caring for the earth and sky important? ¿Por qué es importante cuidar la Tierra y el cielo?**

### Learning Goals

**Social and Emotional Development**
• Child is aware of self in terms of abilities, characteristics and preferences, and respects personal boundaries.

**Language and Communication**
• Child demonstrates an understanding of oral language by responding appropriately.
• Child speaks in complete sentences of four or more words including a subject, verb, and object.

### Vocabulary

| | | | |
|---|---|---|---|
| complete | completar | plastic | plástico |
| respect | respetar | respond | responder |
| sentence | oración | | |

### Differentiated Instruction

 **Extra Support**

**Oral Language and Vocabulary**
**If...**children have difficulty answering questions in complete sentences, **then...**model creating a complete sentence from the answer they offer. Have children repeat your sentence.

 **Enrichment**

**Oral Language and Vocabulary**
Challenge children to make up sentences using today's vocabulary words.

# Let's Start the Day

 **Opening Routines and Transition Tips**

For **Opening Routines** and **Transition Tips** turn to pages 178–181 and visit DLMExpressOnline.com for more ideas.

Read **"A Spring Walk"/**"Una caminata en primavera" from the *Teacher's Treasure Book*, page 187, for your morning Read Aloud.

## Language Time

large group  15 minutes

**Social and Emotional Development** Assess learning by asking children how they will respect other people's space today.

### Oral Language and Vocabulary

✓ **Can children answer questions using complete sentences?**

**Question and Answer About Earth** Talk about ways to help care for Earth.

• Tell children that you will ask them questions about ways they have learned to care for Earth. Explain that they should respond in complete sentences. Help children understand that a complete sentence usually has many words. For example, if you pose a question asking "what should we do..." the answer sentence should repeat "we should...."

• Ask: *What should we do with trash? What should we do with plastic bags? Why should we keep the earth and sky clean?* *¿Qué debemos hacer con la basura? ¿Qué debemos hacer con las bolsas plásticas? ¿Por qué debemos mantener limpios la Tierra y el cielo?*

• Prompt children to think about what earth materials we use and the air we breathe when they are answering why we should care for the earth and sky.

### Phonological Awareness

✓ **Can children segment one-syllable words?**

**Segmenting Phonemes** Display the Dog Puppets. Tell children that the first Dog Puppet will say a word. Then the next Dog Puppet will break apart the word into its smaller sounds.

• Explain that if the puppet correctly segments a word, children should clap and say, "Good job!" If the puppet makes a mistake, children should raise their hands to correct it.

• Have the Dog Puppets segment these words: *bag,* /b/ /a/ /g/; *day,* /d/ /a/; *car,* /k/ /a/ /r/. Choose one to make a mistake children can identify and correct, such as *bag,* /t/ /a/ /g/ or *car,* /k/ /r/.

**ELL** Focus on segmenting words only into onset and rime. Have children repeat the word and then say the first sound and the rest of the word.

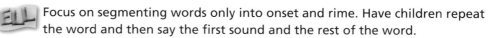

# Center Time

▶ **Center Rotation** Center Time includes teacher-guided activities and independent activities. Refer to the **Learning Centers** on pages 138–139 for activities in additional centers.

  small group 60–90 minutes

## Learning Goals

**Emergent Literacy: Reading**
• Child names most upper- and lowercase letters of the alphabet.

**Emergent Literacy: Writing**
• Child uses scribbles, shapes, pictures, symbols, and letters to represent language.

**Science**
• Child knows the importance of and demonstrates ways of caring for the environment/planet.

**Physical Development**
• Child develops small-muscle strength and control.

**Technology Applications**
• Child uses voice/sound players and recorders, and touch screens correctly.

## ABC Center

### Center Tip

☑ **Track children's letter/sound recognition.**

**Materials** Alphabet/Letter Tiles, Magnetic Wands, voice recorder

**Find the Letter** Place 20 letters randomly on the table. Include *Qq, Ww, Zz,* and any review letters. Children "fish for" (pick up or move) letters using the Magnetic Wands. Remind children how to use the recorder.

• Ask a volunteer to find *Zz.* Ask: **What sound do we say for Z?** *¿Qué sonido tiene la Z?* Repeat with the other letters for the week.

• Periodically ask children to find letters that they know completely in order to give them confidence.

• Have children record themselves naming the letters they have fished from the pile and saying a word that begins with each letter. As they play back their recordings, have them use the wands to push letters back into the pile in the order that they hear them.

**If...**children have difficulty remembering the sound for a letter, **then...**give them a clue by showing them a picture from the *ABC Big Book.* Model saying the picture name, emphasizing the initial sound.

## Writer's Center

### Center Tip

☑ **Track children's ability to form letters on request.**

**Materials** chart paper, crayons

**Class Story** Encourage children to talk about what they learned so far this week about how to care for the earth and sky.

• Write their sentences on chart paper.

• Reread the sentences with children. Track the print and emphasize space between words as you read from left to right.

• Name a letter such as *Ww* and have children look for that letter on the chart and circle it with a unique color crayon.

• Have children write the circled letter below the word in their colors. Repeat with other letters and different colored crayons.

**If...**children have difficulty finding specific letters, **then...**help them by pointing to the word that has that specific letter.

## Differentiated Instruction

 **Extra Support**

**ABC Center**

**If...**children have difficulty remembering the sound of a letter, **then...**have them say the sound softly, then louder, then in a whisper.

 **Enrichment**

**ABC Center**

Challenge children to name two or three other words that begin with their assigned letter.

 **Special Needs**

**Delayed Motor Development**

**If...**children have difficulty holding crayons, **then...**put foam from hair-curlers on the crayons to make them easier to grip.

# Circle Time

**Focus Question**

**Why is caring for the earth and sky important?**

**¿Por qué es importante cuidar la Tierra y el cielo?**

## ✓ Learning Goals

**Language and Communication**
• Child experiments with and produces a growing number of sounds in English words. (ELL)

**Emergent Literacy: Reading**
• Child describes, relates to, and uses details and information from books read aloud.

**Science**
• Child knows the importance of and demonstrates ways of caring for the environment/planet.

### Vocabulary

| | | | |
|---|---|---|---|
| along | juntos | declares | declarar |
| gathered | recoger | glides | deslizarse |
| glistens | brillante | pity | lástima |
| squirms | retorcerse | | |

## Differentiated Instruction

###  Extra Support

**Learn About Letters and Sounds**
**If...**children have difficulty identifying their letter, **then...**let them use the first letter of their names and have them use the *ABC Big Book* to find their matching letter.

###  Enrichment

**Learn About Letters and Sounds**
Challenge children to give each other clues about letter sequence following your model. Children can work in small groups. The child that answers correctly gives the next clue.

## Literacy Time

large group    15 minutes

### 📖 Read Aloud

✓ **Can children relate information learned from a book to their lives?**

**Build Background** Tell children that you will reread the story about Ada, a very special plastic bag. Ask: *What do we do with real plastic bags? ¿Para qué usamos las bolsas de plástico reales?*

**Listen for Understanding** Display the Big Book *Ada, Once Again!* and read the title and the author's name. Ask children to show you how you should hold the book to read. Read the story aloud. Point to the words as you read aloud.

● Ask: *Why is Ada happy in the end? How does the picture help you know she is happy? ¿Por qué está feliz Ada al final? ¿Cómo nos ayuda el dibujo a saber que Ada está feliz?*

**Respond to the Story** Have children discuss page 32 of the story. Explain what the text means and how it relates to recycling. Have children share their experiences with recycling or reusing materials or gardening at home.

**TIP** Remind children that although Ada is acting like a person and showing feelings like a person has, she is part of a make-believe story. Real plastic bags do not have feelings or talk like people.

**ELL** After you read *Ada, Once Again!* pair English learners with native speakers and have them take turns acting out the story as you call out particular lines. Encourage children to mimic your intonation.

*Ada, Once Again!*
*¡Otra vez Ada!*

### Learn About Letters and Sounds

 **Can children identify the correct letter in a sequence?**

**Make an ABC Wall** Tell children that they will make an ABC wall.

● Distribute a crayon and large index card to each child. Assign each child a letter, and print it at the top of each child's card. Include *Qq*, *Ww*, and *Zz*.

● Have children copy the upper- and lowercase forms of their letters on their cards.

● Then ask: *Does anyone have the first letter in the alphabet? ¿Alguien sabe cuál es la primera letra del abecedario?* Prompt children by starting to sing the ABC song over again until they get to a letter someone has. Invite that child to put the letter on the wall. Continue until all the letters are displayed. Help children fasten their cards to a wall or chart paper in ABC order.

● For a challenge, ask students to help you fill in the missing letters from the ABC Wall in order.

# Math Time

## Observe and Investigate

 **Can children count items with one count per item?**

**Pizza Game 2** Demonstrate this game by playing it with children. Each player needs a Pizza Game 2 sheet (*Teacher's Treasure Book,* page 503) and flat, round counters. Choose a target number, such as 5.

- Player One rolls a number cube, and puts that many counters ("toppings) on the sheet's plate, for example, 6. Once Player Two agrees that Player One chose the correct number of counters, Player One moves the counters to one or more of the sheet's pizzas, trying to get 5 on each. If a 6 was rolled, Player One puts 5 on a single pizza and starts another with 1.

- Players take turns. The winner is the first to get the target number on each pizza. Repeat as time permits with a different target number.

- Have children use ordinal terms to tell you what they did first, second, etc.

# ✖✖✖ Social and Emotional Development

## Making Good Choices

 **Do children respect each other's personal spaces?**

**Being Respectful** Display *Making Good Choices Flip Chart* page 32.

- Display a Dog Puppet. Point to one of the children in the illustration who is sitting improperly. Ask: **Who can tell the puppet if this is respectful of the other children's space and the teacher? Why or why not?** *¿Quién puede decirle al títere si lo que hace este niño es respetuoso del espacio de los otros niños y del maestro? ¿Por qué?*

- Have volunteers tell the puppet about a child on the chart, explaining how he or she is respecting or not respecting other children's spaces.

- Ask children why they should sit with enough space between them and listen during class.

- Ask students to think about how they are sitting during this activity. Ask them to make any corrections necessary. Praise children's efforts.

  **ELL** Provide sentence frames to help during the conversation with the Dog Puppet. Use these and others: **The boy is _____ . The girl is _____ .** Model using each frame. Have children repeat the completed frame you provide.

---

**Online Math Activity**

Introduce Ordinal Construction Company, where children learn ordinal positions up to tenth by moving items between floors. Each child should complete the activity this week.

*Making Good Choices Flip Chart, page 32*

---

### Learning Goals

**Social and Emotional Development**
- Child is aware of self in terms of abilities, characteristics and preferences, and respects personal boundaries.

**Mathematics**
- Child counts 1–10 concrete objects correctly.
- Child understands and uses ordinal numbers (such as *first, second, third*) to identify position in a series.

### Vocabulary

| | | | |
|---|---|---|---|
| count | contar | five | cinco |
| four | cuatro | how many | cuántos |
| six | seis | three | tres |

### Differentiated Instruction

**Extra Support**

**Math Time**
**If...**children struggle counting to 5, **then...** model counting 5 counters by moving each counter onto the pizza sheet. Have children count aloud with you.

**Enrichment**

**Math Time**
Have children make up their own rules for the pizza game using counters up to 10.

## Learning Goals

**Social and Emotional Development**
• Child is aware of self in terms of abilities, characteristics and preferences, and respects personal boundaries.

**Language and Communication**
• Child exhibits an understanding of instructional terms used in the classroom.

**Mathematics**
• Child demonstrates that the numerical counting sequence is always the same.
• Child understands and uses ordinal numbers (such as *first, second, third*) to identify position in a series.

### Vocabulary

| eighth | octavo | fifth | quinto |
|--------|--------|-------|--------|
| fourth | cuarto | second | segundo |
| seventh | séptimo | sixth | sexto |
| third | tercero | | |

## Differentiated Instruction

 **Extra Support**

**Math Time**

**If...**children have difficulty identifying ordinal terms, **then...**use the ordinal terms throughout the day, such as when children line up or sit at a table.

 **Enrichment**

**Math Time**

Challenge children to tell about an event that occurred in the classroom or what they did before coming to school using the words *first, second,* and *third*.

 **Special Needs**

**Behavioral/Social/Emotional**

If children become frustrated and act out during math time, redirect them to another, less threatening activity. Children may need to take a break in a quiet corner to calm down.

# Math Time

 large group  20 minutes

**Language and Communication Skills** Use ordinal words to give connected instructions, such as *First, sit down. Second, look at me. Third, pay attention.* *Primero, siéntense. Segundo, mírenme. Tercero, presten atención.*

 **Can children understand that ordinal words are similar to counting words?**

**Lining Up—Who's First?** Help children practice lining up. Call on five to ten children to stand in a line, one behind the other. Have the standing children count off from 1 to 10.

● After children count, gently touch each child in line and say *first, second, third, fourth primero, segundo, tercero, cuarto* and so on.

● Have children sit down and have another group line up by asking: *Who wants to be first? Second? Third? ¿Quién quiere ser el primero? ¿El segundo? ¿El tercero?* Call on children to form another line.

● Continue to review ordinal positions by asking the rest of the class who is first, fourth, sixth, eighth, or ninth in the line.

**Can children identify and use ordinal words?**

**What is First?** Remind children that they can count objects, animals, people, or events using words such as *first, second* and *third*.

● Display *Math and Science Flip Chart* page 60, "First Tree, Second Tree." Discuss the scene. Point out the beginning of the line (at the top) and the end of the line of trees.

● Put your finger on the first 5 trees and use an ordinal number as you point to each to tell its position.

● Then point to the sixth tree and tell children the ordinal number. Continue with the rest of the trees using the ordinal words *seventh, eighth, ninth,* and *tenth.*

● Ask: *How do you know which tree is seventh? Which tree is tenth? ¿Cómo saben qué árbol es el séptimo? ¿Y cómo saben cuál es el décimo?*

● Help children see that just like two always follows one, second always follows first, and so on.

**ELL** Help children equate ordinal words with numbers. Hold up one finger as you say, *One is first.* Hold up two and say, *Two is second.* Have children repeat you. Continue up to five. Repeat with the phrase *This is first* and *This is second,* and so on.

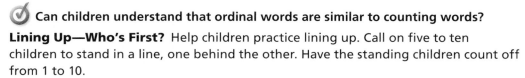

**First Tree, Second Tree**
**Primer árbol, segundo árbol**

*Math and Science Flip Chart, page 60*

# Center Time

► **Center Rotation** Center Time includes teacher-guided activities and independent activities. Refer to the **Learning Centers** on pages 138–139 for activities in additional centers.

small group | 30 minutes

## Math and Science Center

| Center Tip |
| --- |

✓ **Observe children as they identify ordinal positions.**

**Materials** 10 paper cups, marker, a counter, construction-paper squares, glue

**Where Is It?** Turn over the cups and label them from 1 to 10.

- Have children listen and repeat as you use an ordinal number to identify the position of each cup. Point to each cup as you do.

- Hide a counter under one of the cups as children close their eyes. Model how to ask where the counter is hidden: *Is the counter under the sixth cup?* *¿Está la ficha escondida debajo del sexto vaso?* Have children take turns guessing with ordinal words until the counter is found.

- Have children take turns hiding the counter for each other.

**Center Tip**

**If...**children struggle with ordinal words above *fifth,* **then...**let them play the game with only five cups and build up to more.

## Purposeful Play

✓ **Observe children's awareness of their own bodies in a space.**

Children choose an open center for free playtime. Encourage children to be respecful of each other's personal space in the centers.

## Let's Say Good-Bye

large group | 15 minutes

**Read Aloud** Revisit "A Spring Walk"/"Una caminata en primavera" from the *Teacher's Treasure Book,* page 187, for your afternoon Read Aloud. Tell children to picture the words in their minds as you read.

**Home Connection** Refer to the Home Connection activities in the chart on page 135. Remind children to use ordinal words at home with their families. Sing the "Good-bye Song" as children prepare to leave.

### Learning Goals

**Social and Emotional Development**
- Child is aware of self in terms of abilities, characteristics and preferences, and respects personal boundaries.

**Language and Communication**
- Child exhibits an understanding of instructional terms used in the classroom.

**Emergent Literacy: Writing**
- Child uses scribbles, shapes, pictures, symbols, and letters to represent language.

**Mathematics**
- Child understands and uses ordinal numbers (such as *first, second, third*) to identify position in a series.

**Technology Applications**
- Child knows some ways that technology affects people's lives.

### Writing

Recap the day. Say: *Tell me one thing you learned about caring for the earth and sky. Where else could we learn more?* *Díganme algo que hayan aprendido acerca de cuidar la Tierra y el cielo. ¿Dónde podríamos aprender más?* Encourage children to think of books, the library, and computers as sources of more information. Record children's answers on chart paper or an interactive whiteboard. Share the pen with children as you write. Children can write, scribble, or use symbols for their names beside their entries.

**Focus Question**

## Why is caring for the earth and sky important?
## ¿Por qué es importante cuidar la Tierra y el cielo?

 **Learning Goals**

**Language and Communication**
• Child communicates relevant information for the situation (for example, introduces herself; requests assistance).
• Child uses newly learned vocabulary daily in multiple contexts.
• Child understands and uses regular and irregular plural nouns, regular past tense verbs, personal and possessive pronouns, and subject-verb agreement.
• Child uses individual words and short phrases to communicate. (ELL)

### Vocabulary

| | | | |
|---|---|---|---|
| dig | cavar | forest | bosque |
| plant | plantar | shovel | pala |
| tree | árbol | | |

## Differentiated Instruction

 **Extra Support**
*Phonological Awareness*
**If...**children have difficulty segmenting words, **then...**point to the word *room* on the *Rhymes and Chants Flip Chart*. Say: **This starts with R. Say the sound for the letter R. (/r/) Now let's say the rest of the word together.** *Esto comienza con R. Digan el sonido de la letra R. (/r/) Ahora, digamos juntos el resto de la palabra.*

**Enrichment**
*Phonological Awareness*
Challenge children to segment *Ww* words sound by sound, such as *wag, we, web, wet.*

## Let's Start the Day

 **Opening Routines and Transition Tips**
For **Opening Routines** and **Transition Tips** turn to pages 178–181 and visit DLMExpressOnline.com for more ideas.

Read **"What Do Trees Give Us?"/**"¿Qué nos dan los árboles?" from the *Teacher's Treasure Book*, page 268, for your morning Read Aloud.

# Language Time

 large group 15 minutes

 **Social and Emotional Development** Ask children to tell you why they should stay still as they listen and respond without kicking their feet.

### Oral Language and Vocabulary

✓ **Can children respond to questions in complete, correct sentences?**

**Arbor Day** Ask children if any of them have ever heard of Arbor Day or Earth Day. Explain that on these special days, people plant trees and do other things to help care for Earth. Ask children why they think planting trees may be good for Earth. Remind them of all the things we use wood for.

● Display *Oral Language Development Card 70*. Point out the shovel in the picture. Ask: **Who can tell me what is happening in this picture?** *¿Quién puede decirme qué está pasando en esta imagen?* Follow the suggestions on the back of the card.

**ELL** Use *Oral Language Development Card 70* to revisit the verbs *dig* and *plant*. Use actions to demonstrate the words. Have children repeat your actions as they say the words. Ask English language learners to take turns demonstrating and articulating the words for partners during play time.

### Phonological Awareness

✓ **Can children identify two phonemes in words?**

**Segmenting Phonemes** Revisit *Rhymes and Chants Flip Chart* page 32. Remind children how they can say the initial sound for a word and follow with the rest of the word, such as by breaking *bus* into /b/, -us. Point to simple words in the text such as *car, far, ride,* and *big*. Ask volunteers to say the initial sound and then the rest of the word. Challenge children to use each word in a sentence.

*Oral Language Development Card 70*

*Rhymes and Chants Flip Chart, page 32/ page 64*

# Center Time

▶ **Center Rotation** Center Time includes teacher-guided activities and independent activities. Refer to the **Learning Centers** on pages 138–139 for activities in additional centers.

  small group 60–90 minutes

## Pretend and Learn Center

☑ **Track children's ability to share ways to care for Earth.**

**Materials** one clean but used sock per child; markers, fabric paint, fabric scraps, paper, fabric glue

**Making Sock Puppets** Give each child supplies to make a sock puppet. Explain that making puppets is one way to reuse socks that have lost their mates, have holes, or are too small. Encourage children to use their imaginations to decorate their puppets.

● Explain to children that they have just reused these socks in a new way. Ask: **Is this a good way to care for Earth? Why?** *¿Es ésta una buena manera de cuidar la Tierra? ¿Por qué?*

● Have children work in small groups to come up with a short skit about other ways to care for the earth and sky.

● Have children practice and perform their sock puppet skits. Remind them to speak loudly and clearly.

### Center Tip
**If...**children need help decorating a sock puppet, **then...** give hints by asking: *Does your puppet need eyes? A mouth? Hair? ¿El títere necesita ojos? ¿Una boca? ¿Y pelo?*

## Creativity Center

☑ **Track children's abilities to follow three-step directions.**

**Materials** chart paper, nature or garden magazines, scissors, drawing paper, crayons, glue; books about trees

**Planting a Tree Collage** Remind children that they learned that trees are important for Earth. Share that they will "plant" trees in the center by making a collage on a large sheet of paper on an easel.

● Have children *first* find pictures of trees in magazines or books that they like; *second,* cut out pictures from magazines or copy and then cut out pictures from the books; and *third,* glue their trees on the chart paper. Encourage them to find or draw all kinds of trees.

● Encourage children to show appreciation for others' work by being careful not to cover up anyone else's tree on the chart paper.

### Center Tip
**If...**children have difficulty drawing or cutting out trees, **then...**provide tree stencils that they can trace and color directly onto the collage.

## Learning Goals

**Language and Communication**
● Child follows two- and three-step oral directions.

**Emergent Literacy: Reading**
● Child enjoys and chooses reading-related activities.

**Science**
● Child knows the importance of and demonstrates ways of caring for the environment/planet.

**Fine Arts**
● Child expresses emotions or ideas through art.

● Child shares opinions about artwork and artistic experiences.

## Differentiated Instruction

 **Extra Support**
**Pretend and Learn Center**
**If...**children have difficulty thinking of a skit **then...**encourage children to think only of what the puppets can say about caring for the earth and sky.

 **Enrichment**
**Creativity Center**
Challenge children to find two different kinds of trees in magazines and cut them out. Have them tell how they are alike and different.

 **Special Needs**
**Behavioral/Social/Emotional**
**If...**children are uncomfortable working in groups, **then...**let them work in pairs. Encourage them gently to take turns and to incorporate their partners' ideas as well as their own.

# Circle Time

## Focus Question

**Why is caring for the earth and sky important?**

*¿Por qué es importante cuidar la Tierra y el cielo?*

 **Learning Goals**

**Language and Communication**
• Child demonstrates an understanding of oral language by responding appropriately.

**Emergent Literacy: Reading**
• Child names most upper- and lowercase letters of the alphabet.
• Child identifies the letter that stands for a given sound.

**Science**
• Child knows the importance of and demonstrates ways of caring for the environment/planet.

### Vocabulary

| earth | Tierra | energy | energía |
|-------|--------|--------|---------|
| recycle | reciclar | seasons | estaciones |
| soil | tierra | weather | clima |

## Differentiated Instruction

 **Extra Support**

**Read Aloud**
**If...**children have difficulty answering questions, **then...**reread the part of the book that answers the question, and ask it again.

 **Enrichment**

**Read Aloud**
Challenge children to think of other ways to care for the earth or sky that have not just been discussed. List their suggestions on chart paper.

 **Special Needs**

**Vision Loss**
Ask children to provide detailed descriptions of pictures to help sight-impaired peers imagine the pictures. Assign partners who are good at giving descriptions to this task. Encourage the sight-impaired child to help his or her partner in other ways.

## Literacy Time

📖 **Read Aloud**

 large group 15 minutes

✓ **Do children show understanding by responding appropriately?**

**Build Background** Tell children that you will be rereading a book about the earth and sky.

**Listen for Understanding** Display *Concept Big Book 4: The Earth and Sky,* and read the title. Read pages 14–16. Point to photographs as you read aloud.

● Ask: *What do you see here? What does it show you? ¿Qué ven aquí? ¿Qué muestran las fotos?*

**Respond to the Book** Have children discuss the photographs. Ask: *Why do you think the girl has the water off while she is brushing her teeth? What do you know about sharing things? Did you know we share water with everyone in the whole world? Why might it be important to save water? ¿Por qué creen que la niña no deja correr el agua mientras se cepilla los dientes? ¿Qué sabes acerca de compartir? ¿Sabías que compartimos el agua con todas las personas del mundo? ¿Por qué puede ser importante cuidar el agua?*

**TIP** Help children use the picture details by describing what is going on in each picture.

**ELL** After you read the *Concept Big Book,* write any word, letter by letter, that children had trouble understanding. Have children name each letter. Read the word and have children repeat. Explain what it means using pictorial support from the *Concept Big Book.*

## Learn About Letters and Sounds

✓ **Can children match a letter to the initial sound of a picture name?**

**Letter Match** Sing the "ABC Song" with children as you page through the *ABC Big Book.* Review the pages for *Qq, Ww,* and *Zz.* Make the appropriate letter sounds with children, and read the words on the pages aloud again.

● Give each child a sticky note with an upper and lower case *Qq, Ww,* or *Zz.*

● Show children pictures of things whose names begin with *Qq, Ww,* and *Zz,* such as wagon and zebra pictures from the Photo Library CD-ROM. Help children name the items and label the pictures with the correct initial letter.

*The Earth and Sky*
*La Tierra y el cielo*

*ABC Big Book, pages 36, 48, 54*
*Superlibro abecé*

## Building Blocks

**Online Math Activity**

Children can complete Dinosaur Shop 4 and Ordinal Construction Company during computer time or Center Time.

*Making Good Choices Flip Chart, page 32*

# Math Time

## Observe and Investigate

 **Can children quickly recognize the sum of two small groups?**

**Snapshots** This is an adding game using Vehicle Counters. Secretly put three counters in one of your hands and three in the other. Show your closed hands, open them for two seconds, and close them immediately after.

- Ask children how many counters they saw in each hand and how many counters there were altogether. Open both hands and count together to check. Repeat the process with as many counters as possible.

- Model how to make up a verbal problem for adding the counters to 5. For example: *I have 2 counters in this hand and 2 counters in the other hand. When I put the counters together, I have 4 counters altogether. Tengo dos fichas en una mano y dos fichas en la otra. Cuando pongo las fichas juntas, tengo cuatro fichas en total.*

**ELL** Use your fingers to show how to put together an addition problem as you say the numbers. Have children repeat your words and actions.

# ⚉ Social and Emotional Development

## Making Good Choices

 **Are children respectful of other children's space?**

**Being Respectful** Display *Making Good Choices Flip Chart* page 32, "How Do I Sit in Class?" Review the way the children in the picture are respecting or not respecting each other's space.

- Ask children how they can respect people's space in other situations. Then role play a situation with the Dog Puppets and ask children to comment on their correctness. For example, pretend the puppets have to stand in line. Make them stand too close and ask children to help you correct them. Ask: *Why is it important not to take up someone else's space? ¿Por qué es importante no ocupar el espacio de otros?*

- Have pairs discuss the question. Then ask volunteers to explain their reasoning to the puppets. Encourage children to think about how they themselves feel when others stand or sit too close.

- Play the song "Excuse Me"/"Permiso" from the Making Good Choices Audio CD. Ask children how selfishness can be disrespectful of others.

 **Learning Goals**

**Social and Emotional Development**
- Child is aware of self in terms of abilities, characteristics and preferences, and respects personal boundaries.

**Mathematics**
- Child tells how many are in a group of up to 5 objects without counting.
- Child uses concrete objects or makes a verbal word problem to add up to 5 objects.

## Vocabulary

| | | | |
|---|---|---|---|
| altogether | en total | count | contar |
| counters | fichas | how many | cuántos |
| respectful | respetuoso | vehicle | vehículo |

 **Differentiated Instruction**

### ✋ Extra Support
**Observe and Investigate**
**If**...children struggle with counting, **then**...only use up to 5 counters.

### ⭐ Enrichment
**Observe and Investigate**
Challenge children by using a maximum of 10 counters and repeat the game.

### Accommodations for 3's
**Observe and Investigate**
**If**...children struggle counting, **then**...just have them tell you which hand has more counters, and then count with them.

Focus Question
**Why is caring for the earth and sky important?**
**¿Por qué es importante cuidar la Tierra y el cielo?**

## Learning Goals

**Social and Emotional Development**
• Child is aware of self in terms of abilities, characteristics and preferences, and respects personal boundaries.

**Language and Communication**
• Child speaks in a way that is understood by children, teachers, or other adults.

• Child names and describes actual or pictured people, places, things, actions, attributes, and events.

• Child understands or knows the meaning of many thousands of words, many more than he or she uses.

**Social Studies**
• Child understands basic human needs for food, clothing, shelter.

• Child understands basic concepts of buying, selling, and trading.

### Vocabulary

| buy | comprar | consumer | cliente |
|-----|---------|----------|---------|
| money | dinero | pay | pagar |
| shopping | compras | | |

## Differentiated Instruction

**Extra Support**
*Understand and Participate*
**If...**children have difficulty using play money for items, **then...**let them use Farm Animal Counters to trade for items.

**Enrichment**
*Understand and Participate*
Challenge children to name items they would sell if they owned a store. Encourage them to describe each item.

# Social Studies Time

**Language and Communication Skills** Encourage children as they attempt to use new words. Assess how well their speech can be understood by you and other adults in your classroom. Offer gentle corrections and praise effort.

## Oral Language and Academic Vocabulary

✓ **Can children understand why people shop?**

**Talking About Shopping** Ask children if they have ever gone to a store with an adult. Have those children share their experiences. Display clean or play food containers, such as children might see in a store.

• Ask: *Which items would you buy at a store? What does everyone need that you might buy?* (food, clothing) *¿Qué artículos comprarían en una tienda? ¿Qué cosas que necesita todo el mundo podrían comprar? Where can you go to buy bread or flour? ¿Dónde comprarían pan o harina?*

• Explain that most everything we use at school or home comes from a store, and many things come to stores from the earth. Use the *Sequence Card* set "From Field to Table" to illustrate this. Explain to children that an important reason to care for Earth is that it gives us so many things that we need.

Sequence Cards: *"From Field to Table"*

**ELL** Invite children to bring in or draw a picture of special foods that their families buy. Have children describe the items and how they are used.

## Understand and Participate

✓ **Can children understand what it means to be a consumer?**

**Let's Go Shopping** Display appropriate toys for playing "store," such as a cash register, play money, recycled grocery bags, play food, and empty cartons. Explain that a consumer is someone who uses and buys things, like food. Since everyone eats, everyone is a consumer.

• Assign children roles: cashiers, store workers and shoppers. Label the items with colors for prices. Distribute colored play money to each child.

• Tell children that if they want to buy an item, they should look for the color sticker that tells its price. They can only buy an item if they can match the sticker to the color of their play money. As a challenge, ask if children can recognize the numbers printed on their play money.

• Have children take turns shopping for items. Ask: *What did you buy? Did you have enough money to buy all that you wanted? ¿Qué compraste? ¿Tenías suficiente dinero para comprar todo lo que querías?*

• Discuss and record children's shopping experience on chart paper.

# Center Time

▶ **Center Rotation** Center Time includes teacher-guided activities and independent activities. Refer to the **Learning Centers** on pages 138–139 for activities in additional centers.

 **small group** **30 minutes**

## Construction Center

**Center Tip**

 **Monitor children as they make and describe a store.**

**Materials** blocks, books, toys, crayons, paper

**Build a Store** Tell children to use blocks to build a bookstore or a toy store. Have children work in small groups. Ask: *What kind of store will you build? ¿Qué tipo de tienda harán?* Say: *Make a sign for your store. Hagan un letrero para su tienda.*

- Have children describe their store and explain their decisions.

- Invite children to visit each other's stores and play buying and looking for items.

**If...**children need help sharing the blocks and materials, **then...** assign each child a part to build.

## Purposeful Play

 **Observe children as they work in pairs or small groups.**

Children choose an open center for free playtime. Encourage children to pretend that they are shopping at a store. Remind children to respect each other and allow room for all.

# Let's Say Good-Bye

 **large group** **15 minutes**

**Read Aloud** Revisit "What Do Trees Give Us?"/"¿Qué nos dan los árboles?" for your afternoon Read Aloud. Tell children that people plant trees as a way of replacing what we take from the earth.

**Home Connection** Refer to the Home Connection activities listed in the Materials and Resources chart on page 135. Remind children to tell their families what they did in the play store in Social Studies Time. Sing the "Good-bye Song" as children prepare to leave.

## Learning Goals

**Social and Emotional Development**
- Child is aware of self in terms of abilities, characteristics and preferences, and respects personal boundaries.

**Language and Communication**
- Child names and describes actual or pictured people, places, things, actions, attributes, and events.

**Social Studies**
- Child understands basic concepts of buying, selling, and trading.

**Technology Applications**
- Child knows some ways that technology affects people's lives.

## Writing

Recap the day. Have children name something they would like to buy. Ask: *What do you need to buy something? Where would you go to buy it? ¿Por qué necesitan comprar eso? ¿Adónde irían a comprarlo?* Then ask: *If you wanted something but didn't know where to get it, how could you learn more? Si quieren comprar algo pero no saben dónde se vende, ¿cómo podrían averiguarlo?* Encourage children to think of technology, such as the internet or a phone, for finding information. Ask children to draw a picture of something they would buy and label it.

# DAY 4

**Focus Question**

**Why is caring for the earth and sky important?**
**¿Por qué es importante cuidar la Tierra y el cielo?**

## ✓ Learning Goals

**Social and Emotional Development**
• Child is aware of self in terms of abilities, characteristics and preferences, and respects personal boundaries.

**Language and Communication**
• Child demonstrates an understanding of oral language by responding appropriately.

• Child follows basic rules for conversations (taking turns, staying on topic, listening actively).

**Emergent Literacy: Reading**
• Child combines two words to form a compound word.

• Child removes one word from a compound word.

### Vocabulary

folk   folclórico   folktale   cuento folclórico

make-believe   fantasía   real   real

retold   volver a contar   tale   cuento

## Differentiated Instruction

 **Extra Support**

**Oral Language and Vocabulary**
**If…**children have difficulty understanding the concept of folktales, **then…**explain that they are stories that have been retold for many, many years because people enjoy them.

 **Enrichment**

**Oral Language and Vocabulary**
Have children work in small groups to look at illustrated folktales. Invite them to talk about what they see happening in the pictures.

# Let's Start the Day

 **Opening Routines and Transition Tips**

For **Opening Routines** and **Transition Tips** turn to pages 178–181 and visit **DLMExpressOnline.com** for more ideas.

📖 Read **"My Grandmother's Garden"/**"El jardín de mi abuela" from the *Teacher's Treasure Book*, page 266, for your morning Read Aloud.

## Language Time

 large group   15 minutes

👫👫 **Social and Emotional Development** Assess learning by asking children why it's important to give their classmates enough space as they work.

### Oral Language and Vocabulary

✓ **Can children understand a folktale?**

**Folktales** Remind children that they learned about real and make-believe stories. Tell children that today they are going to learn about folktales.

● Explain that a folktale is a favorite tale, or story, that people tell. Folktales are usually make-believe, but they can have real parts. Ask: *What word can we make by deleting a word from the word* folktale? (folk) *What two words can we put together to make the word* folktale? *¿Qué palabra podemos formar si le quitamos una palabra a* folktale? *¿Qué dos palabras tenemos que unir para formar* folktale?

● Explain that people like to tell folktales over again, so stories can be retold for many years. Name a story children are familiar with, such as "Cinderella." Share that you learned that story as a child too.

● Ask: *What kind of story do you like to tell or pass on to a friend? What would it be about? ¿Qué cuento les gustaría contarle a un amigo? ¿De qué se trataría?*

### Phonological Awareness

✓ **Can children segment words by individual phonemes?**

**Segmenting Phonemes** Display the Dog Puppets. Have pairs of children hold the puppets. Whisper a word, such as *not,* in one child's ear. Have the child say the word aloud to his or her puppet.

● Ask the other child, *What is the first sound you hear in the word* not? *¿Cuál es el primer sonido que escuchas en la palabra* not? Repeat with the medial sound. Then ask the first child to supply the last sound in the three-phoneme word.

● Repeat, having children take turns, with words such as *up, it, bag,* and *car.* Provide corrective feedback as needed.

 Display labeled picture cards of a bed, cat, leg, fan and map. Have children segment words with pictorial support.

# Center Time

▶ **Center Rotation** Center Time includes teacher-guided activities and independent activities. Refer to the **Learning Centers** on pages 138–139 for activities in additional centers.

 small group  60–90 minutes

## ABC Center

 **Track children's knowledge of letters and their sounds.**

**Materials** two sets of Alphabet Letter/Tiles

**Play Concentration** Play a version of the game "Concentration."

● Place the tiles face up in random order on the table.

● Give each child a tile and have him or her find the matching tile.

● When all the tiles are matched, have children trace their letters with their fingers.

● Call on each child to say the sound of his or her letters.

### Center Tip

**If...**children have difficulty matching letters to the random tiles, **then...**place the tiles in ABC order.

## Library and Listening Center

 **Track understanding of traditional folktales.**

 **Track understanding of the intonation of English recordings.**

**Materials** illustrated children's books of folktales, audio recordings of folktales

**Browsing Books** Have children browse through other folktale books and listen to folktale recordings. Have children discuss the illustrations with a partner and share what they think is happening in the stories.

● Ask: W*hich is your favorite book or recorded story? Why? ¿Cuál es su libro favorito o su grabación favorita? ¿Por qué?* List children's responses on a Book Log for future reference.

### Center Tip

**If...**children have difficulty listening to stories on CDs, **then...**provide headphones so children can concentrate.

## ✓ Learning Goals

**Language and Communication**
● Child experiments with and produces a growing number of sounds in English words. (ELL)

● Child uses newly learned vocabulary daily in multiple contexts.

**Emergent Literacy: Reading**
● Child names most upper- and lowercase letters of the alphabet.

● Child identifies the letter that stands for a given sound.

## Differentiated Instruction

### ✋ Extra Support
**ABC Center**
**If...**children have difficulty identifying the sound of their letters, **then...**have them say the sounds with you.

### ⭐ Enrichment
**Library and Listening Center**
Have children choose a favorite folktale that they read or listened to and then draw a picture of their favorite character.

### Accommodations for 3's
**ABC Center**
**If...**children have difficulty matching all the letters, **then...**play the game with fewer tiles. Repeat with another group until all letters are matched.

**Focus Question**
## Why is caring for the earth and sky important?
## ¿Por qué es importante cuidar la Tierra y el cielo?

## Learning Goals

**Language and Communication**
• Child demonstrates an understanding of oral language by responding appropriately.

• Child uses nonverbal cues to communicate with others who do not speak his or her home language. (ELL)

**Emergent Literacy: Reading**
• Child combines two words to form a compound word.

• Child removes one word from a compound word.

• Child names most upper- and lowercase letters of the alphabet.

• Child identifies the letter that stands for a given sound.

## Vocabulary

| | | | |
|---|---|---|---|
| afraid | temeroso | country | país |
| journey | viaje | planting | plantar |
| seeds | semillas | weather | tiempo |

## Differentiated Instruction

### Extra Support

**Learn About Letters and Sounds**
**If...**children have difficulty identifying certain sounds, **then...**model correct mouth positions and have them repeat the sounds after you.

### Enrichment

**Learn About Letters and Sounds**
Distribute photos from the Photo Library CD-ROM of objects or animals beginning with *Qq*, *Ww*, and *Zz*. Children can sort the photos by initial sound.

### Special Needs

**Delayed Motor Development**

**If...**children cannot trace letters in the air, **then...**let them trace in sand or shaving cream.

# Literacy Time

large group · 15 minutes

### 📖 Read Aloud

✓ Can children listen and respond appropriately to a story read aloud?

✓ Can children delete words from or combine words into compound words?

**Build Background** Tell children that you will be reading a folktale about a man who planted trees. Ask children what a folktale is.

● Ask: *What different trees can you name? What do trees give us?* *¿Qué tres tipos de árboles conocen? ¿Qué nos dan los árboles?*

● Say: *Think about Johnny Appleseed's name. What does it mean? What two words can we put together to make the word* appleseed? *What word do we get if we delete part of* appleseed? *Piensen en el nombre de Johnny Appleseed (Juan Semillita). ¿Qué dos palabras podemos unir para formar* appleseed? *¿Qué palabra nos queda si quitamos una parte de* appleseed? Tell children to listen to find out what Johnny Appleseed does in the story and how he helps the earth.

**Listen for Enjoyment** Read aloud "The Story of Johnny Appleseed" from the *Teacher's Treasure Book*, page 272. Use the flannel board patterns.

**Respond to the Story** Encourage children to ask questions about the story and to relate their favorite parts to the group.

● Ask: *How did Johnny get the nickname Johnny Appleseed? What did Johnny plant that made trees grow? How did he go from place to place?* *¿Cómo se ganó Juan el sobrenombre de "Juan Semillita"? ¿Qué hizo Juan para que crecieran los árboles? ¿Cómo iba de un lugar a otro?*

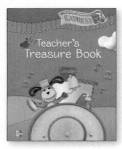

*Teacher's Treasure Book, page 272*

## Learn About Letters and Sounds

✓ Can children identify sounds /kw/, /w/, and /z/ and letters *Qq*, *Ww*, and *Zz*?

**Form Qq, Ww, and Zz** Remind children that they have learned about the sounds and different ways to write *Qq*, *Ww*, and *Zz*.

● Ask children to help you name a word that starts with *Qq*. Say: */kw/, /kw/, is for* **Q** as you show them the proper formation of upper- and lowercase *Qq* on chart paper or an interactive whiteboard.

● Have children trace the letters in the air or on their palms after you have formed them. Then invite a volunteer to come circle uppercase *Q* and another to circle lowercase *q* on the paper or interactive whiteboard.

● Repeat for upper- and lowercase *Ww* and *Zz* as time allows.

 Pair an English learner with a native English speaker to circle the letter and say its sound.

**Online Math Activity**

Children can complete Dinosaur Shop 4 and Ordinal Construction Company during computer time or Center Time.

# Math Time

 large group 15 minutes

### Observe and Investigate

☑ **Can children use concrete models for adding up to 5 objects?**

**Vehicle Shop (Make It Right)** Show children a box with four Vehicle Counters. Tell them you want five, and ask them to help you do so. Follow their suggestions, and count to check.

● Give children their own boxes (or they can cup their hands) and Vehicle Counters. Have them put two vehicles in a box. Tell children the customer wants three vehicles, and ask how they can make it three.

● Check what strategy children use to make it right. Do they add on, counting up from the starting number? Do they have to count from 1 each time? Do they know what number to add on, or are they using trial and error?

● Have children use ordinal terms to tell you what they did first, second, and third to make the right number.

**ELL** Work on ordinal words and the term *vehicle* with children. Display up to five Vehicle Counters as you say, **First vehicle, second vehicle, third vehicle. Which is the second vehicle?** Have children repeat you, answer by pointing, and finish with "This is the second vehicle." Repeat up to *fifth*.

## ⋔⋔ Social and Emotional Development

 large group 15 minutes

### Making Good Choices

☑ **Do children observe physical boundaries?**

**Being Respectful** Display a Dog Puppet. Say: **The puppet needs help recalling what we've learned about respecting each other's space this week.** *El títere necesita ayuda para recordar qué hemos aprendido esta semana acerca de respetar el espacio de otros.*

● Divide children into three groups. Differentiate the groups so the most advanced children are in group three (their topic is an extension of learning so far this week).

● Have the groups discuss the respectful way to: (group one) sit in class, (group two) stand in line, or (group three) work in centers.

● After children have a chance to discuss in their small groups, ask volunteers from each group to explain to the puppet and the large group what their small groups decided.

### Learning Goals

**Social and Emotional Development**
● Child is aware of self in terms of abilities, characteristics and preferences, and respects personal boundaries.

**Mathematics**
● Child understands and uses ordinal numbers (such as *first, second, third*) to identify position in a series.

● Child uses concrete objects or makes a verbal word problem to add up to 5 objects.

### Vocabulary

| add | añadir | counters | fichas |
| count up | contar | customer | cliente |
| shop | tienda | vehicle | vehículo |

### Differentiated Instruction

✋ **Extra Support**
Observe and Investigate
**If...**children have difficulty during Vehicle Shop, **then...**pose problems where the target number is only one more than the starting number.

⭐ **Enrichment**
Observe and Investigate
Challenge children by increasing the number to add by, or alternate posing subtraction problems where the target number is less than the starting number.

**Learning Goals**

**Social and Emotional Development**
• Child is aware of self in terms of abilities, characteristics and preferences, and respects personal boundaries.

**Language and Communication**
• Child exhibits an understanding of instructional terms used in the classroom.

**Mathematics**
• Child understands and uses ordinal numbers (such as *first, second, third*) to identify position in a series.
• Child uses concrete objects or makes a verbal word problem to add up to 5 objects.

## Vocabulary

| | | | |
|---|---|---|---|
| altogether | en total | fifth | quinto |
| first | primero | fourth | cuarto |
| second | segundo | sixth | sexto |
| third | tercero | | |

## Differentiated Instruction

 **Extra Support**

**Math Time**

**If...**children have difficulty using ordinal numbers, **then...**have them count the crackers first using counting numbers.

**Enrichment**

**Math Time**

Challenge children to do subtraction problems by having them eat only some of the crackers they have and asking how many are still in the lake.

**Accommodations for 3's**

**Math Time**

**If...**children eat the fish crackers before counting them, **then...**ask the first question before you distribute any, and distribute additional crackers only as you ask additional questions.

# Math Time

large group / 20 minutes

**Language and Communication Skills** After you model using ordinal numbers, ask children to use ordinal numbers to retell the steps you took to demonstrate the activity.

 **Can children understand and use ordinal numbers correctly?**

**Talk About Ordinal Numbers** Have six children line up in a row. Remind them to line up and stand following their rules for respecting each other's space.

● Point to the first child and say his or name in this sentence: *(Child's name) is first in line/ es el primero o la primera en la fila*. Ask the children seated: *Who is the second child in line? ¿Quién es el segundo o la segunda?*

● Point to the third child and continue.

● Repeat with other children using ordinal positions up to tenth.

**ELL** Display five paper cups numbered 1 to 5. Have children listen as you name the order of the cups aloud, using counting numbers. Then point to each cup as you say the corresponding ordinal number. Have children repeat. For additional suggestions on how to meet the needs of children at the Beginning, Intermediate, Advanced, and Advanced-High levels of English proficiency, see pages 184–187.

 **Can children use concrete models for adding up to 5 objects?**

**Can children identify an object in an ordinal position?**

**Gone Fishing** Tell children that they will pretend to be dinosaurs that eat fish. Distribute five to ten fish crackers per child and have children use blue construction paper as their lake. Tell them not to put the fish in the lake yet.

● Ask: *How many fish are in your lake now?* (zero) *¿Cuántos peces hay en el lago ahora?* Tell them three fish swam near the "dinosaur," and have them add three fish to the "lake."

● Say that two more fish swam near, and have children add two more fish. Ask: *How many fish are there altogether now? ¿Cuántos peces hay en total?* Explain that the dinosaur is going to eat the five fish slowly. Have children eat the crackers one at a time, as you say: *The dinosaur ate the first fish. Then it ate the second fish, El dinosaurio se comió el primer pez. Luego, se comió el segundo pez* and so on.

● After all five crackers are eaten ask: *How many fish are in the lake now? ¿Cuántos peces hay en el lago ahora?* (zero)

● Continue the story, adding various amounts and using ordinal numbers as modeled above, for whatever numbers you wish to review.

**Building Blocks**

**Online Math Activity**

Children can complete Dinosaur Shop 4 and Ordinal Construction Company during computer time or Center Time.

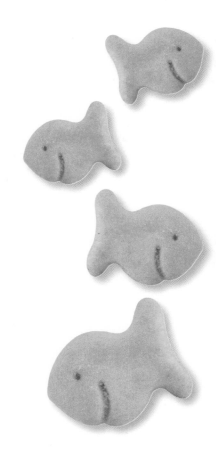

# Center Time

▶ **Center Rotation** Center Time includes teacher-guided activities and independent activities. Refer to the **Learning Centers** on pages 138–139 for activities in additional centers.

  small group · 30 minutes

## Creativity Center

**Center Tip**

✓ **Track children's ability to add up to 5 objects.**

**Materials** red, green, and yellow paint, small circle sponges, construction paper, crayons

**Apple Stories** Show how to sponge-print a line of 1 red and 3 green circles (not touching) to show apples that have fallen on the ground.

- Have children sponge-print a line of 5 circles in any 2 colors and write 5 to show the number of circles. Have children describe how they made 5 from 2 colors. Repeat with another number.

- Encourage children to draw a tree or other details with crayons.

**If...**children need help deciding how many to make red and how many green or yellow, **then...**have them model making 5 using two-color counters.

## ✓ Learning Goals

**Social and Emotional Development**
- Child is aware of self in terms of abilities, characteristics and preferences, and respects personal boundaries.

**Language and Communication**
- Child names and describes actual or pictured people, places, things, actions, attributes, and events.

**Mathematics**
- Child uses concrete objects or makes a verbal word problem to add up to 5 objects.

**Technology Applications**
- Child opens and correctly uses age-appropriate software programs.

- Child names and uses various computer parts (such as mouse, keyboard, CD-ROM, microphone, touch screen).

## Purposeful Play

✓ **Observe children navigating software applications while naming and using hardware.**

Children choose an open center for free playtime. Encourage them to use the computers to work on the math activities. Periodically ask them to name hardware and uses by asking: *What is this called? What do you use this for?* *¿Cómo se llama esto? ¿Para que lo usan?*

## Writing

Recap the day. Have children tell details about Johnny Appleseed. Ask: *Do you think Johnny Appleseed was a nice man? Why do you think people retell his folktale? What kind of trees did he plant?* *¿Piensan que Juan Semillita fue un hombre amigable? ¿Por qué la gente relata este cuento folclórico? ¿Qué tipo de árboles plantó?* Record their answers. Read them back as you track the print, and emphasize the correspondence between speech and print.

# Let's Say Good-Bye

  large group · 15 minutes

 **Read Aloud** Revisit "My Grandmother's Garden"/"El jardín de mi abuela" for your afternoon Read Aloud. Remind children to listen for what in the story comes from the earth and to think about why a garden should be free of litter.

 **Home Connection** Refer to the Home Connection activities listed in the Materials and Resources chart on page 135. Remind children to tell families about what they did *first, second,* and *third* today. Sing the "Good-bye Song" as children prepare to leave.

## DAY 5

# Let's Start the Day

**Focus Question**
**Why is caring for the earth and sky important?**
*¿Por qué es importante cuidar la Tierra y el cielo?*

### Learning Goals

**Social and Emotional Development**
• Child is aware of self in terms of abilities, characteristics and preferences, and respects personal boundaries.

**Language and Communication**
• Child begins and ends conversations appropriately.

**Science**
• Child knows the importance of and demonstrates ways of caring for the environment/planet.

### Vocabulary

| | | | |
|---|---|---|---|
| Earth | Tierra | plastic | plástico |
| recycle | reciclar | toss | lanzar |
| trash | basura | world | mundo |

### Differentiated Instruction

 **Extra Support**
**Oral Language and Vocabulary**
**If...**children have difficulty answering the questions, **then...**use picture clues and read the sentence from the rhyme that answers the question. Then have children respond.

 **Enrichment**
**Oral Language and Vocabulary**
Encourage children to work in pairs. Have pairs choose two sentences from the rhyme to learn and recite to the class.

---

 **Opening Routines and Transition Tips**
For **Opening Routines** and **Transition Tips** turn to pages 178–181 and visit **DLMExpressOnline.com** for more ideas.

Read **"Animal Homes"/**"Hogares de animales" from the *Teacher's Treasure Book*, page 238, for your morning Read Aloud.

# Language Time

 large group · 15 minutes

 **Social and Emotional Development** Assess learning by asking children how they plan to respect others today.

## Oral Language and Vocabulary

**Our Beautiful Earth**

Our beautiful Earth is a wonderful place.
It's like a big house, but built out in space!
Earth is a place we all want to keep clean,
The prettiest planet that we've ever seen!
So turn off the lights before leaving a room.
Gather the trash with a swish of a broom.
Recycle plastic. Don't toss it away!
Save plastic bags to use some other day.
Ask Mom to consider, instead of the car,
A train or a bus when you go near or far.

*Rhymes and Chants Flip Chart, page 32/ page 64*

**Can children respond to questions appropriately?**
**Our Earth** Talk about what children have learned this week about taking care of the earth and sky. Ask: **What do we get from the earth and sky? Who uses things that come from the earth? Who needs a clean earth besides people? What can we do to keep the earth and sky clean?** *¿Qué saben acerca de la Tierra y el cielo? ¿Quiénes usan las cosas que vienen de la Tierra? ¿Quiénes, además de las personas, necesitan un planeta limpio? ¿Qué podemos hacer para para mantener limpios la Tierra y el cielo?*

● Display *Rhymes and Chants Flip Chart* page 32. Read "Our Beautiful Earth" to children. Ask: **Why do you think the poem tells ways to keep Earth beautiful?** *¿Por qué creen el poema habla de las maneras en que podemos mantener la belleza de la Tierra?* Recite the poem again, asking children to join in where they can.

● Ask: **What should you do to lights when you leave a room? What should you do with a plastic bottle?** *¿Qué deben hacer con las luces cuando salen de una habitación? ¿Qué deben hacer con los las botellas plásticas vacías?*

**ELL** As you finish reading a sentence, point to the illustrations to clarify what you read. Show a globe to demonstrate the word *world*.

## Phonological Awareness

**Can children segment words into individual phonemes?**
**Segmenting Phonemes** Remind children that all words are made up of different sounds.

● Ask: **What is the first sound in the word** bus? **What is the second sound? What is the last sound?** *¿Cuál es el primer sonido en la palabra* bus? *¿Cuál es el segundo sonido? ¿Cuál es el último sonido?*

● Have children hold up a finger for each sound they make for *bus*. Ask: **How many sounds is that?** *¿Cuántos sonidos hay?*

● Repeat with the words *bag* and *big*.

# Center Time

▶ **Center Rotation** Center Time includes teacher-guided activities and independent activities. Refer to the **Learning Centers** on pages 138–139 for activities in additional centers.

 small group 60–90 minutes

## Creativity Center

| | Center Tip |
|---|---|

✓ **Monitor children as they decorate a box reusing materials.**

**Materials** old boxes, buttons, bottle caps, newspapers, fabric scraps, glitter, paint, glue

**Treasure Box** Explain to children that they will make their own recycled treasure boxes where they can keep their own "treasures."

- Display the materials. Every child gets a box. Have children use their imaginations to decorate their boxes.

- Encourage children to show their completed boxes and talk about what they reused to decorate them. Ask each child to tell one thing he or she likes about a classmate's box.

- Invite children to talk about what they may keep in their treasure boxes. Children can take their boxes home.

**Center Tip**

**If...**children have difficulty gluing materials onto their boxes, **then...**pair them with children who can help hold materials in place until the glue sticks.

## Writer's Center

**Center Tip**

✓ **Track children's ability to tell and write about their pictures.**

**Materials** drawing paper, crayons

**Our World Pictures** Have children think of other things they can do to care for the earth and sky.

- Have children draw a picture of one thing they would do to keep the earth and sky clean. Have them write their first name at the top of the page.

- Say: **Tell me about your picture.** *Cuéntenme algo acerca de su dibujo.* Write children's responses (a word or a phrase) in pencil block letters. Have children trace over the letters with a crayon and repeat the word or phrase with you.

**Center Tip**

**If...**children have difficulty drawing pictures of actions, **then...**let them draw objects that they have learned are on the earth and in the sky.

---

### ✓ Learning Goals

**Language and Communication**
- Child names and describes actual or pictured people, places, things, actions, attributes, and events.

**Emergent Literacy: Writing**
- Child uses scribbles, shapes, pictures, symbols, and letters to represent language.
- Child experiments with and uses some writing conventions when writing or dictating.

**Fine Arts**
- Child expresses emotions or ideas through art.
- Child shares opinions about artwork and artistic experiences.

---

### Differentiated Instruction

 **Extra Support**
**Writer's Center**
**If...**children have difficulty tracing the letters with a crayon, **then...**let them trace just with their fingers.

 **Enrichment**
**Writer's Center**
Challenge children each to make up a sentence about the picture. Encourage children to write/scribble or dictate their sentences to you.

**Accommodations for 3's**
**Writer's Center**
**If...**children have difficulty writing their names, **then...**write each child's first name on the paper and have the child trace over the letters.

# Circle Time

## Literacy Time

 large group — 15 minutes

### Read Aloud

✓ Can children ask and answer appropriate questions about the book?

✓ Do children demonstrate the importance of caring for our environment?

**Build Background** Tell children that you will reread the story about Ada.

- Ask: **Who is Ada? What does she do?** *¿Quién es Ada? ¿Qué hace?*

**Listen for Understanding** Display *Ada, Once Again!* and read the title.

- Reread pages 18–27. Discuss what Ada is trying to do and why.

- Ask: **Look at the picture. How does it show Ada being unsteady? How does Ada glide? Why does Ada want to be useful?** *¿Cómo muestra que Ada está insegura? ¿Cómo se desliza Ada? ¿Por qué Ada quiere ser útil?*

**Respond and Connect** Have children connect their new learning to their daily lives. Ask: **How do you help the earth? Would you pick up trash in your yard or on the school playground and throw it away? Why? What do you do to help care for the earth and sky?** *¿Cómo pueden ayudar a cuidar el planeta? ¿Recogen basura del jardín o del patio de juegos de la escuela y la tiran? ¿Por qué? ¿Qué hacen para ayudar a cuidar la Tierra y el cielo?*

**TIP** Help children use picture details to tell how Ada is sad and tries to break free from the tree.

*Ada, Once Again!*
*¡Otra vez Ada!*

## Learning Goals

**Emergent Literacy: Reading**
- Child names most upper- and lowercase letters of the alphabet.
- Child identifies the letter that stands for a given sound.
- Child asks and answers questions about books read aloud (such as "Who?" "What?" "Where?").

**Science**
- Child knows the importance of and demonstrates ways of caring for the environment/planet.

### Vocabulary

| | | | |
|---|---|---|---|
| another | otro | glides | deslizarse |
| glistens | brillante | ready | listo |
| stuck | atrapada | unsteady | insegura |
| yelling | gritar | | |

## Differentiated Instruction

### 🖐 Extra Support

**Learn About Letters and Sounds**
**If...**children have difficulty saying the letter sound, **then...**say the picture name and emphasize the beginning letter sound.

### ⭐ Enrichment

**Learn About Letters and Sounds**
Give each child two large index cards. Have children copy two words from the story, one on each card. Children then say the words and start a Word Wall or add to a Word Wall. Add other words each day.

### 💜 Special Needs

**Vision Loss**
Assign children to seeing partners for the letter review. The partner names the picture on the card, and the child with special needs supplies the letter and letter sound.

## Learn About Letters and Sounds

✓ Can children identify at least 20 letters and letter sounds?

**Review Letters and Sounds** Play a game called "Name It, Take It" with children. Mix up the *ABC Picture Cards* and place them in a stack facedown on a table.

- Call on a child to come up and pick the first card. If the child names the letter correctly and says its sound, the card goes at the bottom of the pack.

- If the child cannot name the letter, read the word that begins with it, drawing out the sound. If the child still cannot name the letter after the prompt, he or she keeps the card.

- Repeat until are cards are named or taken.

- Later, use the cards children have kept for individualized review.

**ELL** Have children trace their letters in a tactile material such as sand or shaving cream as they say the sound with you. For additional suggestions on how to meet the needs of children at the Beginning, Intermediate, Advanced, and Advanced-High levels of English proficiency, see pages 184–187.

*ABC Picture Cards*
*Tarjetas abecé de imágenes*

large group 15 minutes

**Online Math Activity**

Children can complete Ordinal Construction Company and Dinosaur Shop 4 during computer time or Center Time.

# Math Time

## Observe and Investigate

✓ **Can children describe numbers and actions with the verbal ordinal terms?**

**Making 5** Display a hula hoop and 5 sets of objects: 5 bean bags, 5 counters, 5 crayons. Tell children they are going to show ways to make 5.

● Make a "throw line" on the floor with masking tape. Explain that you will try to get all 5 objects inside the hoop, but it's OK if some fall outside.

● Stand at the line and throw the objects one at a time. After each throw ask: *Where did the first bean bag land? Where did the second bean bag land? ¿Dónde cayó la primera bolsa de frijoles? ¿Dónde cayó la segunda?*

● Then ask: *How many bean bags are in the hoop? Let's count. How many are outside of the hoop? How many bean bags did I throw altogether? ¿Cuántas bolsas cayeron dentro del aro? Vamos a contar. ¿Cuántas cayeron fuera del aro? ¿Cuántas tiré en total?* (5)

● Call on children to take turns making 5 in the hoop with different objects, and describe where objects land using ordinal terms.

● Have children draw a picture of what they did.

**ELL** Show 4 paper clips of a single color and 1 of another color. Ask: *How many clips are there? Let's count. Now I will add 1.* Choose the second color. Ask: *How many are there altogether?* Have children make a chain of 5.

large group 15 minutes

*Making Good Choices Flip Chart, page 32*

# 👥 Social and Emotional Development

## Making Good Choices

✓ **Are children respectful of each other's space?**

**Being Respectful** Display *Making Good Choices Flip Chart* page 32. Ask: *What did we learn about how to respect other people's spaces? When is it important to respect each other's space? Is it only important at school? ¿Qué hemos aprendido acerca de cómo respetar el espacio de otros? ¿Cuándo es importante respetar el espacio de otros? ¿Sólo en la escuela?*

● Ask children to re-enact the illustration showing the correct way to use their bodies around others.

● Allow children to pick a song from the Making Good Choices Audio CD that they think tells the best message about being respectful.

---

## Learning Goals

**Social and Emotional Development**
• Child is aware of self in terms of abilities, characteristics and preferences, and respects personal boundaries.

**Mathematics**
• Child understands and uses ordinal numbers (such as *first, second, third*) to identify position in a series.

• Child uses concrete objects or makes a verbal word problem to add up to 5 objects.

## Vocabulary

| | | | |
|---|---|---|---|
| fifth | quinto | first | primero |
| fourth | cuarto | how many | cuántos |
| second | segundo | third | tercero |

## Differentiated Instruction

✋ **Extra Support**
**Observe and Investigate**
**If...**children have difficulty identifying how many objects are in the hoop, **then...**give them a colored paper square for every item in the hoop. Repeat for objects outside the hoop using a different colored square.

⭐ **Enrichment**
**Observe and Investigate**
Challenge children by having them make up a story about their hoop pictures.

💛 **Special Needs**
**Cognitive Challenges**
**If...**children struggle with making five, **then...**have them make three.

Focus Question
## Why is caring for the earth and sky important?
## ¿Por qué es importante cuidar la Tierra y el cielo?

 **Learning Goals**

**Social and Emotional Development**
• Child is aware of self in terms of abilities, characteristics and preferences, and respects personal boundaries.

**Language and Communication**
• Child follows two- and three-step oral directions.

**Science**
• Child knows the importance of and demonstrates ways of caring for the environment/planet.

**Fine Arts**
• Child expresses thoughts, feelings, and energy through music and creative movement.

**Physical Development**
• Child coordinates body movements in a variety of locomotive activities (such as walking, jumping, running, hopping, skipping, climbing).
• Child engages in a sequence of movements to perform a task.

### Vocabulary

| | | | |
|---|---|---|---|
| bins | bote | move | mover |
| outdoor | aire libre | recycling | reciclar |
| reusing | reutilizar | trash | basura |

 **Differentiated Instruction**

 **Extra Support**
*Move and Learn*
**If...**children have difficulty hopping on one foot, **then...**let them just jump. Provide positive feedback as they move.

**Enrichment**
*Move and Learn*
Make a straight line with masking tape on the floor or a chalk line outside on the playground. Have children walk on the line; then walk on tiptoes on the line, then crisscross, and so on.

# Outdoor Play

large group 20 minutes

**Personal Safety Skills** Model how to use any indoor or outdoor play equipment properly. Ask children to tell you their rules for safe play.

## Oral Language and Academic Vocabulary

 **Can children tell how and why to care for Earth?**

**Caring for the Outdoors** Take children outdoors for a discussion of caring for the earth and sky. Remind them that they learned about ways to reuse things or steps to take to help care for Earth and keep it clean.

● Ask: *What things can you do to help care for the earth and sky? ¿Qué pueden hacer para ayudar a cuidar la Tierra y el cielo?* (turn off lights, ask to take busses or walk places, throw trash away) *Why is this important? ¿Por qué esto es importante?* (living things need/like a clean Earth; Earth gives us many things)

● Point out trash bins or recycling bins outside around the playground. Ask children to think about whether the area looks clean or dirty. Ask: *Does it look like people are using the bins the right way? How do recycling and reusing help care for the earth? ¿Creen que la gente está usando los botes correctamente? ¿Por qué si reciclamos y volvemos a usar objetos ayudamos a cuidar la Tierra?*

**ELL** Display *Oral Language Development Card* or Photo Library CD-ROM photos to discuss ways to help Earth. Have children tell what they see.

## Move and Learn

✓ **Can children show mastery of gross motor skills?**

**Let's Play Games** Tell children that they will play games where they can run and walk or dance and move their bodies in different ways.

● Provide a large open space for play. Tell children to listen carefully and follow directions to play games.

● Introduce games such as "Follow the Leader." Children can take turns being the leader as they walk slowly, walk fast, hop on one foot, walk moving from side to side, and so on.

● Play music and let children dance or play musical chairs.

● Play other games that include motor activities such as "Red Light, Green Light," "Freeze Tag," and relay races (where children pass a ball under their legs or over their heads and run to a specific spot).

**TIP** Modify activities according to the needs of individual children.

# Center Time

▶ **Center Rotation** Center Time includes teacher-guided activities and independent activities. Refer to the **Learning Centers** on pages 138–139 for activities in additional centers.

small group    30 minutes

## Construction Center

| | Center Tip |

✓ **Monitor children as they make a recycling center.**

**Materials** boxes, blocks, recyclable materials, index cards, markers

**Build a Recycling Center** Tell children that they will use blocks, empty boxes, and other art materials to build a recycling center. If possible, take a trip to a recycling center, show pictures, or explain that there are special containers and trucks for different materials: newspaper and magazines, glass and plastic, paper and cardboard.

**Center Tip**

**If...**children have difficulty planning their construction, **then...**show them pictures of recycling centers to give them guidance.

- Have children work in pairs to build one kind of container. Help children label their construction. Allow more than one of the same kind of container. Have children describe what they made.

- Make a big sign for "Our Class Recycling Center," and have children decorate it using found objects such as for their treasure boxes.

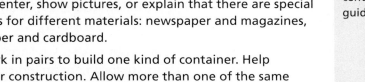

## Purposeful Play

✓ **Observe children's awareness of personal boundaries as they play.**

Children choose an open center for free playtime. Encourage children to play in their "recycling center" and pretend that they are sorting bags like Ada to be made into something new.

## Let's Say Good-Bye

large group    15 minutes

 **Read Aloud** Revisit "Animal Homes"/"Hogares de animales" for your afternoon Read Aloud. Remind children that animals need a clean Earth and sky too.

 **Home Connection** Refer to the Home Connection activities listed in the Materials and Resources chart on page 135. Remind children to show or tell their families what games they played outdoors today. Sing the "Good-bye Song" as children prepare to leave.

---

### ✓ Learning Goals

**Social and Emotional Development**
• Child is aware of self in terms of abilities, characteristics and preferences, and respects personal boundaries.

**Language and Communication**
• Child names and describes actual or pictured people, places, things, actions, attributes, and events.

**Science**
• Child knows the importance of and demonstrates ways of caring for the environment/planet.

### Writing

Recap the day and week. Say: *Tell me one thing you learned about how to care for the earth and sky. Mencionen lo que aprendieron acerca de cómo cuidar la Tierra y el cielo.* Record answers on chart paper or the interactive whiteboard. Have each child write his or her name beside the entry.

In general, the purpose of assessing young children in the early childhood classroom is to collect information necessary to make important decisions about their developmental and educational needs. Because assessment is crucial to making informed teaching decisions, it is necessarily a vital component of *DLM Early Childhood Express.* The guidelines and forms found online allow the teacher to implement assessment necessary in the pre-kindergarten classroom.

Effective assessment is an ongoing process that always enhances opportunities for optimal growth, development, and learning. The process of determining individual developmental and educational needs tailors early childhood education practices and provides a template for setting individual and program goals.

Pre-kindergarten assessment should be authentic; that is, it should be a natural, environmental extension of the classroom. Assessments should be incorporated into classroom activities whenever possible, not completed as separate, pull-out activities in which the teacher evaluates the student one-on-one. Whenever possible, assessment should evaluate children's real knowledge in the process of completing real activities. For example, observing children as they equally distribute snacks would be a better assessment of their ability to make groups than observing an exercise in which children group counters would be.

It is also important to note that assessments should be administered over time, as environmental influences can greatly impact single outcomes. If a pre-kindergarten child is tired or ill, for example, the child may not demonstrate knowledge of a skill that has actually been mastered. It is also important to consider the length of assessment for children of this age, as attention spans are still developing and can vary greatly based on environmental influences. Most assessments should be completed within half an hour.

If possible, use multiple types of assessment for the same content area when working with pre-kindergarten children. Some children may be able to demonstrate mastery kinesthetically if they are not able to use expressive language well; others may not process auditory instruction adequately, but will be able to complete an assessment after observing someone model the task. It is vital that the assessment process should never make the child anxious or scared.

## Informal Assessment

**INFORMAL** assessments rely heavily on observational and work-sampling techniques that continually focus on child performance, processes, and product over selected periods of time and in a variety of contexts.

**ANECDOTAL** assessments are written descriptions that provide a short, objective account of an event or an incident. Only the facts are reported—where, what, when, and how. Anecdotal records are especially helpful when trying to understand a child's behavior or use of skills. These recordings can be used to share the progress of individual children and to develop and individualize curriculum.

The Anecdotal Observational Record Form can be used at any time to document an individual child's progress toward a goal or signs indicating the need for developmental or medical evaluation. Observations can reflect the focused skills for the week, but are not limited to those skills. You may pair the form with video or audio recordings of the child to complete an anecdotal record.

*Anecdotal Observational Record Form*

**CHECKLISTS** are lists of skills or behaviors arranged into disciplines or developmental domains and are used to determine how a child exhibits the behaviors or skills listed. Teachers can quickly and easily observe groups of children and check the behaviors or skills each child is demonstrating at the moment.

*Weekly Assessment*

Weekly Assessments measure progress toward specific guidelines that are addressed in the weekly curriculum. The Performance Assessment Checklist measures progress toward the guidelines of the entire curriculum. It is intended to be used three times per year.

*Performance Assessment Checklist*

When using either type of checklist, it is important to remember that the skills and behaviors on the list are only guidelines. Each child is unique and has his or her own developmental timetable. It is also important to remember that the checklist only documents the presence or absence of a specific skill or behavior during the time of observation. It does not necessarily mean the skill is consistently present or lacking, though consistency may be noted when the skill has been observed over time.

**PORTFOLIO** assessments are collections of thoughtfully selected work samples, or artifacts, and accompanying reflections indicative of the child's learning experiences, efforts, and progress toward and/or attainment of established curriculum goals. They are an authentic, performance-based method to allow teachers to analyze progress over time. As children choose work samples for their portfolios, they become involved in their own learning and assessment and begin to develop the concept of evaluating their own work.

Although early childhood activities tend to focus on processes as opposed to products, there are numerous opportunities to collect samples of children's work. Items to collect include drawings, tracings, cuttings, attempts to print their names, and paintings. You may also include informal assessments of a child's ability to recognize letters, shapes, numbers, and rhyming words.

## Formal Assessment

**FORMAL** assessments involve the use of standardized tests. They are administered in a prescribed manner and may require completion within a specified amount of time. Standardized tests result in scores that are usually compared to the scores of a normative group. These tests generally fall into the following categories: achievement tests, readiness tests, developmental screening tests, intelligence tests, and diagnostic tests.

## Assessing Children with Special Needs

Children with special needs may require a more thorough initial assessment, more frequent on-going assessments, and continuous adaptation of activities. Assessment is essentially the first task for the teacher or caregiver in developing the individualized instruction program required for children with disabilities.

## Assessing Children Who Are English Language Learners

Whenever possible, assessments should be given in both the child's first language and in English.

# Celebrate the Unit

**Focus Question**

**What can I learn about the earth and sky?**

# Earth and Sky Festival

## Stage a Festival for Other Classes

- Invite children to share what they learned by holding an Earth and Sky Festival for other classes.

- Before the festival, record children singing the song "Twinkle, Twinkle Little Star." Have them sing more than one verse and play the recording softly as background music during the Earth and Sky Festival.

- Organize the classroom into four areas, focusing each area on one of the weekly themes for the unit: My World, Outside My Window, Day and Night, and Taking Care of the World. In each area, display the appropriate focus question and have children display examples of their completed work, such as:

  **nature scrapbooks**

  **3-D object mural**

  **reused sock puppets**

  **recycling center**

  **writing pieces, drawings, and other creative work**

- Invite pairs of children to take visitors from other classes around the festival. Encourage children to talk about the displays, explain what they learned, and answer questions. Children can use their sock puppets to act out ways to care for the earth and sky for their visitors.

- Provide "sunrise and sunset snacks" for all to enjoy at the festival, such as orange juice and cups of dry cereal (sunrise snacks) and graham crackers and milk (sunset snacks). Check for food allergies before serving snacks.

## Evaluate and Inform

- ✓ Review the informal observation notes you recorded for each child during the four weeks of the unit. Identify areas in which individual children will need additional support.

- ✓ Send a summary of your observation notes home with children. Encourage parents to respond to the summary with questions or comments.

- ✓ Review dated samples of children's work in their portfolios. Copy some of these samples to send home to families along with the observation summary.

- ✓ Send home the Unit 7 My Library Book, *Good Morning, Earth!,* for children to read with their families.

# Celebrar la unidad

**Pregunta esencial**

¿Qué puedo aprender sobre la Tierra y el cielo?

## Festival de la Tierra y el cielo

### Lleve a cabo un festival para otras clases

- Invite a los niños a llevar a cabo un "Festival de la Tierra y el cielo" para que compartan lo que aprendieron con las demás clases.

- Antes del festival, grabe a los niños cantando la melodía "Twinkle, Twinkle Little Star". Durante el Festival de la Tierra y el cielo, pídales a los niños que canten más de una estrofa, mientras usted reproduce la grabación a bajo volumen, como fondo musical.

- Organice a la clase en cuatro áreas, asignándole a cada área uno de los temas semanales de la unidad: Mi mundo, Por la ventana, El día y la noche, y Cuidamos el mundo. En cada área, presente la pregunta de enfoque correspondiente y pídales a los niños que exhiban ejemplos de sus trabajos completados, como:

  **álbumes de recortes sobre la naturaleza**

  **mural de objetos en tercera dimensión**

  **títeres con calcetas recicladas**

  **centro de reciclaje**

  **piezas de escritura, dibujos y otros trabajos creativos**

- Forme parejas de niños y pídales que les muestren el festival a los visitantes. Anímelos a hablar sobre los trabajos exhibidos, a explicar lo que aprendieron y a responder las preguntas de los visitantes. Los niños pueden usar los títeres de calcetas para actuar ante los visitantes demostrando cómo cuidar a la Tierra y el cielo.

- Ofrezca "bocadillos del amanecer y el anochecer" para que los disfruten todos los asistentes al festival, como jugo de naranja y tazas con cereal seco (bocadillos del amanecer) y galletas Graham con leche (bocadillos del anochecer). Antes de servir los bocadillos, verifique que no haya alergias a ciertos alimentos entre la clase.

### Evaluar e informar

- ✓ Revise las observaciones informales que anotó para cada niño durante las cuatro semanas de la unidad. Identifique las áreas en las que cada niño podría requerir un apoyo adicional.

- ✓ Dé a los padres de los niños el resumen respectivo de sus observaciones. Insístales que respondan a este informe con preguntas o comentarios.

- ✓ Revise las muestras fechadas que hay en el portafolios de trabajo de cada niño. Haga copias de algunas de estas muestras para que las vean sus padres junto con el resumen de observaciones.

- ✓ Deles a los niños el librito de la Unidad 7 para leer con sus familias.

# Appendix

# About the Authors

**NELL K. DUKE, ED.D.,** is Professor of Teacher Education and Educational Psychology and Co-Director of the Literacy Achievement Research Center at Michigan State University. Nell Duke's expertise lies in early literacy development, particularly among children living in poverty, and integrating literacy into content instruction. She is the recipient of a number of awards for her research and is co-author of several books including *Literacy and the Youngest Learner: Best Practices for Educators of Children from Birth to 5* and *Beyond Bedtime Stories: A Parent's Guide to Promoting Reading, Writing, and Other Literacy Skills From Birth to 5.*

**DOUG CLEMENTS** is SUNY Distinguished Professor of Education at the University of Buffalo, SUNY. Previously a preschool and kindergarten teacher, Clements currently researchs the learning and teaching of early mathematics and computer applications. He has published over 100 research studies, 8 books, 50 chapters, and 250 additional publications, including co-authoring the reports of President Bush's National Mathematics Advisory Panel and the National Research Council's book on early mathematics. He has directed twenty projects funded by the National Science Foundation and Department of Education's Institute of Education Sciences.

**JULIE SARAMA** Associate Professor at the University at Buffalo (SUNY), has taught high school mathematics and computer science, gifted and talented classes, and early childhood mathematics. She directs several projects funded by the National Science Foundation and the Institute of Education Sciences. Author of over 50 refereed articles, 4 books, 30 chapters, 20 computer programs, and more than 70 additional publications, she helped develop the Building Blocks and Investigations curricula and the award-winning Turtle Math. Her latest book is *Early Childhood Mathematics Education Research: Learning Trajectories for Young Children.*

**WILLIAM TEALE** is Professor of Education at the University of Illinois at Chicago. Author of over one hundred publications on early literacy learning, the intersection of technology and literacy education, and children's literature, he helped pioneer research in emergent literacy. Dr. Teale has worked in the area of early childhood education with schools, libraries, and other organizations across the country and internationally. He has also directed three U.S. Department of Education-funded Early Reading First projects that involve developing model preschool literacy curricula for four-year-old children from urban, low-income settings in Chicago.

## Contributing Authors

**Kimberly Brenneman,** PhD, is an Assistant Research Professor of Psychology at Rutgers University. She is also affiliated with the Rutgers Center for Cognitive Science (RuCCS) and the National Institute for Early Education Research (NIEER). Brenneman is co-author of *Preschool Pathways to Science (PrePS): Facilitating Scientific Ways of Thinking, Talking, Doing, and Understanding* and is an educational advisor for PBS's *Sid the Science Kid* television show and website. Research interests include the development of scientific reasoning and methods to improve instructional practices that support science and mathematics learning in preschool.

**Peggy Cerna** is an independent Early Childhood Consultant. She was a bilingual teacher for 15 years and then served as principal of the Rosita Valley Literacy Academy, a Pre-Kindergarten through Grade 1 school in Eagle Pass, Texas. Cerna then opened Lucy Read Pre-Kindergarten Demonstration School in Austin, Texas, which had 600 Pre-Kindergarten students. During her principalship at Lucy Read, Cerna built a strong parental community with the collaboration of the University of Texas, AmeriCorps, and Austin Community College. Her passion for early literacy drove her to create book clubs where parents were taught how to read books to their children.

**Dan Cieloha** is an educator with more than 30 years' experience in creating, implementing, and evaluating experientially based learning materials, experiences, and environments for young children. He believes that all learners must be actively and equitably involved in constructing, evaluating, and sharing what they learn. He has spearheaded the creation and field-testing of a variety of learning materials including *You & Me: Building Social Skills in Young Children*. He is also president of the Partnership for Interactive Learning, a leading nonprofit organization dedicated to the development of children's social and thinking skills.

**Paula A. Jones,** M.Ed., is an Early Childhood Consultant at the state and national levels. As a former Early Childhood Director for the Lubbock Independent School District, she served as the Head Start Director and co-founded three of their four Early Childhood campuses which also became a model design and Best Practices Program for the Texas Education Agency. She was a contributing author for the first Texas Prekindergarten Guidelines, served as president for the Texas Association of Administrators and Supervisors of Programs for Young Children, and is a 2010 United Way Champions for Children Award winner.

**Bobbie Sparks** is a retired educator who has taught biology and middle school science as well as being the K-12 district science consultant for a suburban district. At Harris County Department of Education she served as the K-12 science consultant in Professional Development. During her career as K-12 science consultant, Sparks worked with teachers at all grade levels to revamp curriculum to meet the Texas science standards. She served on Texas state committees to develop the TEKS standards as well as committees to develop items for tests for teacher certification in science.

**Rita Abrams** is a composer, lyricist, educator, and author whose music has won two Emmy Awards, multiple ASCAP Awards, and a variety of others including Parents' Choice, American Education Foundation, and Associated Press. As a teacher she sang her international hit, "Mill Valley," with the Strawberry Point School Third Grade Class. Since then, Abrams has continued to blend her classical music background, special education graduate work, and early childhood teaching experience into a prolific recording career including myriad children's albums, videos and film scores. She also creates musical theatre for both children and adults.

# Opening Routines

Below are a few suggested routines to use for beginning your day with your class. You can rotate through them, or use one for a while before trying a new approach. You may wish to develop your own routines by mixing and matching ideas from the suggestions given.

## 1. Days of the Week

Ask children what day of the week it is. When they respond, tell them that you are going to write a sentence that tells everyone what day of the week it is. Print "Today is Monday." on the board. If you have a helper chart, have children assist you in finding the name of the day's helper. Print: "Today's helper is Miguel." Ask the helper to come forward and find the Letter Tiles or ABC Picture Cards that spell his or her name.

As the year progresses, you might want to have the helper find the letters that spell the day of the week. Eventually some children may be able to copy the entire sentence with Letter Tiles or ABC Picture Cards.

moon

iguana   icicle

giraffe   girl

umbrella   unicycle

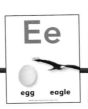
egg   eagle

leaf

## 2. Calendar Search

Print "Today is _____." on the board. Ask children to help you fill in the blank. Print the day of the week in the blank. Invite children to look at the calendar to determine today's date. Write the date under the sentence that tells what day of the week it is. Invite children to clap out the syllables of both the sentence and the date.

Review the days of the week and the months of the year using the "Days of the Week Song"/"Canción de los días de la semana" and the "Months of the year"/ "Los meses del año."

Ask children what day of the week it was yesterday. When they respond, ask them what day it is today. Place a seasonal sticker on today's date. Have children follow your lead and recite "Yesterday was Monday, September 12. Today is Tuesday, September 13. Tomorrow will be Wednesday, September 14."

## 3. Feelings

Make happy- and sad-faced puppets for each child by cutting yellow circles from construction paper and drawing happy and sad faces on them. Laminate the faces, and glue them to tongue depressors. Cover two large coffee cans. On one can glue a happy face, and write the sentence "I feel happy today." Glue the sad face to the second can, and write the sentence "I feel sad today."

Give each child a happy- and a sad-faced puppet. Encourage children to tell how they feel today and to hold up the appropriate puppet. Encourage children to come forward and place their puppets in the can that represents their feelings. Later in the year you can add puppets to represent other emotions.

You can vary this activity by using a graph titled "How I Feel Today"/"Como me siento hoy." Have children place their puppets in the appropriate column on the graph instead of in the cans.

## 4. Pledge of Allegiance/ Moment of Silence

Have children locate the United States flag. Recite the Pledge of Allegiance to the U.S. flag. Then allow a minute for a moment of silence.

Discuss these activities with children, allowing them to volunteer reasons the Pledge of Allegiance is said and other places they have seen the Pledge recited.

## 5. Coming to Circle

Talk with children about being part of a class family. Tell children that as part of a class family they will work together, learn together, respect each other, help each other, and play together. Explain that families have rules so that jobs get done and everyone stays safe. Let children know they will learn rules for their classroom. One of those rules is how they will come together for circle. Sing "This is the Way We Come to Circle" (to the tune of "This is the Way We Wash Our Clothes").

*This is the way we come to circle.*
*Come to circle, come to circle.*
*This is the way we come to circle,*
*So early in the morning.*

*This is the way we sit right down,*
*Sit right down, sit right down.*
*This is the way we sit right down,*
*So early in the morning.*

*This is the way we fold our hands,*
*Fold our hands, fold our hands.*
*This is the way we fold our hands,*
*So early in the morning.*

# Transition Tips

Sing songs or chants such as those listed below while transitioning between activities:

## 1. I Am Now in Pre-K

**To the tune of "I'm a Little Teapot"**

*I am now in Pre-K,*
*I can learn.*
*I can listen. I can take a turn.*
*When the teacher says so,*
*I can play.*
*Choose a center and together we'll play.*

## 2. Did You Clean Up?

**To the tune of "Are You Sleeping, Are You Sleeping, Brother John?"**

*Did you clean up?*
*Did you clean up?*
*Please make sure.*
*Please make sure.*
*Everything is picked up.*
*Everything is picked up.*
*Please. Thank you!*
*Please. Thank you!*

**Chant: Red, Yellow, Green**
*Red, yellow, green*
*Stop, change, go*
*Red, yellow, green*
*Stop, change, go*
*Green says yes.*
*And red says no.*
*Yellow says everybody wait in a row.*
*Red, yellow, green*
*Stop, change, go*
*Red, yellow, green*
*Stop, change, go*

## 3. The Five Senses Song

**To the tune of "If You're Happy and You Know It"**

*I can see with my eyes every day* (clap clap)
*I can see with my eyes every day* (clap clap)
*I can see with my eyes*
*I can see with my eyes*
*I can see with my eyes every day* (clap clap)
(Repeat with smell with my nose, hear with my ears, feel with my hands, and taste with my mouth.)

## 4. Eat More Vegetables

**To the tune of "Row, Row, Row Your Boat"**

*Eat, eat, eat more,*
*Eat more vegetables.*
*Carrots, carrots, carrots, carrots*
*Eat more vegetables.*
(Repeat with broccoli, lettuce, celery, and spinach.)

## 5. Circle Time

**To the tune of "Here We Go 'Round the Mulberry Bush"**

*This is the way we come to circle*
*Come to circle, come to circle.*
*This is the way we come to circle*
*So early in the morning.*

*This is the way we sit right down,*
*Sit right down, sit right down.*
*This is the way we sit right down,*
*So early in the morning.*

Play a short game such as one of the following to focus children's attention:

### Name That Fruit!

Say: *It's red on the outside and white on the inside. It rhymes with chapel!*

Children answer, "Apple!" and then repeat twice, "Apple/Chapel."

Repeat with other fruits, such as cherry and banana.

### I Spy

Use a flashlight to focus on different letters and words in the classroom. Have children identify them.

### Monkey See Monkey Do

Choose one child to be the monkey leader. He or she will act out a motion such as twist, jump, clap, or raise hand, and the rest of the monkeys say the word and copy the motion.

### Let's Play Pairs

Distribute one *ABC Picture Card* to each child. Draw letters from an additional set of cards. The child who has the matching letter identifies it and goes to the center of his or her choice.

### That's My Friend!

Take children's name cards with their pictures from the wall and distribute making sure no one gets his or her own name. When you call a child's name, she or he has to say something positive about the child on the card and end with "That's my friend!"

### Name Game

Say: *If your name begins with ___, you may choose a center.* Have the child say his or her name as he or she gets up. Repeat the child's name, emphasizing the beginning sound.

# Center Management

Learning Centers provide children with additional opportunities to practice or extend each lesson's skills and concepts either individually or in small groups. The activities and materials that are explored in the centers not only promote oral language but also help develop children's social skills as they work together. The use of these Learning Centers encourages children to explore their surroundings and make their own choices.

## Teacher's Role

The Learning Centers allow time for you to:

- Observe children's exploration of the centers.
- Assess children's understanding of the skills and concepts being taught.
- Provide additional support and encouragement to children who might be having difficulty with specific concepts or skills. If a child is having difficulty, model the correct approach.

## Classroom Setup

The materials and activities in the centers should support what children are learning. Multiple experiences are necessary for children's comprehension. The centers should also engage them in learning by providing hands-on experiences. Every time children visit a center and practice skills or extend concepts being taught in the lessons, they are likely to broaden their understanding or discover something new.

In order to support children's learning, the materials and activities in the Learning Centers should change every week. It is important that all the children have a chance to explore every center throughout each week. Be sure they rotate to different centers and do not focus on only one activity. You might also consider adding new materials to the centers as the week progresses. This will encourage children to expand on their past work. Modify or add activities or materials based on your classroom needs.

It is crucial that children know what is expected of them in each center. To help children understand the expectation at each center, display an "I can" statement with an illustration or photograph of a student completing the activity. Discuss these expectations with children in advance, and reinforce them as needed. These discussions might include reviewing your typical classroom rules and talking about the limited number of children allowed in each center. Remind them that they may work individually or in small groups.

# Library and Listening Center

Children should feel free throughout the day to explore books and other printed materials. Create a comfortable reading area in the room, and fill it with as many children's books as possible. Include a number of informational books that tell why things happen and books of rhymes, poems, and songs, as well as storybooks and simple alphabet books.

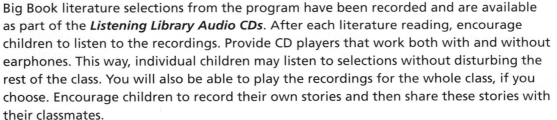

Before beginning each unit in the program, bring in books about the specific concepts or themes in a unit. Encourage children to bring in books they have enjoyed and would like to share with classmates. Even though they may not be actually reading, have children visit the area often. Here they can practice their book handling, apply their growing knowledge of print awareness, and look at pictures and talk about them. Have them read the books to you or to classmates.

Big Book literature selections from the program have been recorded and are available as part of the *Listening Library Audio CDs*. After each literature reading, encourage children to listen to the recordings. Provide CD players that work both with and without earphones. This way, individual children may listen to selections without disturbing the rest of the class. You will also be able to play the recordings for the whole class, if you choose. Encourage children to record their own stories and then share these stories with their classmates.

As you set up the Learning Centers, here are a few ideas you might want to implement in your classroom.

- Create a separate Workshop Center sign-up chart for children to use when choosing a center to explore.

- Provide an area for children who want to be alone to read or to simply reflect on the day's activities.

- Separate loud areas and quiet areas.

- Hang posters or art at eye level for the children.

- Place on shelves materials, such as books or art supplies, that are easily accessible to the children.

# English Language Learners

## Teaching the English Language Learner

### Stages of English-Language Proficiency

An effective learning environment is an important goal of all educators. In a supportive environment, all English learners have the opportunity to participate and to learn. The materials in this guide are designed to support children while they are acquiring English, allowing them to develop English-language reading skills and the fluency they need to achieve in the core content areas as well.

This guide provides direction in supporting children in four stages of English proficiency: Beginning, Intermediate, Advanced, and Advanced-High. While children at a beginning level by definition know little English and will probably have difficulty comprehending English, by the time they progress to the intermediate or early advanced levels of English acquisition, their skills in understanding more complex language structures will have increased. These stages can be described in general terms as follows:

**BEGINNING AND INTERMEDIATE** Children identified at these levels of English-language proficiency demonstrate dramatic growth. During these stages, children progress from having no receptive or productive English to possessing a basic command of English. They are learning to comprehend and produce one- or two-word responses to questions, are moving to phrases and simple sentences using concrete and immediate topics, and are learning to interact in a limited fashion with text that has been taught. They progress to responding with increasing ease to more varied communication tasks using learned material, comprehending a sequence of information on familiar topics, producing basic statements and asking questions on familiar subjects, and interacting with a variety of print. Some basic errors are found in their use of English syntax and grammar.

**ADVANCED** Children who have reached the Advanced level of English-language proficiency have good comprehension of overall meaning and are beginning to demonstrate increased comprehension of specific details and concepts. They are learning to respond in expanded sentences, are interacting more independently with a variety of text, and in using newly acquired English vocabulary to communicate ideas orally and in writing. They demonstrate fewer errors in English grammar and syntax than at the beginning and early intermediate levels.

**ADVANCED-HIGH** Children who are identified at this level of English-language proficiency demonstrate consistent comprehension of meaning, including implied and nuanced meaning, and are learning the use of idiomatic and figurative language. They are increasingly able to respond using detail in compound and complex sentences and sustain conversation in English. They are able to use standard grammar with few errors and show an understanding of conventions of formal and informal usage.

It is important to provide an instructional scaffold for phonemic awareness, phonics, words structure, language structures, comprehension strategies and skills, and grammar, usage, and mechanics so that children can successfully learn to read while advancing along the continuum of English acquisition. For example, at the Beginning level, you might ask children for *yes* or *no* answers when answering questions about selection comprehension or grammar. Children at the Advanced-High level should be asked to provide answers in complete and expanded sentences. By the time children achieve an Advanced level, their knowledge of English will be more sophisticated because they are becoming more adept at comprehending English and using techniques such as making inferences or using persuasive language.

The following charts illustrate how to use sentence stems with children at each level of English-language proficiency:

## Teaching Sentence Stems

- Write the sentence stems on the board, chart paper, or sentence strips. Choose stems that are appropriate for the four general levels of English proficiency.

- Model using the sentence stem(s) for the comprehension strategy or skill.

- Read each phrase as you insert the appropriate words to express an idea. Have children repeat the sentences after you. For Beginning and Intermediate children, use the stems within the questions you ask them.

**Linguistic Pattern:** *I predict that* _____.

| Beginning | Intermediate | Advanced | Advanced-High |
|---|---|---|---|
| Simple questions about the text. Yes-or-no responses or responses that allow children to point to an object or picture. | Simple questions about the text which allow for one- or two-word responses or give children two options for a response to select from. | Questions that elicit a short response or a complete simple sentence using the linguistic pattern. | Have children make predictions on their own. Children should use the linguistic pattern and respond with a complete complex sentence. |

## Practicing Sentence Stems

- To give children multiple opportunities to generate the language they have just been taught, have them work in pairs or small groups and utilize cooperative learning participation strategies to facilitate this communicative practice.

- Pair children one level of proficiency above or below the other. For example, have Beginning children work with Intermediate level children.

- Use differentiated prompts to elicit the responses that incorporate the linguistic patterns and structures for the different proficiency levels. See the following sample of prompts and responses.

| Beginning | Intermediate | Advanced | Advanced-High |
|---|---|---|---|
| Do you predict _____? <br><br> *Yes/No* | Do you predict _____ or _____? <br><br> *I predict* _____. | What do you predict _____? <br><br> *I predict* _____. | Give a prediction about _____. <br><br> *I predict* _____. |

- Select some common cooperative learning participation strategies to teach to children. Once they have learned some language practice activities, they can move quickly into the various routines. See the examples on the next page.

# English Language Learners

## My Turn, Your Turn

Children work in pairs.

1. The teacher models a sentence and the whole group repeats, or echoes it.

2. One child generates an oral phrase, and the partner echoes it.

3. Partners switch and alternate roles so that each child has a chance to both generate and repeat phrases.

## Talking Stick

Children work in small groups. This strategy allows every child to have an opportunity to speak several times and encourages more reflective or reticent participants to take a turn. Children can "pass" only one time.

1. The teacher charts sentence graphic organizers and linguistic patterns children will use in their responses.

2. The teacher models use of linguistic patterns from the lesson.

3. The teacher asks a question or gives a prompt, and then passes a stick, eraser, stuffed animal, or any other designated object to one child.

4. A child speaks, everyone listens, and then the child passes the object on to the person next to him or her.

5. The next child speaks, everyone listens, and the process continues until the teacher or facilitator gives a signal to return the object.

## Think-Pair-Share

This strategy allows children time for processing ideas by building in sufficient wait time to process the question and frame an answer. It is an appropriate strategy to use during small- or large-group discussions or lessons, giving all children a chance to organize their thoughts and have a turn sharing their responses with a partner. It also allows for small group verbal interaction to practice language before sharing with the larger group.

1. After reading or listening to a section of text, the teacher presents a question or task. It is helpful to guide with a specific prompt, modeling the language to be used in the response.

2. Children think about their responses for a brief, designated amount of time.

3. Partners share and discuss their responses with each other.

4. An adaptation can be to have each child share his or her partner's response within a small group to promote active listening.

## Teaching Vocabulary

Building the background knowledge and a context for children to learn new words is critical in helping children understand new vocabulary. Primary language can be a valuable tool for preteaching, concept development, and vocabulary. Cognates, or words similar in English counterparts, often provide an opportunity for bridging the primary language and English. Also, children who have background knowledge about a topic can more easily connect the new information they are learning with what they already know than children without a similar context from which to work. Therefore, giving children background information and encouraging them to make as many connections as possible with the new vocabulary word they encounter will help them better understand the selection they are about to read.

In addition to building background knowledge, visual displays such as pictures, graphs, charts, maps, models, or other strategies offer unambiguous access to new content. They provide a clear and parallel correspondence between the visual objects and the new vocabulary to be learned. Thus, because the correlation is clear, the negotiation of meaning is established. Additionally, this process must be constant and reciprocal between you and each child if the child is to succeed in effectively interacting with language.

Included in this guide is a routine for teaching vocabulary words. In addition to this routine, more detailed explanations of the ways to teach vocabulary are as follows:

**REAL OBJECTS AND REALIA:** Because of the immediate result visuals have on learning language, when explaining a word such as *car,* the best approach is simply to show a real car. As an alternative to the real object, you can show realia. Realia are toy versions of real things, such as plastic eggs to substitute for real eggs, or in this case, a toy car to signify a real car. A large, clear picture of an automobile can also work if it is absolutely recognizable.

If, however, the child has had no experience with the item in the picture, more explanation might be needed. For example, if the word you are explaining is a zoo animal such as an *ocelot,* and children are not familiar with this animal, one picture might be insufficient. They might confuse this animal with a cat or any one of the feline species. Seeing several clear pictures, then, of each individual type of common feline and comparing their similarities and differences might help clarify meaning in this particular instance. When children make a connection between their prior knowledge of the word *cat* with the new word *ocelot,* it validates their newly acquired knowledge, and thus they process learning more quickly.

**PICTURES:** Supplement story illustrations with visuals such as those found in the ***Photo Library CD, ABC Picture Cards,*** magazine pictures, and picture dictionaries. Videos, especially those that demonstrate an entire setting such as a farm or zoo, or videos where different animals are highlighted in the natural habitat, for instance, might be helpful. You might also wish to turn off the soundtrack to avoid a flood of language that children might not be able to understand. This way children can concentrate on the visual-word meaning correlation.

**PANTOMIME:** Language is learned through modeling within a communicative context. Pantomiming is one example of such a framework of communication. Some words, such as *run* and *jump,* are appropriate for pantomiming. Throughout this guide, you will find suggestions for pantomiming words like *sick* by coughing, sneezing, and holding your stomach. If children understand what you are trying to pantomime, they will more easily engage in the task of learning.

# Letter Formation Guide

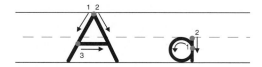

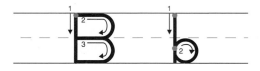

**A** Starting point, slanting down left
Starting point, slanting down right
Starting point, across the middle: capital *A*

**a** Starting point, around left all the way
Starting point, straight down,
touching the circle: small *a*

**B** Starting point, straight down
Starting point, around right and in
at the middle, around right and in
at the bottom: capital *B*

**b** Starting point, straight down, back
up, around right all the way: small *b*

C c

**C** Starting point, around left to
stopping place: capital *C*

**C** Starting point, around left to
stopping place: small *c*

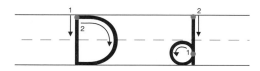

**D** Starting point, straight down
Starting point, around right and in
at the bottom: capital *D*

**d** Starting point, around left all the way
Starting point, straight down, touching
the circle: small *d*

**E** Starting point, straight down
Starting point, straight out
Starting point, straight out
Starting point, straight out: capital *E*

**e** Starting point, straight out, up and
around to the left, curving down
and around to the right: small *e*

**F** Starting point, straight down
Starting point, straight out
Starting point, straight out: capital *F*

**f** Starting point, around left and straight down
Starting point, straight across: small *f*

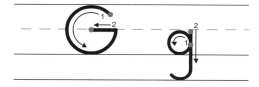

**G** Starting point, around left, curving up and
around
Straight in: capital *G*

**g** Starting point, around left all the way
Starting point, straight down, touching the
circle, around left to stopping place: small *g*

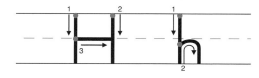

**H** Starting point, straight down
Starting point, straight down
Starting point, across the middle: capital *H*

**h** Starting point, straight down, back
up, around right, and straight down: small *h*

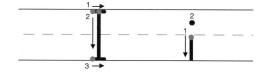

**I** Starting point, across
Starting point, straight down
Starting point, across: capital *I*

**i** Starting point, straight down
Dot exactly above: small *i*

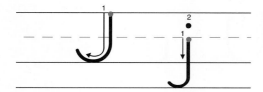

**J** Starting point, straight down, around left to stopping place: capital *J*

**j** Starting point, straight down, around left to stopping place Dot exactly above: small *j*

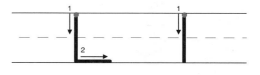

**K** Starting point, straight down
Starting point, slanting down left, touching the line, slanting down right: capital *K*

**k** Starting point, straight down
Starting point, slanting down left, touching the line, slanting down right: small *k*

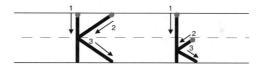

**L** Starting point, straight down, straight out: capital *L*

**l** Starting point, straight down: small *l*

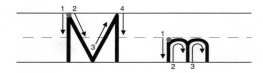

**M** Starting point, straight down
Starting point, slanting down right to the point, slanting back up to the right, straight down: capital *M*

**m** Starting point, straight down, back up, around right, straight down, back up, around right, straight down: small *m*

**N** Starting point, straight down
Starting point, slanting down right, straight back up: capital *N*

**n** Starting point, straight down, back up, around right, straight down: small *n*

**O** Starting point, around left all the way: capital *O*

**o** Starting point, around left all the way: small *o*

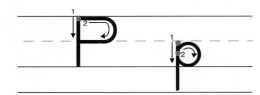

**P** Starting point, straight down
Starting point, around right and in at the middle: capital *P*

**p** Starting point, straight down
Starting point, around right all the way, touching the line: small *p*

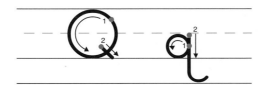

**Q** Starting point, around left all the way
Starting point, slanting down right: capital *Q*

**q** Starting point, around left all the way
Starting point, straight down, touching the circle, curving up right to stopping place: small *q*

**R** Starting point, straight down
Starting point, around right and in at the middle, touching the line, slanting down right: capital *R*

**r** Starting point, straight down, back up, curving around right to stopping place: small *r*

# Letter Formation Guide

**S** Starting point, around left, curving right and down around right, curving left and up: capital S

**s** Starting point, around left, curving right and down around right, curving left and up to stopping place: small s

**T** Starting point, straight across
Starting point, straight down: capital T

**t** Starting point, straight down
Starting point, across short: small t

**U** Starting point, straight down, curving around right and up, straight up: capital U

**u** Starting point, straight down, curving around right and up, straight up, straight back down: small u

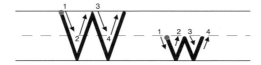

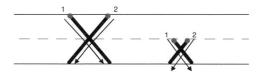

**V** Starting point, slanting down right, slanting up right: capital V

**v** Starting point, slanting down right, slanting up right: small v

**W** Starting point, slanting down right, slanting up right, slanting down right, slanting up right: capital W

**w** Starting point, slanting down right, slanting up right, slanting down right, slanting up right: small w

**X** Starting point, slanting down right
Starting point, slanting down left: capital X

**X** Starting point, slanting down right
Starting point, slanting down left: small x

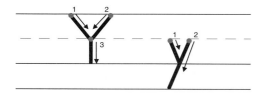

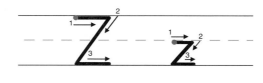

**Y** Starting point, slanting down right, stop
Starting point, slanting down left, stop
Starting point, straight down: capital Y

**y** Starting point, slanting down right
Starting point, slanting down left, connecting the lines: small y

**Z** Starting point, straight across, slanting down left, straight across: capital Z

**z** Starting point, straight across, slanting down left, straight across: small z

# Number Formation Guide

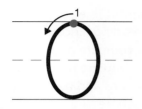

**0** Starting point, curving left all the way around to starting point: *0*

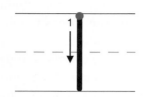

**1** Starting point, straight down: *1*

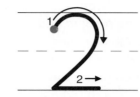

**2** Starting point, around right, slanting left and straight across right: *2*

**3** Starting point, around right, in at the middle, around right: *3*

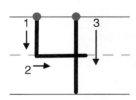

**4** Starting point, straight down
Straight across right
Starting point, straight down, crossing line: *4*

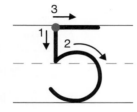

**5** Starting point, straight down, curving around right and up
Starting point, straight across right: *5*

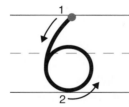

**6** Starting point, slanting left, around the bottom curving up, around right and into the curve: *6*

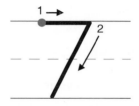

**7** Starting point, straight across right, slanting down left: *7*

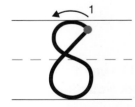

**8** Starting point, curving left, curving down and around right, slanting up right to starting point: *8*

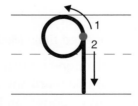

**9** Starting point, curving around left all the way, straight down: *9*

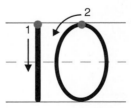

**10** Starting point, straight down
Starting point, curving left all the way around to starting point: *10*

# Vocabulary Development

Vocabulary development is a key part of **The DLM Early Childhood Express**. Children learn new words through exposure during reading and class discussion. They build language and vocabulary through activities using key words and phrases and by exploring selected vocabulary. After vocabulary words have been introduced, encourage children to use the words in sentences. Again, providing linguistic structures gives children a context for using new vocabulary and building oral language and gives you the opportunity to assess children's understanding of new words. For example, use sentence patterns such as the following:

- A _____ can _____.
- A _____ is a _____.
  (Use this for classification activities. *A tulip is a flower. A rabbit is an animal.*)
- The _____ is _____.
  (Use for describing. *The rabbit is soft.*)

Define words in ways children in your class can understand. When possible, show pictures of objects or actions to help clarify the meanings of words. Provide examples or comparisons to help reinforce the meanings of words and to connect new words to previously learned words. For example, say *The rabbit's FUR is soft like COTTON.* Connect words to categories. For example, say: *Pears are fruits. Are apples fruits? What else is a fruit?* Demonstrate the meaning of words when possible.

During reading, be sure children feel comfortable asking questions and sharing their reactions to what you are reading. Encourage children to share explanations, make predictions, compare and contrast ideas, sequence story events, and describe what you are reading. Encourage children's engagement by modeling reactions and responses while reading. For example, say *I like the part where _____ did _____.* or *This story is about _____.* Support children who are reluctant to speak by using linguistic structures that encourage them to talk about stories and use vocabulary words. You might use the following linguistic structures:

- This story is about _____.
- First _____.
- Next _____.
- Last _____. (Use this for retelling stories.)
- The _____ is the same as _____.
- The _____ is different from _____.
- We read about _____.

Model asking questions before, during, and after reading:

- I wonder what this story is going to be about.
- Who is _____?
- What is _____?
- What did _____ do?
- Why did _____ do _____?
- What happened first? Middle? Last?

Be sure to ask open-ended questions. Unlike questions that simply require a *yes* or *no* or one-word answer, open-ended questions encourage children to think about responses and use new vocabulary in sentences.

Throughout the day, create opportunities for children to talk to each other as they share daily experiences, discuss and explain what they are doing, and talk about what they are learning.

# Vocabulary Words by Topic

## Animals

alligator/caimán
ant/horminga
anteater/oso hormiguero
bat/murciélago
bear/oso
beaver/castor
bee/abeja
beetle/escarabajo
bobcat/lince
butterfly/mariposa
camel/camello
cat/gato
chicken/gallina/pollo
chipmunk/ardilla
cow/vaca
crab/cangrejo
deer/venado/ciervo
dog/perro
dolphin/delfin
donkey/burro
dragonfly/libélula
duck/pato
eagle/águila
elephant/elefante
flamingo/flamingo
fly/mosca
fox/zorro
frog/rana
giraffe/jirafa
goat/cabra
gorilla/gorila
grasshopper/saltamontes
hamster/hámster
hippopotamus/hipopótamo
horse/caballo
kangaroo/canguro
koala/coala

ladybug/catarina
leopard/leopardo
lion/león
llama/llama
lobster/langosta
monkey/mono
moose/alce
mosquito/mosquito
mouse/ratón
octopus/pulpo
opossum/zarigüeya
owl/búho
panda/oso panda
parakeet/periquito
peacock/pavo real
pelican/pelicano
penguin/pingüino
pig/cerdo
polar bear/oso polar
porcupine/puerco espín
rabbit/conejo
raccoon/mapache
rhinoceros/rinoceronte
robin/petirrojo
salamander/salamandra
sea horse/caballo de mar
shark/tiburón
sheep/oveja
skunk/mofeta/zorrillo
snake/serpiente
squirrel/ardilla
starfish/estrella de mar
swan/cisne
tiger/tigre
toad/sapo
turkey/pavo
turtle/tortuga
walrus/morsa

whale/ballena
zebra/cebra

## Colors and Shapes

blue/azul
green/verde
red/rojo
yellow/amarillo
circle/círculo
diamond/diamante
oval/óvalo
rectangle/rectángulo
square/cuadrado
triangle/triángulo

## Signs

deer crossing/cruce de venado
handicapped parking/
    estacionamiento para inválidos
railroad crossing/paso del tren
school crossing/cruce escolar
speed limit/limite de velocidad
stop sign/señal de alto
traffic light/semáforo
yield sign/señal de ceder el paso

## Earth

beach/playa
blizzard/tormenta de nieve
cloud/nube
coral reef/arrecife de coral
desert/desierto
dry season/temporada seca
fall/otoño
fog/niebla
forest/bosque
geyser/géiser
glacier/glaciar

hail/granizo
hurricane/huracán
ice/hielo
island/isla
lake/lago
lightning/relámpago
mountain/montaña
ocean/océano
plain/llano
rain/lluvia
rain forest/selva tropical
rainy season/temporada de lluvias
rapids/rápidos
river/río
snow/nieve
spring/primavera
stream/arroyo
summer/verano
sun/sol
tornado/tornado
tundra/tundra
volcano/volcán
waterfall/cascada
wind/viento
winter/invierno

## Human Body

ankle/tobillo
arm/brazo
body/cuerpo
ear/oreja
elbow/codo
eyes/ojos
feet/pies
fingers/dedos
hair/pelo
hands/manos

# Vocabulary Words by Topic

head/cabeza
hearing/oído
heel/talón
hips/caderas
knee/rodilla
legs/piernas
mouth/boca
nose/nariz
sense/sentido
shoulders/hombros
sight/vista
smell/olfato
taste/gusto
teeth/dientes
toes/dedos de los pies
touch/ tacto

## Plants

cactus/cactus
carrot/zanahoria
clover/trébol
cornstalk/planta de maíz
dandelion/diente de león
fern/helecho
grapevine/parra
grass/hierba
lettuce/lechuga
lilac bush/lila de monte
marigold/caléndula
moss/musgo
oak tree/árbol de roble
onion/cebolla
orange tree/naranjo
palm tree/palma
pine tree/pino
poison ivy/hiedra venenosa
rice/arroz
rose/rosa

seaweed/alga marina
sunflower/girasol
tomato/tomate
tulip/tulipán
water lily/nenúfar
wheat/trigo

## Clothing

belt/cinturón
blouse/blusa
boots/botas
boy's swimsuit/traje de baño para
  niños
coat/abrigo
dress/vestido
earmuffs/orejeras
girl's swimsuit/traje de baño para
  niñas
gloves/guantes
hat/sombrero
jacket/chaqueta
jeans/pantalones vaqueros
mittens/manoplas
pajamas/pijama
pants/pantalones
raincoat/impermeable
robe/bata
scarf/bufanda
shirt/camisa
shoes/zapatos
shorts/pantalones cortos
skirt/falda
slippers/pantuflas
socks/calcetines
sweat suit/chandal
sweater/suéter
tie/corbata
vest/chaleco

## Food

apples/manzanas
bacon/tocino
bagels/roscas de pan
bananas/plátanos
beans/frijoles
beef/carne
beets/betabel
blueberries/arándanos
bread/pan
broccoli/brécol
butter/mantequilla
cake/pastel
cantaloupe/cantalupo
carrots/zanahoria
cauliflower/coliflor
celery/apio
cereal/cereal
cheese/queso
cherries/cerezas
chicken/pollo
clams/almejas
cookies/galletas
corn/maíz
cottage cheese/requesón
crackers/galletas saladas
cream cheese/queso crema
cucumbers/pepinos
eggs/huevos
figs/higos
fish/pescado
grapefruit/toronja
grapes/uvas
green peppers/pimientos verdes
ham/jamón
ice-cream cone/cono de helado
jelly/gelatina
lemons/limones

lettuce/lechuga
limes/limas
macaroni/macarrones
milk/leche
mushrooms/champiñones
nuts/nueces
onions/cebollas
orange juice/jugo de naranja
oranges/naranjas
peaches/duraznos
peanut butter/crema de cacahuete
pears/peras
peas/guisantes
pie/tarta
pineapples/piñas
plums/ciruelas
pork chop/chuleta de puerco
potatoes/papas
radishes/rábanos
raisins/pasas
rice/arroz
rolls/panecillos
salad/ensalada
sausage/salchicha
shrimp/camarón
soup/sopa
spaghetti/espaguetis
squash/calabaza
strawberries/fresas
sweet potatoes/camotes
tomatoes/tomates
watermelon/sandía
yogurt/yogur

## Recreation

archery/tiro el arco
badminton/bádminton
baseball/béisbol
basketball/baloncesto
biking/ciclismo
boating/paseo en bote
bowling/boliche
canoeing/piragüismo
climbing/montañismo
croquet/croquet
discus/disco
diving/buceo
fishing/pesca
football/fútbol
golf/golf
gymnastics/gimnasia
hiking/excursionismo
hockey/hockey
horseback riding/equitación
ice-skating/patinaje sobre hielo
in-line skating/patines en línea
lacrosse/lacrosse
pole-vaulting/salto con pértiga
running/atletismo
scuba diving/buceo
shot put/lanzamiento de peso
skiing/esquí
soccer/fútbol
surfing/surfing
swimming/natación
T-ball/T-ball
tennis/tenis
volleyball/voleibol
walking/caminar
waterskiing/esquí acuático
weight lifting/levantamiento

## School

auditorium/auditorio
book/libro
cafeteria/cafetería
cafeteria table/mesa de cafetería
calculator/calculadora
chair/silla
chalk/tiza
chalkboard/pizarrón
chart paper/rotafolio
classroom/aula
computer/computadora
construction paper/papel para
   construir
crayons/crayones
desk/escritorio
easel/caballete
eraser/borrador
globe/globo
glue/pegamento
gym/gimnasio
hallway/vestíbulo
janitor's room/conserjería
learning center/centro de
   aprendizaje
library/biblioteca
markers/marcadores
music room/salón de música
notebook paper/papel de cuaderno
nurse's office/enfermería
paint/pintura
paintbrush/pincel
pen/pluma
pencil/lápiz
pencil sharpener/sacapuntas
playground/patio de recreo
principal's office/oficina del
   director

ruler/regla
science room/salón de ciencias
scissors/tijeras
stairs/escaleras
stapler/grapadora
supply room/almacén
tape/cinta adhesiva

## Toys

ball/pelota
balloons/globos
bike/bicicleta
blocks/cubos
clay/arcilla
coloring book/libro para colorear
doll/muñeca
doll carriage/careola de muñecas
dollhouse/casa de muñecas
farm set/juego de la granja
game/juego
grocery cart/carro de compras
hats/sombreros
in-line skates/patines
instruments/instrumentos
jump rope/cuerda para saltar
kite/cometa
magnets/imanes
marbles/canicas
puppet/títere
puzzle/rompecabezas
scooter/motoneta
skateboard/patineta
slide/tobogán
stuffed animals/peluches
tape recorder/grabadora
top/trompo
toy cars/carro de juguete
toy trucks/camión de juguete

train set/juego de tren
tricycle/triciclo
wagon/vagón
yo-yo/yó-yó

## Equipment

baggage cart/carro para equipaje
baseball/béisbol
bat/bate
mitt/manopla
basketball/pelota de baloncesto
basketball net/canasta
blueprints/planos
computer/computadora
drafting tools/borradores
bow/arco
arrow/flecha
bowling ball/pelota de boliche
bowling pin/bolos de boliche
bridle/freno
saddle/silla de montar
saddle pad/montura
broom/escoba
bulldozer/aplanadora
canoe/canoa
paddle/paleta
cash register/caja registradora
computer/computadora
crane/grúa
dishwasher/lavaplatos
drill/taladro
drum/tambor
drumsticks/palillos
dryer/secadora
dustpan/recogedor
figure skates/patinaje artistico

# Vocabulary Words by Topic

football/balón
shoulder pads/hombreras
football helmet/casco
goggles/gafas
golf ball/pelota de golf
golf clubs/palo de golf
tee/tee
hammer/martillo
handcuffs/esposas
badge/placa
hat/gorra
hockey stick/palo de hockey
hockey puck/disco de hockey
ice skates/patines
hoe/azadón
hose/manguera
coat/chaqueta
hat/sombrero
sprinkler/rociador
iron/plancha
ironing board/tabla de planchar
lawn mower/cortacéspedes
mail pouch/bolsa de correo
mirror/espejo
probe/sonda
pick/pico
mop/estropajo
paintbrush/brocha de pintar
piano/piano
pliers/alicates
rake/rastrillo
roller skates/patines
saw/sierra
screwdriver/desarmador
scuba tank/tanque de buceo
mask/máscara
flippers/aletas
shovel/pala

sketch pad/cuaderno para dibujo
palette/paleta
skis/esquís
ski boots/botas para esquiar
poles/palos
soccer ball/balón de fútbol
shoes/zapatos de tenis
stepladder/escalera doble
stethoscope/estetoscopio
surfboard/tabla de surf
tennis ball/pelota de tenis
tennis racket/raqueta de tenis
tractor/tractor
vacuum cleaner/aspiradora
washer/lavadora
water skis/esquís acuáticos
rope/cuerda
life jacket/chaleco salvavidas
watering can/regadera
wheelbarrow/carretilla
wrench/llave inglesa

## Home

basement/sótano
bathroom/baño
bathroom sink/lavabo
bathtub/bañera
bed/cama
bedroom/recámara/habitación
blanket/cobija/manta
chair/silla
circuit breaker/cortocircuito
dresser/cómoda
electrical outlet/enchufe
end table/mesa auxiliar
fireplace/chimenea
furnace/horno
kitchen/cocina

kitchen chair/silla de cocina
kitchen sink/fregadero
kitchen table/mesa de cocina
lamp/lámpara
light switch/interruptor de la luz
living room/sala
medicine cabinet/botiquín
nightstand/mesilla de noche
pillow/almohada
refrigerator/refrigerador
shower/ducha
smoke alarm/alarma de incendios
sofa/sofá
stove/estufa
thermostat/termostato
toilet/el baño
water heater/calentador de agua

## Occupations

administrative assistant/asistente
    administrativo
air traffic controller/controlador
    aéreo
airline pilot/piloto
architect/arquitecto
artist/artista
astronaut/astronauta
athlete/atleta
author/autor
ballerina/bailarina
banker/banquero
bus driver/conductor de autobús
camera operator/operador de
    cámara
carpenter/carpintero
cashier/cajero
chef/jefe de cocina
computer technician/técnico en

computación
cosmetologist/cosmetólogo
dancer/bailarín
dentist/dentista
doctor/doctor
electrician/electricista
engineer/ingeniero
farmer/granjero
firefighter/bombero
forest ranger/guardabosques
lawyer/abogado
manicurist/manicurista
musician/músico
nurse/enfermera
paramedic/paramédico
photographer/fotógrafo
police officer/policía
postal worker/empleado postal
real estate agent/corridor de
    bienes raíces
refuse collector/recolector de
    basura
reporter/reportero
school crossing guard/guarda
    escolar
server/mesero
ship captain/capitán de barco
singer/cantante
skater/patinador
teacher/maestro
truck driver/conductor de camión
veterinarian/veterinario
weaver/tejedora

## Structures

adobe/casa de adobe
airplane hangar/hangar de avión
airport/aeropuerto
apartment building/edificio de
    departamentos/edificio de pisos
arena/arena
art museum/museo de arte
bakery/panadería
bank/banco
barn/granero
bridge/peunte
bus shelter/parada cubierta
city hall/ayuntamiento
clothing store/tienda de ropa
condominium/condominio
courthouse/tribunal
covered bridge/puente cubierto
dam/presa
dock/muelle
drawbridge/puente levadizo
duplex/dúplex
fire station/estación de bomberos
flower shop/floristeria
garage/garaje
gas station/gasolinera
gazebo/mirador
grain elevator/elevador de granos
grocery store/supermercado
hospital/hospital
house/casa
library/biblioteca
log cabin/cabaña de madera
marina/marina
monument/monumento
movie theater/cine
opera house/teatro de la ópera
palace/palacio

parking garage/estacionamiento
pizza shop/pizzaría
police station/estación de policía
power plant/central eléctrica
pyramid/pirámide
restaurant/restaurante
school/escuela
shelter house/albergue
shopping mall/centro comercial
skyscraper/rascacielos
stadium/estadio
swimming pool/alberca/piscina
tent/tienda
toy store/juguetería
train station/estación del tren
windmills/molino de viento

## Transportation

airplane/avión
bicycle/bicicleta
bus/autobús
canoe/canoa
car/coche
four-wheel-drive vehicle/coche con
    doble tracción
helicopter/helicóptero
hot air balloon/globo de aire
    caliente
kayak/kayac
moped/ciclomotor
motor home/casa motora
motorboat/lancha motora
motorcycle/motocicleta
pickup truck/camioneta
rowboat/bote de remos
sailboat/velero
school bus/camión escolar

semitrailer truck/camión con semi-
    remolque
ship/barco
submarine/submarino
subway/metro
taxi/taxi
train/tren
van/furgoneta

# Learning Trajectories for Math

Children follow natural developmental progressions in learning. Curriculum research has revealed sequences of activities that are effective in guiding children through these levels of thinking. These developmental paths are the basis for *Building Blocks* learning trajectories.

## Learning Trajectories for Primary Grades Mathematics

Learning trajectories have three parts: a mathematical goal, a developmental path along which children develop to reach that goal, and a set of activities matched to each of the levels of thinking in that path that help children develop the next higher level of thinking. The **Building Blocks** learning trajectories give simple labels, descriptions, and examples of each level. Complete learning trajectories describe the goals of learning, the thinking and learning processes of children at various levels, and the learning activities in which they might engage. This document provides only the developmental levels.

The following provides the developmental levels from the first signs of development in different strands of mathematics through approximately age 8. Research shows that when teachers understand how children develop mathematics understanding, they are more effective in questioning, analyzing, and providing activities that further children's development than teachers who are unaware of the development process. Consequently, children have a much richer and more successful math experience in the primary grades.

Each of the following tables, such as "Counting," represents a main developmental progression that underlies the learning trajectory for that topic.

For some topics, there are "subtrajectories"—strands within the topic. In most cases, the names make this clear. For example, in Comparing and Ordering, some levels are "Composer" levels and others involve building a "Mental Number Line." Similarly, the related subtrajectories of "Composition" and "Decomposition" are easy to distinguish. Sometimes, for clarification, subtrajectories are indicated with a note in italics after the title. For example, Parts and Representing are subtrajectories within the Shape Trajectory.

## Frequently Asked Questions (FAQ)

1. Why use learning trajectories? Learning trajectories allow teachers to build the mathematics of children—the thinking of children as it develops naturally. So, we know that all the goals and activities are within the developmental capacities of children. Finally, we know that the activities provide the mathematical building blocks for success.

2. When are children "at" a level? Children are at a certain level when most of their behaviors reflect the thinking—ideas and skills—of that level. Most levels are levels of thinking. However, some are merely "levels of attainment" and indicate a child has gained knowledge. For example, children must learn to name or write more numerals, but knowing more numerals does not require more complex thinking.

3. Can children work at more than one level at the same time? Yes, although most children work mainly at one level or in transition between two levels. Levels are not "absolute stages." They are "benchmarks" of complex growth that represent distinct ways of thinking.

4. Can children jump ahead? Yes, especially if there are separate subtopics. For example, we have combined many counting competencies into one "Counting" sequence with subtopics, such as verbal counting skills. Some children learn to count to 100 at age 6 after learning to count objects to 10 or more, some may learn that verbal skill earlier. The subtopic of verbal counting skills would still be followed.

5. How do these developmental levels support teaching and learning? The levels help teachers, as well as curriculum developers, assess, teach, and sequence activities. Through planned teaching and encouraging informal, incidental mathematics, teachers help children learn at an appropriate and deep level.

6. Should I plan to help children develop just the levels that correspond to my children's ages? No! The ages in the table are typical ages children develop these ideas. (These are rough guides only.) These are "starting levels" not goals. We have found that children who are provided high-quality mathematics experiences are capable of developing to levels one or more years beyond their peers.

# Developmental Levels for Counting

The ability to count with confidence develops over the course of several years. Beginning in infancy, children show signs of understanding numbers. With instruction and number experience, most children can count fluently by age 8, with much progress in counting occurring in kindergarten and first grade. Most children follow a natural developmental progression in learning to count with recognizable stages or levels. This developmental path can be described as part of a learning trajectory.

| Age Range | Level Name | Level | Description |
|---|---|---|---|
| 1–2 | Precounter | 1 | At the earliest level a child shows no verbal counting. The child may name some number words with no sequence. |
| 1–2 | Chanter | 2 | At this level, a child may sing-song or chant indistinguishable number words. |
| 2 | Reciter | 3 | At this level, the child may verbally count with separate words, but not necessarily in the correct order. |
| 3 | Reciter (10) | 4 | A child at this level may verbally count to 10 with some correspondence with objects. He or she may point to objects to count a few items, but then lose track. |
| 3 | Corresponder | 5 | At this level, a child may keep one-to-one correspondence between counting words and objects—at least for small groups of objects laid in a line. A corresponder may answer "how many" by recounting the objects. |
| 4 | Counter (Small Numbers) | 6 | At around 4 years of age, the child may begin to count meaningfully. He or she may accurately count objects in a line to 5 and answer the "how many" question with the last number counted. When objects are visible, and especially with small numbers, the child begins to understand cardinality (that numbers tell how many). |
| 4 | Producer (Small Numbers) | 7 | The next level after counting small numbers is to count out objects to 5. When asked to show four of something, for example, this child may give four objects. |
| 4 | Counter (10) | 8 | This child may count structured arrangements of objects to 10. He or she may be able to write or draw to represent 1–10. A child at this level may be able to tell the number just after or just before another number, but only by counting up from 1. |
| 5 | Counter and Producer—Counter to (10+) | 9 | Around 5 years of age, a child may begin to count out objects accurately to 10 and then beyond to 30. He or she has explicit understanding of cardinality (that numbers tell how many). The child may keep track of objects that have and have not been counted, even in different arrangements. He or she may write or draw to represent 1 to 10 and then 20 and 30, and may give the next number to 20 or 30. The child also begins to recognize errors in others' counting and is able to eliminate most errors in his or her own counting. |

| Age Range | Level Name | Level | Description |
|---|---|---|---|
| 5 | Counter Backward from 10 | 10 | Another milestone at about age 5 is being able to count backward from 10 to 1, verbally, or when removing objects from a group. |
| 6 | Counter from N (N+1, N–1) | 11 | Around 6 years of age, the child may begin to count on, counting verbally and with objects from numbers other than 1. Another noticeable accomplishment is that a child may determine the number immediately before or after another number without having to start back at 1. |
| 6 | Skip Counting by 10s to 100 | 12 | A child at this level may count by 10s to 100 or beyond with understanding. |
| 6 | Counter to 100 | 13 | A child at this level may count by 1s to 100. He or she can make decade transitions (for example, from 29 to 30) starting at any number. |
| 6 | Counter On Using Patterns | 14 | At this level, a child may keep track of a few counting acts by using numerical patterns, such as tapping as he or she counts. |
| 6 | Skip Counter | 15 | At this level, the child can count by 5s and 2s with understanding. |
| 6 | Counter of Imagined Items | 16 | At this level, a child may count mental images of hidden objects to answer, for example, "how many" when 5 objects are visible and 3 are hidden. |
| 6 | Counter On Keeping Track | 17 | A child at this level may keep track of counting acts numerically, first with objects, then by counting counts. He or she counts up one to four more from a given number. |
| 6 | Counter of Quantitative Units | 18 | At this level, a child can count unusual units, such as "wholes" when shown combinations of wholes and parts. For example, when shown three whole plastic eggs and four halves, a child at this level will say there are five whole eggs. |
| 6 | Counter to 200 | 19 | At this level, a child may count accurately to 200 and beyond, recognizing the patterns of ones, tens, and hundreds. |
| 7 | Number Conserver | 20 | A major milestone around age 7 is the ability to conserve number. A child who conserves number understands that a number is unchanged even if a group of objects is rearranged. For example, if there is a row of ten buttons, the child understands there are still ten without recounting, even if they are rearranged in a long row or a circle. |
| 7 | Counter Forward and Back | 21 | A child at this level may count in either direction and recognize that sequence of decades mirrors single-digit sequence. |

# Learning Trajectories for Math

## Developmental Levels for Comparing and Ordering Numbers

Comparing and ordering sets is a critical skill for children as they determine whether one set is larger than another in order to make sure sets are equal and "fair." Prekindergartners can learn to use matching to compare collections or to create equivalent collections. Finding out how many more or fewer in one collection is more demanding than simply comparing two collections. The ability to compare and order sets with fluency develops over the course of several years. With instruction and number experience, most children develop foundational understanding of number relationships and place value at ages four and five. Most children follow a natural developmental progression in learning to compare and order numbers with recognizable stages or levels. This developmental path can be described as part of a learning trajectory.

| Age Range | Level Name | Level | Description |
|---|---|---|---|
| 2 | Object Corresponder | 1 | At this early level, a child puts objects into one-to-one correspondence, but may not fully understand that this creates equal groups. For example, a child may know that each carton has a straw, but does not necessarily know there are the same numbers of straws and cartons. |
| 2 | Perceptual Comparer | 2 | At this level, a child can compare collections that are quite different in size (for example, one is at least twice the other) and know that one has more than the other. If the collections are similar, the child can compare very small collections. |
| 3 | First-Second Ordinal Counter | 3 | At this level the child can identify the "first" and often "second" object in a sequence. |
| 3 | Nonverbal Comparer of Similar Items | 4 | At this level, a child can identify that different organizations of the same number are equal and different from other sets (1–4 items). For example, a child can identify ••• and •ᐧ• as equal and different from •• or ᐧ•. |
| 4 | Nonverbal Comparer of Dissimilar Items | 5 | At this level, a child can match small, equal collections of dissimilar items, such as shells and dots, and show that they are the same number. |
| 4 | Matching Comparer | 6 | As children progress, they begin to compare groups of 1–6 by matching. For example, a child gives one toy bone to every dog and says there are the same number of dogs and bones. |

| Age Range | Level Name | Level | Description |
|---|---|---|---|
| 4 | Knows-to-Count Comparer | 7 | A significant step occurs when the child begins to count collections to compare. At the early levels, children are not always accurate when a larger collection's objects are smaller in size than the objects in the smaller collection. For example, a child at this level may accurately count two equal collections, but when asked, says the collection of larger blocks has more. |
| 4 | Counting Comparer (Same Size) | 8 | At this level, children make accurate comparisons via counting, but only when objects are about the same size and groups are small (about 1–5 items). |
| 5 | Counting Comparer (5) | 9 | As children develop their ability to compare sets, they compare accurately by counting, even when a larger collection's objects are smaller. A child at this level can figure out how many more or less. |
| 5 | Ordinal Counter | 10 | At this level, a child identifies and uses ordinal numbers from "first" to "tenth." For example, the child can identify who is "third in line." |
| 6 | Counting Comparer (10) | 11 | This level can be observed when the child compares sets by counting, even when a larger collection's objects are smaller, up to 10. A child at this level can accurately count two collections of 9 items each, and says they have the same number, even if one collection has larger blocks. |
| 6 | Mental Number Line to 10 | 12 | As children move into this level, they begin to use mental images and knowledge of number relationships to determine relative size and position. For example, a child at this level can answer which number is closer to 6, 4 or 9 without counting physical objects. |
| 6 | Serial Orderer to 6+ | 13 | At this level, the child orders lengths marked into units (1–6, then beyond). For example, given towers of cubes, this child can put them in order, 1 to 6. |
| 7 | Place Value Comparer | 14 | Further development is made when a child begins to compare numbers with place value understanding. For example, a child at this level can explain that "63 is more than 59 because six tens is more than five tens, even if there are more than three ones." |
| 7 | Mental Number Line to 100 | 15 | Children demonstrate the next level when they can use mental images and knowledge of number relationships, including ones embedded in tens, to determine relative size and position. For example, when asked, "Which is closer to 45, 30 or 50?" a child at this level may say "45 is right next to 50, but 30 isn't." |
| 8+ | Mental Number Line to 1,000s | 16 | At about age 8, children may begin to use mental images of numbers up to 1,000 and knowledge of number relationships, including place value, to determine relative size and position. For example, when asked, "Which is closer to 3,500—2,000 or 7,000?" a child at this level may say "70 is double 35, but 20 is only fifteen from 35, so twenty hundreds, 2,000, is closer." |

## Developmental Levels for Recognizing Number and Subitizing (Instantly Recognizing)

The ability to recognize number values develops over the course of several years and is a foundational part of number sense. Beginning at about age two, children begin to name groups of objects. The ability to instantly know how many are in a group, called *subitizing,* begins at about age three. By age eight, with instruction and number experience, most children can identify groups of items and use place values and multiplication skills to count them. Most children follow a natural developmental progression in learning to count with recognizable stages or levels. This developmental path can be described as part of a learning trajectory.

| Age Range | Level Name | Level | Description |
|---|---|---|---|
| 2 | Small Collection Namer | 1 | The first sign occurs when the child can name groups of 1 to 2, sometimes 3. For example, when shown a pair of shoes, this young child says, "two shoes." |
| 3 | Maker of Small Collections | 2 | At this level, a child can nonverbally make a small collection (no more than 4, usually 1 to 3) with the same number as another collection. For example, when shown a collection of 3, the child makes another collection of 3. |
| 4 | Perceptual Subitizer to 4 | 3 | Progress is made when a child instantly recognizes collections up to 4 and verbally names the number of items. For example, when shown 4 objects briefly, the child says "4." |
| 5 | Perceptual Subitizer to 5 | 4 | This level is the ability to instantly recognize collections up to 5 and verbally name the number of items. For example, when shown 5 objects briefly, the child says "5." |
| 5 | Conceptual Subitizer to 5 | 5 | At this level, the child can verbally label all arrangements to about 5, when shown only briefly. For example, a child at this level might say, "I saw 2 and 2, and so I saw 4." |
| 5 | Conceptual Subitizer to 10 | 6 | This step is when the child can verbally label most arrangements to 6 shown briefly, then up to 10, using groups. For example, a child at this level might say, "In my mind, I made 2 groups of 3 and 1 more, so 7." |
| 6 | Conceptual Subitizer to 20 | 7 | Next, a child can verbally label structured arrangements up to 20 shown briefly, using groups. For example, the child may say, "I saw 3 fives, so 5, 10, 15." |
| 7 | Conceptual Subitizer with Place Value and Skip Counting | 8 | At this level, a child is able to use groups, skip counting, and place value to verbally label structured arrangements shown briefly. For example, the child may say, "I saw groups of tens and twos, so 10, 20, 30, 40, 42, 44, 46…46!" |
| 8+ | Conceptual Subitizer with Place Value and Multiplication | 9 | As children develop their ability to subitize, they use groups, multiplication, and place value to verbally label structured arrangements shown briefly. At this level, a child may say, "I saw groups of tens and threes, so I thought, 5 tens is 50 and 4 threes is 12, so 62 in all." |

# Learning Trajectories for Math

## Developmental Levels for Composing (Knowing Combinations of Numbers)

Composing and decomposing are combining and separating operations that allow children to build concepts of "parts" and "wholes." Most prekindergartners can "see" that two items and one item make three items. Later, children learn to separate a group into parts in various ways and then to count to produce all of the number "partners" of a given number. Eventually children think of a number and know the different addition facts that make that number. Most children follow a natural developmental progression in learning to compose and decompose numbers with recognizable stages or levels. This developmental path can be described as part of a learning trajectory.

| Age Range | Level Name | Level | Description |
|---|---|---|---|
| 4 | Pre-Part-Whole Recognizer | 1 | At the earliest levels of composing, a child only nonverbally recognizes parts and wholes. For example, when shown 4 red blocks and 2 blue blocks, a young child may intuitively appreciate that "all the blocks" includes the red and blue blocks, but when asked how many there are in all, the child may name a small number, such as 1. |
| 5 | Inexact Part-Whole Recognizer | 2 | A sign of development is that the child knows a whole is bigger than parts, but does not accurately quantify. For example, when shown 4 red blocks and 2 blue blocks and asked how many there are in all, the child may name a "large number," such as 5 or 10. |
| 5 | Composer to 4, then 5 | 3 | At this level, a child knows number combinations. A child at this level quickly names parts of any whole, or the whole given the parts. For example, when shown 4, then 1 is secretly hidden, and then shown the 3 remaining, the child may quickly say "1" is hidden. |
| 6 | Composer to 7 | 4 | The next sign of development is when a child knows number combinations to totals of 7. A child at this level quickly names parts of any whole, or the whole when given parts, and can double numbers to 10. For example, when shown 6, then 4 are secretly hidden, and then shown the 2 remaining, the child may quickly say "4" are hidden. |
| 6 | Composer to 10 | 5 | This level is when a child knows number combinations to totals of 10. A child at this level may quickly name parts of any whole, or the whole when given parts, and can double numbers to 20. For example, this child would be able to say "9 and 9 is 18." |
| 7 | Composer with Tens and Ones | 6 | At this level, the child understands two-digit numbers as tens and ones, can count with dimes and pennies, and can perform two-digit addition with regrouping. For example, a child at this level may explain, "17 and 36 is like 17 and 3, which is 20, and 33, which is 53." |

## Developmental Levels for Adding and Subtracting

Single-digit addition and subtraction are generally characterized as "math facts." It is assumed children must memorize these facts, yet research has shown that addition and subtraction have their roots in counting, counting on, number sense, the ability to compose and decompose numbers, and place value. Research has also shown that learning methods for addition and subtraction with understanding is much more effective than rote memorization of seemingly isolated facts. Most children follow an observable developmental progression in learning to add and subtract numbers with recognizable stages or levels. This developmental path can be described as part of a learning trajectory.

| Age Range | Level Name | Level | Description |
|---|---|---|---|
| 1 | Pre +/− | 1 | At the earliest level, a child shows no sign of being able to add or subtract. |
| 3 | Nonverbal +/− | 2 | The first sign is when a child can add and subtract very small collections nonverbally. For example, when shown 2 objects, then 1 object being hidden under a napkin, the child identifies or makes a set of 3 objects to "match." |
| 4 | Small Number +/− | 3 | This level is when a child can find sums for joining problems up to 3 + 2 by counting with objects. For example, when asked, "You have 2 balls and get 1 more. How many in all?" the child may count out 2, then count out 1 more, then count all 3: "1, 2, 3, 3!" |
| 5 | Find Result +/− | 4 | **Addition** Evidence of this level in addition is when a child can find sums for joining (you had 3 apples and get 3 more; how many do you have in all?) and part-part-whole (there are 6 girls and 5 boys on the playground; how many children are there in all?) problems by direct modeling, counting all, with objects. For example, when asked, "You have 2 red balls and 3 blue balls. How many in all?" the child may count out 2 red, then count out 3 blue, then count all 5.<br>**Subtraction** In subtraction, a child can also solve take-away problems by separating with objects. For example, when asked, "You have 5 balls and give 2 to Tom. How many do you have left?" the child may count out 5 balls, then take away 2, and then count the remaining 3. |

| Age Range | Level Name | Level | Description |
|---|---|---|---|
| 5 | Find Change +/− | 5 | **Addition** At this level, a child can find the missing addend (5 + _ =7) by adding on objects. For example, when asked, "You have 5 balls and then get some more. Now you have 7 in all. How many did you get?" The child may count out 5, then count those 5 again starting at 1, then add more, counting "6, 7," then count the balls added to find the answer, 2.<br><br>**Subtraction** A child can compare by matching in simple situations. For example, when asked, "Here are 6 dogs and 4 balls. If we give a ball to each dog, how many dogs will not get a ball?" a child at this level may count out 6 dogs, match 4 balls to 4 of them, then count the 2 dogs that have no ball. |
| 5 | Make It +/− | 6 | A significant advancement occurs when a child is able to count on. This child can add on objects to make one number into another without counting from 1. For example, when told, "This puppet has 4 balls, but she should have 6. Make it 6," the child may put up 4 fingers on one hand, immediately count up from 4 while putting up 2 fingers on the other hand, saying, "5, 6," and then count or recognize the 2 fingers. |
| 6 | Counting Strategies +/− | 7 | This level occurs when a child can find sums for joining (you had 8 apples and get 3 more…) and part-part-whole (6 girls and 5 boys…) problems with finger patterns or by adding on objects or counting on. For example, when asked "How much is 4 and 3 more?" the child may answer "4…5, 6, 7!" Children at this level can also solve missing addend (3 + _ = 7) or compare problems by counting on. When asked, for example, "You have 6 balls. How many more would you need to have 8?" the child may say, "6, 7 [puts up first finger], 8 [puts up second finger]. 2!" |
| 6 | Part-Whole +/− | 8 | Further development has occurred when the child has part-whole understanding. This child can solve problems using flexible strategies and some derived facts (for example, "5 + 5 is 10, so 5 + 6 is 11"), can sometimes do start-unknown problems ( _ + 6 = 11), but only by trial and error. When asked, "You had some balls. Then you get 6 more. Now you have 11 balls. How many did you start with?" this child may lay out 6, then 3, count, and get 9. The child may put 1 more, say 10, then put 1 more. The child may count up from 6 to 11, then recount the group added, and say, "5!" |

| Age Range | Level Name | Level | Description |
|---|---|---|---|
| 6 | Numbers-in-Numbers +/− | 9 | Evidence of this level is when a child recognizes that a number is part of a whole and can solve problems when the start is unknown ( _ + 4 = 9) with counting strategies. For example, when asked, "You have some balls, then you get 4 more balls, now you have 9. How many did you have to start with?" this child may count, putting up fingers, "5, 6, 7, 8, 9." The child may then look at his or her fingers and say, "5!" |
| 7 | Deriver +/− | 10 | At this level, a child can use flexible strategies and derived combinations (for example, "7 + 7 is 14, so 7 + 8 is 15") to solve all types of problems. For example, when asked, "What's 7 plus 8?" this child thinks: 7 + 8 = 7 [ 7 + 1] = [7 +7] + 1 = 14 + 1 = 15. The child can also solve multidigit problems by incrementing or combining 10s and 1s. For example, when asked "What's 28 + 35?" this child may think: 20 + 30 = 50; + 8 = 58; 2 more is 60, and 3 more is 63. He or she can also combine 10s and 1s: 20 + 30 = 50. 8 + 5 is like 8 plus 2 and 3 more, so it is 13. 50 and 13 is 63. |
| 8+ | Problem Solver +/− | 11 | As children develop their addition and subtraction abilities, they can solve by using flexible strategies and many known combinations. For example, when asked, "If I have 13 and you have 9, how could we have the same number?" this child may say, "9 and 1 is 10, then 3 more makes 13. 1 and 3 is 4. I need 4 more!" |
| 8+ | Multidigit +/− | 12 | Further development is shown when children can use composition of 10s and all previous strategies to solve multidigit +/− problems. For example, when asked, "What's 37 − 18?" this child may say, "Take 1 ten off the 3 tens; that's 2 tens. Take 7 off the 7. That's 2 tens and 0…20. I have one more to take off. That's 19." Or, when asked, "What's 28 + 35?" this child may think, 30 + 35 would be 65. But it's 28, so it's 2 less…63. |

# Learning Trajectories for Math

## Developmental Levels for Multiplying and Dividing

Multiplication and division build on addition and subtraction understanding and are dependent upon counting and place-value concepts. As children begin to learn to multiply, they make equal groups and count them all. They then learn skip counting and derive related products from products they know. Finding and using patterns aid in learning multiplication and division facts with understanding. Children typically follow an observable developmental progression in learning to multiply and divide numbers with recognizable stages or levels. This developmental path can be described as part of a learning trajectory.

| Age Range | Level Name | Level | Description |
|---|---|---|---|
| 2 | Non-quantitative Sharer "Dumper" | 1 | Multiplication and division concepts begin very early with the problem of sharing. Early evidence of these concepts can be observed when a child dumps out blocks and gives some (not an equal number) to each person. |
| 3 | Beginning Grouper and Distributive Sharer | 2 | Progression to this level can be observed when a child is able to make small groups (fewer than 5). This child can share by "dealing out," but often only between 2 people, although he or she may not appreciate the numerical result. For example, to share 4 blocks, this child may give each person a block, check that each person has one, and repeat this. |
| 4 | Grouper and Distributive Sharer | 3 | The next level occurs when a child makes small equal groups (fewer than 6). This child can deal out equally between 2 or more recipients, but may not understand that equal quantities are produced. For example, the child may share 6 blocks by dealing out blocks to herself and a friend one at a time. |
| 5 | Concrete Modeler ×/÷ | 4 | As children develop, they are able to solve small-number multiplying problems by grouping—making each group and counting all. At this level, a child can solve division/sharing problems with informal strategies, using concrete objects—up to 20 objects and 2 to 5 people—although the child may not understand equivalence of groups. For example, the child may distribute 20 objects by dealing out 2 blocks to each of 5 people, then 1 to each, until the blocks are gone. |
| 6 | Parts and Wholes ×/÷ | 5 | A new level is evidenced when the child understands the inverse relation between divisor and quotient. For example, this child may understand "If you share with more people, each person gets fewer." |
| 7 | Skip Counter ×/÷ | 6 | As children develop understanding in multiplication and division, they begin to use skip counting for multiplication and for measurement division (finding out how many groups). For example, given 20 blocks, 4 to each person, and asked how many people, the children may skip count by 4, holding up 1 finger for each count of 4. A child at this level may also use trial and error for partitive division (finding out how many in each group). For example, given 20 blocks, 5 people, and asked how many each should get, this child may give 3 to each, and then 1 more. |
| 8+ | Deriver ×/÷ | 7 | At this level, children use strategies and derived combinations to solve multidigit problems by operating on tens and ones separately. For example, a child at this level may explain "7 × 6, five 7s is 35, so 7 more is 42." |
| 8+ | Array Quantifier | 8 | Further development can be observed when a child begins to work with arrays. For example, given 7 × 4 with most of 5 × 4 covered, a child at this level may say, "There are 8 in these 2 rows, and 5 rows of 4 is 20, so 28 in all." |
| 8+ | Partitive Divisor | 9 | This level can be observed when a child is able to figure out how many are in each group. For example, given 20 blocks, 5 people, and asked how many each should get, a child at this level may say, "4, because 5 groups of 4 is 20." |
| 8+ | Multidigit ×/÷ | 10 | As children progress, they begin to use multiple strategies for multiplication and division, from compensating to paper-and-pencil procedures. For example, a child becoming fluent in multiplication might explain that "19 times 5 is 95, because 20 fives is 100, and 1 less five is 95." |

## Developmental Levels for Measuring

Measurement is one of the main real-world applications of mathematics. Counting is a type of measurement which determines how many items are in a collection. Measurement also involves assigning a number to attributes of length, area, and weight. Prekindergarten children know that mass, weight, and length exist, but they do not know how to reason about these or to accurately measure them. As children develop their understanding of measurement, they begin to use tools to measure and understand the need for standard units of measure. Children typically follow an observable developmental progression in learning to measure with recognizable stages or levels. This developmental path can be described as part of a learning trajectory.

| Age Range | Level Name | Level | Description |
|---|---|---|---|
| 3 | Length Quantity Recognizer | 1 | At the earliest level, children can identify length as an attribute. For example, they might say, "I'm tall, see?" |
| 4 | Length Direct Comparer | 2 | In this level, children can physically align 2 objects to determine which is longer or if they are the same length. For example, they can stand 2 sticks up next to each other on a table and say, "This one's bigger." |
| 5 | Indirect Length Comparer | 3 | A sign of further development is when a child can compare the length of 2 objects by representing them with a third object. For example, a child might compare the length of 2 objects with a piece of string. Additional evidence of this level is that when asked to measure, the child may assign a length by guessing or moving along a length while counting (without equal-length units). For example, the child may move a finger along a line segment, saying 10, 20, 30, 31, 32. |
| 6 | Serial Orderer to 6+ | 4 | At this level, a child can order lengths, marked in 1 to 6 units. For example, given towers of cubes, a child at this level may put them in order, 1 to 6. |
| 6 | End-to-End Length Measurer | 5 | At this level, the child can lay units end-to-end, although he or she may not see the need for equal-length units. For example, a child might lay 9-inch cubes in a line beside a book to measure how long it is. |
| 7 | Length Unit Iterater | 6 | A significant change occurs when a child iterates a single unit to measure. He or she sees the need for identical units. The child uses rulers with help. |
| 7 | Length Unit Relater | 7 | At this level, a child can relate size and number of units. For example, the child may explain, "If you measure with centimeters instead of inches, you'll need more of them because each one is smaller." |
| 8+ | Length Measurer | 8 | As a child develops measurement ability, they begin to measure, knowing the need for identical units, the relationships between different units, partitions of unit, and the zero point on rulers. At this level, the child also begins to estimate. The children may explain, "I used a meterstick 3 times, then there was a little left over. So, I lined it up from 0 and found 14 centimeters. So, it's 3 meters, 14 centimeters in all." |
| 8+ | Conceptual Ruler Measurer | 9 | Further development in measurement is evidenced when a child possesses an "internal" measurement tool. At this level, the child mentally moves along an object, segmenting it, and counting the segments. This child also uses arithmetic to measure and estimates with accuracy. For example, a child at this level may explain, "I imagine one meterstick after another along the edge of the room. That's how I estimated the room's length to be 9 meters." |

# Learning Trajectories for Math

## Developmental Levels for Recognizing Geometric Shapes

Geometric shapes can be used to represent and understand objects. Analyzing, comparing, and classifying shapes help create new knowledge of shapes and their relationships. Shapes can be decomposed or composed into other shapes. Through their everyday activities, children build both intuitive and explicit knowledge of geometric figures. Most children can recognize and name basic two-dimensional shapes at four years of age. However, young children can learn richer concepts about shape if they have varied examples and nonexamples of shape, discussions about shapes and their characteristics, a wide variety of shape classes, and interesting tasks. Children typically follow an observable developmental progression in learning about shapes with recognizable stages or levels. This developmental path can be described as part of a learning trajectory.

| Age Range | Level Name | Level | Description |
|---|---|---|---|
| 2 | Shape Matcher— Identical | 1 | The earliest sign of understanding shape is when a child can match basic shapes (circle, square, typical triangle) with the same size and orientation. |
| 2 | Shape Matcher— Sizes | 2 | A sign of development is when a child can match basic shapes with different sizes. |
| 2 | Shape Matcher— Orientations | 3 | This level of development is when a child can match basic shapes with different orientations. |
| 3 | Shape Recognizer— Typical | 4 | A sign of development is when a child can recognize and name a prototypical circle, square, and, less often, a typical triangle. For example, the child names this a square. ☐ Some children may name different sizes, shapes, and orientations of rectangles, but also accept some shapes that look rectangular but are not rectangles. Children name these shapes "rectangles" (including the nonrectangular parallelogram). |
| 3 | Shape Matcher— More Shapes | 5 | As children develop understanding of shape, they can match a wider variety of shapes with the same size and orientation. |
| 3 | Shape Matcher— Sizes and Orientations | 6 | The child matches a wider variety of shapes with different sizes and orientations. |
| 3 | Shape Matcher— Combinations | 7 | The child matches combinations of shapes to each other. |
| 4 | Shape Recognizer— Circles, Squares, and Triangles | 8 | This sign of development is when a child can recognize some nonprototypical squares and triangles and may recognize some rectangles, but usually not rhombi (diamonds). Often, the child does not differentiate sides/corners. The child at this level may name these as triangles. |
| 4 | Constructor of Shapes from Parts— Looks Like *Representing* | 9 | A significant sign of development is when a child represents a shape by making a shape "look like" a goal shape. For example, when asked to make a triangle with sticks, the child may create the following: △. |

| Age Range | Level Name | Level | Description | |
|---|---|---|---|---|
| 5 | Shape Recognizer— All Rectangles | 10 | As children develop understanding of shape, they recognize more rectangle sizes, shapes, and orientations of rectangles. For example, a child at this level may correctly name these shapes "rectangles." | |
| 5 | Side Recognizer *Parts* | 11 | A sign of development is when a child recognizes parts of shapes and identifies sides as distinct geometric objects. For example, when asked what this shape is, the child may say it is a quadrilateral (or has 4 sides) after counting and running a finger along the length of each side. | |
| 5 | Angle Recognizer *Parts* | 12 | At this level, a child can recognize angles as separate geometric objects. For example, when asked, "Why is this a triangle," the child may say, "It has three angles" and count them, pointing clearly to each vertex (point at the corner). | |
| 5 | Shape Recognizer— More Shapes | 13 | As children develop, they are able to recognize most basic shapes and prototypical examples of other shapes, such as hexagon, rhombus (diamond), and trapezoid. For example, a child can correctly identify and name all the following shapes: | |
| 6 | Shape Identifier | 14 | At this level, the child can name most common shapes, including rhombi, without making mistakes such as calling ovals circles. A child at this level implicitly recognizes right angles, so distinguishes between a rectangle and a parallelogram without right angles. A child may correctly name all the following shapes: | |
| 6 | Angle Matcher *Parts* | 15 | A sign of development is when the child can match angles concretely. For example, given several triangles, the child may find two with the same angles by laying the angles on top of one another. | |

| Age Range | Level Name | Level | Description | |
|---|---|---|---|---|
| 7 | Parts of Shapes Identifier | 16 | At this level, the child can identify shapes in terms of their components. For example, the child may say, "No matter how skinny it looks, that's a triangle because it has 3 sides and 3 angles." | |
| 7 | Constructor of Shapes from Parts—Exact Representing | 17 | A significant step is when the child can represent a shape with completely correct construction, based on knowledge of components and relationships. For example, when asked to make a triangle with sticks, the child may create the following: | |
| 8 | Shape Class Identifier | 18 | As children develop, they begin to use class membership (for example, to sort) not explicitly based on properties. For example, a child at this level may say, "I put the triangles over here, and the quadrilaterals, including squares, rectangles, rhombi, and trapezoids, over there." | |
| 8 | Shape Property Identifier | 19 | At this level, a child can use properties explicitly. For example, a child may say, "I put the shapes with opposite sides that are parallel over here, and those with 4 sides but not both pairs of sides parallel over there." | |
| 8 | Angle Size Comparer | 20 | The next sign of development is when a child can separate and compare angle sizes. For example, the child may say, "I put all the shapes that have right angles here, and all the ones that have bigger or smaller angles over there." | |
| 8 | Angle Measurer | 21 | A significant step in development is when a child can use a protractor to measure angles. | |
| 8 | Property Class Identifier | 22 | The next sign of development is when a child can use class membership for shapes (for example, to sort or consider shapes "similar") explicitly based on properties, including angle measure. For example, the child may say, "I put the equilateral triangles over here, and the right triangles over here." | |
| 8 | Angle Synthesizer | 23 | As children develop understanding of shape, they can combine various meanings of angle (turn, corner, slant). For example, a child at this level could explain, "This ramp is at a 45° angle to the ground." | |

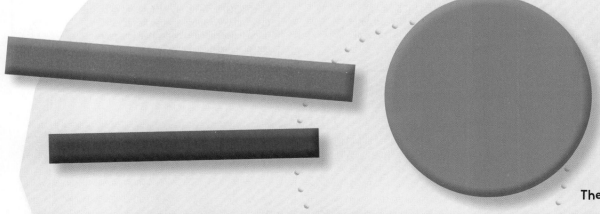

# Learning Trajectories for Math

## Developmental Levels for Composing Geometric Shapes

Children move through levels in the composition and decomposition of two-dimensional figures. Very young children cannot compose shapes but then gain ability to combine shapes into pictures, synthesize combinations of shapes into new shapes, and eventually substitute and build different kinds of shapes. Children typically follow an observable developmental progression in learning to compose shapes with recognizable stages or levels. This developmental path can be described as part of a learning trajectory.

| Age Range | Level Name | Level | Description |
|---|---|---|---|
| 2 | Pre-Composer | 1 | The earliest sign of development is when a child can manipulate shapes as individuals, but is unable to combine them to compose a larger shape. |
| 3 | Pre-Decomposer | 2 | At this level, a child can decompose shapes, but only by trial and error. |
| 4 | Piece Assembler | 3 | Around age 4, a child can begin to make pictures in which each shape represents a unique role (for example, one shape for each body part) and shapes touch. A child at this level can fill simple outline puzzles using trial and error. |
| 5 | Picture Maker | 4 | As children develop, they are able to put several shapes together to make one part of a picture (for example, 2 shapes for 1 arm). A child at this level uses trial and error and does not anticipate creation of the new geometric shape. The children can choose shapes using "general shape" or side length, and fill "easy" outline puzzles that suggest the placement of each shape (but note that the child is trying to put a square in the puzzle where its right angles will not fit). |
| 5 | Simple Decomposer | 5 | A significant step occurs when the child is able to decompose ("take apart" into smaller shapes) simple shapes that have obvious clues as to their decomposition. |

| Age Range | Level Name | Level | Description |
|---|---|---|---|
| 5 | Shape Composer | 6 | A sign of development is when a child composes shapes with anticipation ("I know what will fit!"). A child at this level chooses shapes using angles as well as side lengths. Rotation and flipping are used intentionally to select and place shapes. |
| 6 | Substitution Composer | 7 | A sign of development is when a child is able to make new shapes out of smaller shapes and uses trial and error to substitute groups of shapes for other shapes in order to create new shapes in different ways. For example, the child can substitute shapes to fill outline puzzles in different ways. |
| 6 | Shape Decomposer (with Help) | 8 | As children develop, they can decompose shapes by using imagery that is suggested and supported by the task or environment. |
| 7 | Shape Composite Repeater | 9 | This level is demonstrated when the child can construct and duplicate units of units (shapes made from other shapes) intentionally, and understands each as being both multiple, small shapes and one larger shape. For example, the child may continue a pattern of shapes that leads to tiling. |
| 7 | Shape Decomposer with Imagery | 10 | A significant sign of development is when a child is able to decompose shapes flexibly by using independently generated imagery. |
| 8 | Shape Composer—Units of Units | 11 | Children demonstrate further understanding when they are able to build and apply units of units (shapes made from other shapes). For example, in constructing spatial patterns, the child can extend patterning activity to create a tiling with a new unit shape—a unit of unit shapes that he or she recognizes and consciously constructs. For example, the child may build Ts out of 4 squares, use 4 Ts to build squares, and use squares to tile a rectangle. |
| 8 | Shape Decomposer — Units of Units | 12 | As children develop understanding of shape, they can decompose shapes flexibly by using independently generated imagery and planned decompositions of shapes that themselves are decompositions. |

## Developmental Levels for Comparing Geometric Shapes

As early as four years of age, children can create and use strategies, such as moving shapes to compare their parts or to place one on top of the other, for judging whether two figures are the same shape. From Pre-K to Grade 2, they can develop sophisticated and accurate mathematical procedures for comparing geometric shapes. Children typically follow an observable developmental progression in learning about how shapes are the same and different with recognizable stages or levels. This developmental path can be described as part of a learning trajectory.

| Age Range | Level Name | Level | Description |
|---|---|---|---|
| 3 | "Same Thing" Comparer | 1 | The first sign of understanding is when the child can compare real-world objects. For example, the children may say two pictures of houses are the same or different. |
| 4 | "Similar" Comparer | 2 | This sign of development occurs when the child judges two shapes to be the same if they are more visually similar than different. For example, the child may say, "These are the same. They are pointy at the top." |
| 4 | Part Comparer | 3 | At this level, a child can say that two shapes are the same after matching one side on each. For example, a child may say, "These are the same" (matching the two sides). |
| 4 | Some Attributes Comparer | 4 | As children develop, they look for differences in attributes, but may examine only part of a shape. For example, a child at this level may say, "These are the same" (indicating the top halves of the shapes are similar by laying them on top of each other). |
| 5 | Most Attributes Comparer | 5 | At this level, the child looks for differences in attributes, examining full shapes, but may ignore some spatial relationships. For example, a child may say, "These are the same." |
| 7 | Congruence Determiner | 6 | A sign of development is when a child determines congruence by comparing all attributes and all spatial relationships. For example, a child at this level may say that two shapes are the same shape and the same size after comparing every one of their sides and angles. |
| 7 | Congruence Superposer | 7 | As children develop understanding, they can move and place objects on top of each other to determine congruence. For example, a child at this level may say that two shapes are the same shape and the same size after laying them on top of each other. |
| 8+ | Congruence Representer | 8 | Continued development is evidenced as children refer to geometric properties and explain with transformations. For example, a child at this level may say, "These must be congruent because they have equal sides, all square corners, and I can move them on top of each other exactly." |

## Developmental Levels for Spatial Sense and Motions

Infants and toddlers spend a great deal of time learning about the properties and relations of objects in space. Very young children know and use the shape of their environment in navigation activities. With guidance they can learn to "mathematize" this knowledge. They can learn about direction, perspective, distance, symbolization, location, and coordinates. Children typically follow an observable developmental progression in developing spatial sense with recognizable stages or levels. This developmental path can be described as part of a learning trajectory.

| Age Range | Level Name | Level | Description |
|---|---|---|---|
| 4 | Simple Turner | 1 | An early sign of spatial sense is when a child mentally turns an object to perform easy tasks. For example, given a shape with the top marked with color, the child may correctly identify which of three shapes it would look like if it were turned "like this" (90 degree turn demonstrated), before physically moving the shape. |
| 5 | Beginning Slider, Flipper, Turner | 2 | This sign of development occurs when a child can use the correct motions, but is not always accurate in direction and amount. For example, a child at this level may know a shape has to be flipped to match another shape, but flips it in the wrong direction. |
| 6 | Slider, Flipper, Turner | 3 | As children develop spatial sense, they can perform slides and flips, often only horizontal and vertical, by using manipulatives. For example, a child at this level may perform turns of 45, 90, and 180 degrees. For example, a child knows a shape must be turned 90 degrees to the right to fit into a puzzle. |
| 7 | Diagonal Mover | 4 | A sign of development is when a child can perform diagonal slides and flips. For example, children at this level may know a shape must be turned or flipped over an oblique line (45 degree orientation) to fit into a puzzle. |
| 8 | Mental Mover | 5 | Further signs of development occur when a child can predict results of moving shapes using mental images. A child at this level may say, "If you turned this 120 degrees, it would be just like this one." |

# Learning Trajectories for Math

## Developmental Levels for Patterning and Early Algebra

Algebra begins with a search for patterns. Identifying patterns helps bring order, cohesion, and predictability to seemingly unorganized situations and allows one to make generalizations beyond the information directly available. The recognition and analysis of patterns are important components of young children's intellectual development because they provide a foundation for the development of algebraic thinking. Although prekindergarten children engage in pattern-related activities and recognize patterns in their everyday environment, research has revealed that an abstract understanding of patterns develops gradually during the early childhood years. Children typically follow an observable developmental progression in learning about patterns with recognizable stages or levels. This developmental path can be described as part of a learning trajectory.

| Age Range | Level Name | Level | Description |
|---|---|---|---|
| 2 | Pre-Patterner | 1 | A child at the earliest level does not recognize patterns. For example, a child may name a striped shirt with no repeating unit a "pattern." |
| 3 | Pattern Recognizer | 2 | At this level, the child can recognize a simple pattern. For example, a child at this level may say, "I'm wearing a pattern" about a shirt with black and white stripes. |
| 4 | Pattern Fixer | 3 | At this level the child fills in missing elements of a pattern, first with ABABAB patterns. When given items in a row with an item missing, such as ABAB_BAB, the child identifies and fills in the missing element (A). |
| 4 | Pattern Duplicator AB | 4 | A sign of development is when the child can duplicate an ABABAB pattern, although the children may have to work alongside the model pattern. For example, given objects in a row, ABABAB, the child may make his or her own ABABAB row in a different location. |
| 4 | Pattern Extender AB | 5 | At this level the child extends AB repeating patterns. For example, given items in a row—ABABAB—the child adds ABAB to the end of the row. |
| 4 | Pattern Duplicator | 6 | At this level, the child is able to duplicate simple patterns (not just alongside the model pattern). For example, given objects in a row, ABBABBABB, the child may make his or her own ABBABBABB row in a different location. |
| 5 | Pattern Extender | 7 | A sign of development is when the child can extend simple patterns. For example, given objects in a row, ABBABBABB, he or she may add ABBABB to the end of the row. |
| 7 | Pattern Unit Recognizer | 8 | At this level, a child can identify the smallest unit of a pattern. For example, given objects in a row with one missing, ABBAB_ABB, he or she may identify and fill in the missing element. |

# Developmental Levels for Classifying and Analyzing Data

Data analysis contains one big idea: classifying, organizing, representing, and using information to ask and answer questions. The developmental continuum for data analysis includes growth in classifying and counting to sort objects and quantify their groups. Children eventually become capable of simultaneously classifying and counting; for example, counting the number of colors in a group of objects. Children typically follow an observable developmental progression in learning about patterns with recognizable stages or levels. This developmental path can be described as part of a learning trajectory.

| Age Range | Level Name | Level | Description |
|---|---|---|---|
| 2 | Similarity Recognizer | 1 | The first sign that a child can classify is when he or she recognizes, intuitively, two or more objects as "similar" in some way. For example, "that's another doggie." |
| 2 | Informal Sorter | 2 | A sign of development is when a child places objects that are alike in some attribute together, but switches criteria and may use functional relationships as the basis for sorting. A child at this level might stack blocks of the same shape or put a cup with its saucer. |
| 3 | Attribute Identifier | 3 | The next level is when the child names attributes of objects and places objects together with a given attribute, but cannot then move to sorting by a new rule. For example, the child may say, "These are both red." |
| 4 | Attribute Sorter | 4 | At the next level the child sorts objects according to given attributes, forming categories, but may switch attributes during the sorting. A child at this stage can switch rules for sorting if guided. For example, the child might start putting red beads on a string, but switches to spheres of different colors. |
| 5 | Consistent Sorter | 5 | A sign of development is when the child can sort consistently by a given attribute. For example, the child might put several identical blocks together. |
| 6 | Exhaustive Sorter | 6 | At the next level, the child can sort consistently and exhaustively by an attribute, given or created. This child can use terms "some" and "all" meaningfully. For example, a child at this stage would be able to find all the attribute blocks of a certain size and color. |

| Age Range | Level Name | Level | Description |
|---|---|---|---|
| 6 | Multiple Attribute Sorter | 7 | A sign of development is when the child can sort consistently and exhaustively by more than one attribute, sequentially. For example, a child at this level can put all the attribute blocks together by color, then by shape. |
| 7 | Classifier and Counter | 8 | At the next level, the child is capable of simultaneously classifying and counting. For example, the child counts the number of colors in a group of objects. |
| 7 | List Grapher | 9 | In the early stage of graphing, the child graphs by simply listing all cases. For example, the child may list each child in the class and each child's response to a question. |
| 8+ | Multiple Attribute Classifier | 10 | A sign of development is when the child can intentionally sort according to multiple attributes, naming and relating the attributes. This child understands that objects could belong to more than one group. For example, the child can complete a two-dimensional classification matrix or form subgroups within groups. |
| 8+ | Classifying Grapher | 11 | At the next level the child can graph by classifying data (e.g., responses) and represent it according to categories. For example, the child can take a survey, classify the responses, and graph the result. |
| 8+ | Classifier | 12 | A sign of development is when the child creates complete, conscious classifications logically connected to a specific property. For example, a child at this level gives a definition of a class in terms of a more general class and one or more specific differences and begins to understand the inclusion relation. |
| 8+ | Hierarchical Classifier | 13 | At the next level, the child can perform hierarchical classifications. For example, the child recognizes that all squares are rectangles, but not all rectangles are squares. |
| 8+ | Data Representer | 14 | Signs of development are when the child organizes and displays data through both simple numerical summaries such as counts, tables, and tallies, and graphical displays, including picture graphs, line plots, and bar graphs. At this level the child creates graphs and tables, compares parts of the data, makes statements about the data as a whole, and determines whether the graphs answer the questions posed initially. |